Make-Believe Presidents
Illusions of Power from McKinley to Carter

Make-Believe Presidents

Illusions of Power from McKinley to Carter

Nicholas von Hoffman

Pantheon Books
New York

Grateful acknowledgment is made to the following for permission to reprint previously published material:

American Civil Liberties Union: Excerpts from Zecharial Chafee, Jr., *Thirty-five Years with Freedom of Speech,* Roger N. Baldwin Civil Liberties Foundation pamphlet (May 1952), pp. 6–7.

Johns Hopkins University Press: Excerpts from *The Economic Thought of Woodrow Wilson* (Baltimore: Johns Hopkins University Press, 1943), pp. 80, 94, 122, 132.

The New Republic: Poem by Langston Hughes reprinted from *The New Republic,* November 4, 1934, p. 9. Copyright © 1934 by The New Republic, Inc.

The New York Times: Editorial of August 8, 1964. Copyright © 1964 by The New York Times Company.

Library of Congress Cataloging in Publication Data

von Hoffman, Nicholas.
  Make-Believe Presidents.

  Includes bibliographical references and index.
  1. Presidents—United States—History. 2. Executive power—United States—History. 3. United States—Politics and government—20th century. I. Title.
JK511.V66   1978   353.03'13   77-88764
ISBN 0-394-41081-5

Manufactured in the United States of America

First Edition

To Deborah
Two weeks and twenty more pages

Acknowledgments

Without the research, editing, and criticisms of Susan Dooley this book would have been a year longer in the writing and far inferior to what I hope it is. Her help has been invaluable. I also want to thank Virginia Barber for the enormous amount of time and trouble she has taken in going over the manuscript in order to make many helpful suggestions. Last, I owe many thanks to André Schiffrin, the managing director of Pantheon Books, both for his editorial help and for the discussions of ideas which shaped and formed the work. The errors, mistakes, and deficiencies are, of course, mine.

Contents

Make-Believe Presidents

Part 1

What we have to discuss is, not wrongs which individuals intentionally do—I do not believe there are a great many of those—but the wrongs of a system. . . . The truth is, we are all caught in a great economic system which is heartless.

Woodrow Wilson

1

The Captive Presidency

The first noteworthy act of his presidency was Jerry Ford having his picture taken in his peejays as he picked up the morning paper from his Alexandria, Virginia, front door and ambled back into his kitchen to toast himself an English muffin. In a similar vein Jimmy Carter's first act upon taking the oath of office was to walk down Pennsylvania Avenue, hand in hand with his wife, a plebeian gesture which won him much praise. The presidency was being cut down to size by both men; the imperial office was being dismantled and returned to its original republican state before Franklin Roosevelt, Lyndon Johnson, and Richard Nixon entertained pretensions and usurped powers it does not constitutionally have. Two good men would make us whole again, would bind up the wounds of a stricken nation, to use the cliché exhumed from an earlier period of patriotic rhetoric.

The Lesson of Vietnam, and the Lesson of Watergate, then, is not to distort our system by letting the presidency grow imperial, but to make sure the office is hereafter conferred on good family folk of humble, worthy, and deserving character. If you know right from wrong, you know what went wrong, and you'll see to it that no president ever again can do what a Johnson or a Nixon did. Flawed men, the both of them; once their problem was diagnosed as moral, their tragedy became Shakespearean.

Macbeth, whom Lyndon Johnson was compared with in the satirical play *MacBird,* and Richard III, whom Richard Nixon doubtless will be compared to, are men whose personal traits, not whose politics, bring them down. It's their characters, their lusts, their weaknesses as men that the playwright uses to tell again the ancient story of the fall of kings. It makes good theater to relate this tale of bigger-than-life people who find their way to their deaths on a stage without a backdrop, who exist and play out their tragedies without context, who perish, not victims of society nor creatures of historical forces greater than themselves, but just the opposite—those kings have only themselves to blame.

The treatment accorded the two bad presidents is oddly out of joint with modern perception, in which the background is as important as the foreground, which explains crime, neurosis, and obesity by environment, which regards a person's context as inseparably necessary as Hindus consider a person's karma. This is the epoch in which there are no big men, only large organizations and tall buildings. No one is larger than life, because life isn't large so much as it's interrelated, interdependent, complex, multifaceted, and the dozen other words we use to explain that nothing is simple enough to just let us say, He did it. It is this failure to see the two in a political or institutional context that makes them fascinating as characters but incomprehensible as personages in the historical pageant.

Johnson and Nixon have been turned into the bad kings of Shakespearean drama. Johnson's pride, his loudness, his dirty mouth, and his cocksure personality make it plausible to call Vietnam Johnson's War, especially when we recall the equally cocksure retinue of the Best and the Brightest who collaborated with him. He is made into the Emperor Tiberius of the imperial presidency, so that, maniac that he was, he could be said to have used the formal powers of his office to tell his lies and commit his murders. Miser, self-confessed paranoid, introspective holder of grudges, more Mephistophelean spider than man, Nixon lends himself to such dramatization more easily: a moral mutant who tried to overthrow the Constitution for his own foul purposes which we'll never fully understand. Grand drama but hopelessly overdone, oversimplified, and overstated except for the audience captivated by the magic of the action on stage. That's why Europeans, who don't sit in the amphitheater of American public affairs, found the reasons proffered for Nixon's defenestration so puzzling and so unconvincing. They never lost sight of the background against which these two men read their lines.

While it momentarily escaped us, they continued to understand that even the despots and dictators of the twentieth-century totalitarian state find their power significantly less than absolute. Only the kings of theatrical fiction or Johnson/Nixon hold such sway they can execute their wicked schemes by announcing their will: two badmen at the control module of the world's greatest power acting out their morose personal needs at the expense of an impotent planet.

When the principal players' characters and morals get too much emphasis, politics and all social meaning recede and disappear. Only people who have read a lot of Revolutionary War history can think of George Washington as a domestic political leader. For the rest of us, he's too good to be political, just as Nixon is too bad. The translation of Abraham Lincoln into a kind of secular Christ figure who died for the sins of slavery in order that a purified and redeemed nation might burst the stones apart and ascend has made it extraordinarily difficult for nonhistorians to think of this man as a politician. His goodness has been so enlarged and dwelt upon that we cannot see him as a human actor on the scene. Christians have exactly the same problem in comprehending Jesus, the God-man. To give exaggerated importance to a few actors and the moral content of their acts makes it impossible to fathom their politics or our own. There are meanings other than right and wrong, and sometimes more important ones.

But since we have declared the major events in the United States between 1963 and 1974 to be more in the domain of theology than civics, we must explain how the two major political parties nominated Beelzebub and Belial and the voters thrice elected them. What was the mechanism by which they were able to put a big, healthy, modern country under an evil spell? The answer is conspiracy. Ultimately all moralists are driven to explain the actions of politics by conspiracy.

Ordinarily the devotees of conspiracy theory are the young, the insane, and the excessively pure of heart, but in the instance of Watergate everybody bought it—the courts, the House Judiciary Committee, the *New York Times.* The dreadful duo's election victories were owing to the way they and their accomplices deceived us. Books were written on how their dishonest advertising men packaged the candidates. But go back over the speeches and the old TV news footage and it's not so obvious these men were prettified past recognition. Lyndon Johnson's ears stuck out just as far as his principles, and the New, New, New Dick Nixon's nose swooped just as low as his ever did.

Nixon, the unindicted, pardoned co-conspirator, who should know better, has encouraged the conspiracy thesis by his cloudy suggestions that the CIA plotted to do him in. Because the Watergate burglary was messed up by the ex-CIA personnel who tried to commit it, some of Nixon's supporters have wondered if he had been set up, if the burglars hadn't been ordered by the agency to fail so as to catch Nixon in the disaster that would consume him. If that's what happened, it was one of the greatest carom billiard shots of all time.

There is a more cosmopolitan CIA-conspiracy hypothesis. It holds that Alexander Butterfield, one of the few White House aides to know of Nixon's taping arrangements, was a CIA operative under orders from the topmost shadows in the Langley headquarters to blurt out word of the system's existence to staff investigators of the Senate Watergate Committee. Unfortunately, no believable evidence exists to support the hypothesis, but even if the CIA had conspired, the plot would have failed.

Most conspiracies do fail. They misfire because they are attempts to make up for, by clandestine manipulation, what the conspirators lack in real power. Those who can win elections or influence government actions in other, more ordinary ways don't dabble in plots. It was precisely that kind of weakness that motivated the no-account, rich-trash millionaires to sponsor the only classic type conspiracy against the United States government in modern times. The incident occurred in the early 1930s when agents from some members of the Mellon, Pew, Morgan, and other families among the very rich sought to install Marine Maj. Gen. Smedley Darlington Butler as a dictator. Butler, perhaps the most popular military hero of that epoch, was to use the American Legion as his base to force President Roosevelt to make him "secretary of general affairs," a to-be-created post that would take over the real powers of the presidency while FDR would be limited to a ceremonial role until he could be forced to resign for reasons of health. In picking General Butler, the plotters had badly misjudged their man. Far from sympathizing with the conspiracy, the old marine, who was rather favorably disposed toward the New Deal, led the conspirators on only to expose them. A congressional investigation was held. John W. McCormack, who many years later would become the Speaker of the House of Representatives, chaired the committee investigating the bizarre little affair. "Those fellows were afraid that Roosevelt would take their money away by taxes," McCormack remarked long afterward. "They were desperate and sought to take power and frighten Roosevelt into doing what they wanted. . . . If General Butler had not been the patriot he was, and if they had been able to maintain secrecy, the plot certainly might very well have succeeded, having in mind the conditions existing at the time."[1]

That apparently no serious thought was ever given to prosecuting the conspirators indicates that the potential targets of the plot thought too little of it to try to punish its perpetrators. Had the plotters been able to collect themselves to the extent of delivering a coup, they probably would have found that few of the rich would have supported them, especially in the early years of Roosevelt's administration, when much of big-time corporate capitalism looked upon the Squire of Hyde Park with some favor. Had this medley of imbeciles and eccentrics gotten

10

power, they would shortly have had to sneak out the back door of the White House for lack of any kind of support.

When Americans talk about conspiracies—the Communist conspiracy being put aside as a special case—they usually mean the conspiracy of their government against them, not dissident citizens conspiring against established authority. These aren't conspiracies, properly speaking, but what are perceived as betrayals, and in this Nixon isn't the first president to be accused, only the first to be run out of office. A significant fraction of every living generation of Americans has felt betrayed by a president. For our grandparents and great-grandparents, it was Woodrow Wilson and America's entry into the abattoir of Europe in 1917–18; for our parents it was Franklin D. Roosevelt and the 1941–45 war; for those yet younger it was Johnson/Nixon and the ten years of death in Vietnam. By 1968 when Nixon assumed office, the lifetime political experiences of many Americans had exhausted the credit of any new president. For them there was no margin of tolerance left; one gross deception and they would never forgive him.

At the 1916 Democratic National Convention at St. Louis, the keynote speaker, Martin Glynn, entertained the delegates by listing the times in American history when the country didn't respond to provocation by going to war. With each incident Glynn named, the audience would chant, "What did we do? What did we do?" And Glynn would answer back, "We didn't go to war." The next afternoon, another speaker in praise of Wilson touched off a twenty-one-minute floor demonstration by saying, "Without orphaning a single American child, without widowing a single American mother, without firing a single gun, without shedding a single drop of blood—" And that same night, the Great Commoner, William Jennings Bryan, who had earlier resigned as Wilson's secretary of state because he thought the president was taking the country to war, was invited by unanimous consent to talk to the convention. "My friends, I have differed with our President on some of the methods employed, but I join with the American people in thanking God that we have a President who does not want this nation plunged into this war,"[2] he said, and it was on that understanding that many voted for Wilson that year. When the President, or "Big Slick," as some of his disillusioned former supporters were to call him, went to Congress less than seven months after election day and asked for a declaration of war, it detonated an angry bitterness—and the last armed insurrection against the United States of America by a body of its citizens. By itself, the Green Corn Rebellion, as this revolt by poor blacks, Indians, and white sharecroppers in rural Oklahoma was called, wasn't serious enough to frighten the administration in Washington, but it serves as an indicator of how vast and how violent was the reaction by some to this war Wilson said we would be spared.

The conviction that politics is prone to be a low-life, dishonest occupation long antedates Wilson. From the inception of the Republic, Americans have loved their country and hated their government, revered the presidency and despised those who sought to occupy it. Twentieth-century politics has merely reinforced the cultural bias against the men and women who give their lives to political endeavor. Even those who supported the war can't have been unaware that what Wilson promised and what he delivered were greatly at variance; he taught those who agreed with him as much as those who didn't to listen to presidential utterances with a certain skepticism.

Within twenty-five years the nation would repeat the experience with Franklin D. Roosevelt. Once the war had started, he didn't have to contend with an organized peace party denouncing him for having gone back on his pledge that American boys would not again be sent to fight on foreign shores. Nevertheless, the feeling that the president had been less than honest, that he had tricked the electorate, was widespread if without an organized political party to express it. The belief that they had been dishonestly dealt with afflicted some, particularly those who opposed FDR for his economic policies anyway, to the point that they suspected him of conspiring to egg the Japanese into the attack on Pearl Harbor. The idea of the conspiratorial presidency had been born and it would, in the decades after

1945, change from being considered a paranoid obsession of the far right to a belief held by those of every persuasion and none.

The fear of concentrating power in Washington long predates him, but what had happened by FDR's time was that presidents had become captives of the government over which they theoretically presided. Only fitfully and episodically recognized by the office's occupants, the hedging in of the presidency has accompanied the augmentation of the central power that began back in the 1880s. From the first modern sort of intervention in the private sector, the Interstate Commerce Commission, presidents learned they would not be allowed to use the new power created by the legislative branch directly, but would have to operate through bureaus and commissions which they could manipulate and influence but not control. This government that we know so well for its expanse and expense was not suddenly called into being by the New Deal and the economic catastrophe of the early 1930s. It had been evolving and developing for decades as an answer to economic and social problems that did not yield to the nineteenth-century formula of keeping the public sector small and the private sector large and separate. The new arrangement wasn't the simple engorgement of public power in the executive branch to the cost of everyone else. Although apparently under presidential authority, the newly created federal powers were widely and intricately shared by bureaucrats and a myriad of special constituencies, a fact recognized in indignant surprise by those who exclaim that federal regulators are controlled by the regulatees. That is the way it is supposed to be, the way the system was designed. Richard Nixon didn't sufficiently appreciate that. He didn't understand that the formal powers of his office, written in the Constitution and the law, are often little more than ceremonial and can be used only when the countervailing powers in the system assent. All presidents enter the job thinking the buttons on the Oval Office desk are there to be punched at will; all but Mr. Nixon learn that the wires leading away from them have been snipped and accommodate themselves to the limitations. Mr. Nixon did not, and his downfall issued less from any illegal act he may have committed, than from a lawful use of his office that threatened to destroy a vast system of shared and intertwined political power.

Even before Watergate, many of Nixon's opponents believed he was conspiring to alter the political system. In part this was because the man who became the Milhous around America's neck was so deeply unlovable. Nixon might have said, as William Howard Taft did in 1912 when he was about to become one of the few presidents ever defeated for reelection, "I think I might as well give up so far as being a candidate is concerned. There are so many people in the country who don't like me. Without knowing much about me, they don't like me—apparently on the Dr. Fell principle . . . they don't exactly know the reason, but it is on the principle;

> " 'I don't like you, Dr. Fell,
> The reason why I cannot tell,
> But this I know and know full well,
> I don't like you, Dr. Fell.' "[3]

Taft, who was as dear a man as ever lived in the White House, did himself an injustice. Nixon, on the other hand, had to deal not only with those who disliked him instinctively, but also those who knew full well why they didn't care for this Dr. Fell. This latter group was a politically diverse crowd with as little in common as Abbie Hoffman's Yippies and the Young Americans for Freedom, a right-wing organization that regarded Nixon as little better than a Socialist. Nor did the people and groups of such variegated background and motive come together to sack Nixon because of a shared shock and indignation at his uniquely awful acts in the history of the American presidency. The Nixon people were aware that there was nothing unique about many of the things their man had done. The history of the twentieth-century presidency is laced with occurrences which might have served Nixon as precedents, but his

side didn't present their case well—not that any argument
would have saved their man from the gallows. Even in the
aftermath, pro-Nixon polemicists like Victor Lasky were so
fixated on the Kennedy clan that they couldn't get past shouting, "Look who did it first!"

In the modern era Theodore Roosevelt was probably the
president who did it first, commencing with a bit of tax-dodging
the great Rough Rider never satisfactorily explained. He was
also accused of riding roughly over other people's privacy and
resorting to political blackmail every bit as nasty as the Liddy-
Hunt proposal to trap Democratic party leaders with call girls
and hidden cameras aboard a yacht at the 1972 Miami convention. It was thought, though never proven, that Teddy was
using the Secret Service to keep track of which congressmen
were patrons of Washington's bordellos and was using the information to keep the miscreants in line on key votes. True or
not—and this was in 1908, before the day of hidden micro-
phones—enough people in Congress believed it to tack an
amendment onto a bill restricting the Secret Service activities
to catching counterfeiters and guarding the president.[4]

Nixon's problem, if we compare him to the incomparable
Teddy, may have been that he advanced his constitutional
claim to do things like impound funds appropriated by Congress in too timid and mumbling a fashion. When Roosevelt did
such things, he gloried in his disregard of due legislative process
and prerogative. There was no murmuring defensiveness such
as Nixon displayed after he'd ordered the Cambodian invasion
when the Rough Rider described how he wrenched the then
province of Panama away from the Republic of Colombia to
build his still-controversial canal:

> The Panama Canal I naturally take special interest in because
> I started it.
> There are plenty of other things I started merely because the
> time had come that whoever was in power would have started
> them. But the Panama Canal would not have started if I had not
> taken hold of it, because if I had followed the traditional or

conservative method I should have submitted an admirable state paper occupying a couple of hundred pages detailing all of the facts to Congress and asking Congress' consideration of it.

In that case there would have been a number of excellent speeches made on the subject in Congress; the debate would be proceeding at this moment with great spirit and the beginning of work on the canal would be fifty years in the future.

Fortunately the crisis came at a period when I could act unhampered. Accordingly, I took the isthmus, started the canal and then left Congress not to debate the canal, but to debate me. . . .[5]

Nixon elected to try the same thing but lost and got canned. Theodore Roosevelt and Richard Nixon are quite unalike as persons and as historical figures, but these instances illustrate something that holds for all presidents: what they get away with and succeed in accomplishing depends not on how good or bad they are, but on what else they've managed to have going for them. They put TR on Mount Rushmore because his high crimes and misdemeanors were regarded as brilliant, as visionary leadership by the majority coalition he had put himself at the head of; they put Nixon in San Clemente after his politics had failed. Like TR, Nixon built a majority coalition, a gigantic coalition, but by arrogance, inadvertence, miscalculation, and misunderstanding he built it against himself.

This answers the Nixonites' question as to why the Kennedys could get away with it unimpeached and they could not. The answer is what they were screaming at the time: it was all politics. In addition to cheating on his taxes and settling grudges by the misuse of government agencies, Nixon's policies were getting him into deeper trouble than his morals.

No one of the groups in alienated opposition to him would have been strong enough to bring down Nixon or any president. It was his ability to estrange himself from so many parts of the society that made Nixon quite remarkable. Ordinarily you can say that if a president tees off labor, he will pick up a certain stratum of business support, and if he annoys the lumber industry, he can expect to get smiles from the environmentalists.

Nixon had a way of winning enemies without getting his enemies' enemies for friends. In a crazy manner this explains the enormous variety of the names on his enemies list. By the time he was finished he'd gotten everyone—left, right, and center—down on him.

Different segments of the right lost their taste for Nixon at different times. Some never forgave him the New Economic Policy, which brought with it, besides devaluation of the currency, an act all good conservatives see as a sign of the coming decline and fall, the imposition of wage and price controls. But anyone familiar with Nixon's record knew he wasn't much of an orthodox free-market man. It was in foreign policy that so many felt he had doublecrossed them. In fact, he had told them what he would do, that he would make a rapprochement with China, long before he met Henry Kissinger. In an October, 1967, article in *Foreign Affairs* which subsequently appeared in *Reader's Digest,* Nixon wrote, "Taking the long view, we simply cannot afford to leave China forever outside the family of nations, there to nurture its fantasies, cherish its hates, and threaten its neighbors. There is no place on this small planet for a billion of its potentially most able people to live in angry isolation."[6]

In the end Nixon got the blame for recognizing Red China while Henry Kissinger got the credit for pulling off a long-overdue and necessary diplomatic triumph. The blame for the disadvantageous sale of wheat to Russia also went to old droopy-jowls, who had his membership card in the hate-commie-bait-commie club lifted, while Kissinger was recognized as the architect of peace in Vietnam. At least he was by those who considered it peace and not the first war America ever lost. Those who thought the latter tended to lay that melancholy accomplishment at RMN's feet also. Men like former Central Intelligence Agency director William Colby felt we lost the war because our fighters were stabbed in the back, much as the German general staff claimed after World War I the army hadn't lost to the enemy but to the craven civilian politicians who betrayed it from the rear. As the peaceniks and the warniks came into an ironic unity of opposition, so did a seeming infinity of other miffed interests, some small but others too powerful to alienate save at great risk.

Nixon's relations with the entire bureaucracy over which he presided were those of guerrilla warfare, with the president repeatedly saying things like "one half the time of government officials is spent writing papers to each other. . . . We have no discipline in this bureaucracy. We never fire anybody. We never reprimand anybody. We always promote the sons-of-bitches that kick us in the ass . . . we are going to quit being a bunch of God damn soft-headed managers."[7] By June of 1972 the ill-will, contempt, and anger between the head of the executive branch of government and the people who compose it was described by White House aide Michael Balzano thus: "President Nixon doesn't run the bureaucracy; the civil service and the unions do. It took him three years to find out what was going on in the bureaucracy. And God forbid if any president is defeated after the first term, because then the bureaucracy has another three years to play games with the next president."[8]

In Kissinger, Nixon had found a man who had less use for the bureaucracy than he. They shared the belief that if you want to get anything done you have to end-run the administrative and organizational structures set up to do it. Which accounts for goings-on such as happened at the Strategic Arms Limitation Treaty (SALT) conference when the chief Russian negotiator was aware of American proposals the chief American ambassador, Gerard Smith, hadn't known about himself. The Russians didn't get the information by stealing it. Nixon and Kissinger were conducting their own, private, higher-level negotiations with the Russians and not telling the State Department.[9]

But a miffed bureaucracy was not the only group that, when things went sour, refused to come to Nixon's aid. Many Republicans didn't either. Their apathy is explained in some part by Nixon's treatment of his party. As famously partisan as he could be, Nixon was more cognizant than most that you need a party to get you nominated, but getting elected is something you do on your own. "Anytime you talk Democrats versus Republicans, we lose," he once remarked. In addition, as the first president since Zachary Taylor to be elected to a first term with both houses of Congress in the other party's hands, by 1970 Nixon knew what political scientists don't, which is that it doesn't make that much difference. What a president needs is what during the 1970 elections the Nixon people called an "ideological majority." What he needed in Congress wasn't a majority of Republicans but a majority of votes, which is why he could go ahead in 1970 and quietly support Sen. Scoop Jackson of Washington and in 1972 do it again with Jim East-land of Mississippi. Presidents at least as far back as Franklin Roosevelt have done the same thing, but no president prior to Nixon made it so clear that, for the White House at least, the two parties weren't the Republicans and the Democrats but the Presidential Party and the other party, composed of some Democrats, some Republicans, and a lot of other people and other interests. As Nixon elbowed and kicked his friends and supporters out of the way in his determination to get to the gallows, the other party increasingly became the Congressional Party, the party which has nothing much in common among its members but a need and a dedication to make sure the presidency is hedged about with limitations. Under Ford and Carter, the strength of this set of antagonisms has waxed and waned, but even with the Georgia peanut farmer and the control of both ends of Pennsylvania Avenue by the same party, the struggle has not ended.

Nixon repeatedly said during the last year and subsequently from exile that he was fighting for the integrity of his office. His words have been dismissed as self-serving by a thoughtless political jury which presumes that everything which is self-serving is also false. This goes along with the idea that everything a politician says in public is either wholly not true or a misleading distortion. Even Nixon, who did far more lying in public than was good for him, spoke the truth, or some reasonable facsimile thereof, most of the time. Only people with infallible memories dare lie with any frequency, and modern public figures who are on camera so much really can't disguise themselves very successfully. Nixon, who was old-fashioned in his attempts to control when and how the TV camera might be used on him, still had to submit to a good deal of cinema-verité journalism. Hence the Nixon who so often appeared on the TV screen was not the calculated poseur he was made out to be. Who would contrive by artifice and deception to be the graceless, unappealing human who would drop into our living rooms? You can lie about specific names and dates and make up a certain number of specious arguments that even you don't believe in, but when you log as much tube time as Nixon did, the essential person and his genuine concerns must show themselves. The Nixon of the tapes and the transcripts wasn't a surprising, schizophrenic departure from the public man we'd been having to watch for years.

In part, at least, the battle he put up against Congress and the Special Prosecutor getting the goods on him was, as he said, to protect executive privilege, to keep the powers of his office intact. Not that anyone was listening. What had happened to Wall Street and the rest of that part of the business world that had backed him against the domestic radicals? Why didn't they hear and assist him? After they read the 1972 election results they may have decided the threat from the streets was over and they didn't need a Republican who twice imposed price controls. The full-page ads in the *New York Times* and the *Wall Street Journal,* which businessmen have recourse to when they have something they think is important on their minds, weren't forthcoming. Nixon's only organized support came from the Reverend Sun Myung Moon's peculiar sect of goose-stepping Baptists and a retired Orthodox rabbi from Taunton, Massachusetts. Baruch Korff's National Citizens Committee for Fairness to the Presidency was received with disbelief and sometimes with irritation by those who expect the rabbinate to keep its eyes closed and hew to Hubert Humphrey and the old New Deal.

It's impossible not to think that the refusal to help came as a reaction to what the then-Democratic Majority Leader Tip O'Neill called a "plain, old-fashioned, god damn shakedown" of businessmen for campaign money. Here's O'Neill's view of what happened to George Steinbrenner III, chairman of the American Ship Building Company, who, by the time the scandals had been concluded, had to plead guilty to two felony counts:

> . . . George Steinbrenner. He's a helluva guy. I called him up and I said, "George, old pal, what's the matter? Why don't we hear from you anymore? Is something the matter? . . ." So what does Steinbrenner say to me? He said, "Geez, Tip, I want to come to see you and tell you what's going on." And he came into my office. He said, "Gee, they are holding lumber over my head." They got him between the IRS, the Justice Department, the Commerce Department. He was afraid he'd lose his business. . . . He said Stan's [Maurice Stans, ex–Secretary of Commerce and top money-raiser for the Committee to Re-Elect the President, or CREEP] people wanted a hundred thousand dollars for Nixon's campaign. . . . I guess he had no choice. This Maurice Stans. He has to be the lousiest bastard ever to live. Now, I was getting this from all over. Guys began to come in and see me and say, "Tip, I'm having trouble with a contract. I never had trouble before. It's legitimate business. They tell me to see Stans. What can I do?" . . . I said to myself somewhere in the 1972 campaign . . . "This fellow is going to get himself impeached." The strange thing about it is that I never gave much thought to the Watergate break-in. . . . I never thought it was important. I was concentrating on the shakedown of these fellas like Steinbrenner.[10]

There was nothing strange about the Tipster's never thinking of the burglary. He'd been around; he was, in the best sense of the expression, a smart pol and he understood there had to be graver reasons than that for tossing a president. A massive and systematic shakedown of corporate America certainly would constitute one. But how big was this effort? Herbert E. Alexander of the Citizens' Research Foundation, generally considered *the* expert on campaign financing, writes,

The 1972 campaign, businessmen pointed out, had brought extraordinary pressure. It was the first campaign in memory, for example, in which solicitations were so widely made by so high a former government official as Maurice Stans, who as Secretary of Commerce had close association with many of the businessmen he was soliciting. One might have to hearken back to the days of Mark Hanna and his systematic assessment of corporations for funds in support of William McKinley for a historic parallel. . . .[11]

But in the election of 1896 all Hanna did was scare businessmen with the reminder that if the Republicans lost, William Jennings Bryan, Populism, and the excesses of the Commune of Paris would take over the executive branch. He couldn't extort money by use of the government. There was a Democratic president in the White House. A goodly number of businessmen were no less scared of George McGovern for the same reasons. Indeed it was this exaggerated fear of McGovern, the Bolshevik who was going to confiscate the property of the rich, pay everybody $1,000, and put welfare mothers up at the Holiday Inn, that helps explain the lack of interest in the Watergate burglary until after the election. Better an extortionist in the White House than a Communist. It's doubtful that many business people are possessed of this kind of cynical acumen, nor need they have been to help account for the massive disinclination in the media and elsewhere to poke around the burglary. Social psychology teaches how selective perception can be, so that until McGovern was safely defeated, people were too distracted by the threat of what he represented to look closely at Nixon's disquieting behavior.

Nixon's administration was hardly the first to use the patronage powers of the federal government to get itself reelected. That was one of the reasons for the enactment of civil-service legislation in the last quarter of the nineteenth century. Franklin Roosevelt was similarly accused of taking advantage of the much-enlarged federal government in his time for the same purposes, although he does not seem to have done so. Lyndon Johnson tried in a hit-or-miss way, but according to Jeb Stuart Magruder, who had been assigned to see what predecessor presidents had done, there was "nothing of the magnitude of the present administration's activities to use federal resources to ensure re-election."[12]

It appears that attempts were made to compile lists of government contractors and suppliers to put the bite on them. In the same way, new contracts were to be awarded to those who made contributions, if kickback is too strong a word, to the campaign. This activity was bunched together under the delightful title of the "Responsiveness Program." The language is a little murky but the meaning is clear in a memo to H. R. Haldeman from Fred Malek, an important patronage manager in the Nixon inner group, dated December, 1971, as they were cranking up plans for the campaign:

> . . . we have already initiated programs to derive greater political benefit from grants, communications, and personnel. . . . These White House directed efforts will control the key Executive Branch operations having the highest potential political payoff. In addition, we should take action to ensure that the day-to-day Departmental operations are conducted as much as possible to support the President's re-election. Since it is impossible for the White House to directly control day-to-day activities, we must establish management procedures to ensure that the Departments systematically identify opportunities and utilize resources for maximum political benefit.[13]

The records make it much less clear whether Mr. Malek was ever able to come close to mobilizing all of Washington's potential power for these unworthy objects. Many meetings were held in various departments to get the great fleecing machine rolling, but bureaucratic inefficiency is no respector of motives. It frustrates wicked intentions just as surely as it sludges up good ones.

However, contractors and corporations dependent for one reason or another on good treatment by the government can't be sure that the machinery really is rusty enough to protect them. You don't need many Steinbrenners loose in the country-club locker rooms bitching and moaning they're being blackjacked for the word to get around, and we have the Tipster telling us the word was getting around. Obviously there was a climate of intimidation that could scare businessmen even though they weren't directly threatened. The testimony of American Airlines president George Spater to the Senate Watergate Committee bears that out: " . . . most contributions from the business community are not volunteered to see a competitive advantage, but are made in response to pressure for fear of competitive disadvantage that might result if they are not made. The process degrades both the donor and the donee."[14] For men like Spater, the degradation must have been amplified by the elaborate ruses that had to be worked out to cover the trail of illegal corporate contributions. In American Airlines' case, the money had to go to the Swiss bank account of a Lebanese who then transferred it to another bank whence it was converted into cash and ultimately delivered in an unmarked envelope to the Nixon people. Contrary to their reputation in some quarters, many businessmen do think twice about breaking the law. Some of them think it's wrong, and others suffer the anguish and timidity characteristic of white-collar crime.

Executives in the same corporation have been known to fight each other over violating the election laws. Take the case with the Gulf Oil Corporation, which for many years maintained an account with the Bank of Nova Scotia in the Bahamas as a means of laundering cash to make illegal political contributions. Joseph Bounds, former executive vice-president, opposed former board chairman W. K. Whiteford until, according to a federal court document,

> in 1961, he complained to Whiteford that he did not like "the Bahamian set-up," indicating uneasiness as to his vulnerability. Whiteford told him that was what he was getting paid for and he had better do it or be fired. Bounds' discontent led to a confrontation with Whiteford in Pittsburgh on October 4, 1961. . . . At . . . the meeting at the Duquesne Club, where some spirits were consumed, Bounds . . . said he now wanted early retirement. A violent argument ensued, in the course of which Bounds, according to his account of the affair, "decked" White-

ford. The next day Whiteford told Bounds he should fire him except for the difficulty of explaining such a move to Mr. R. K. Mellon [a major stockholder].[15]

This incident long antedates Watergate, although Gulf continued violating the election laws through 1972 and had to plead guilty for it. The Bounds-Whiteford brawl, however, gives us enough of a look at what was going on in the executive suite to show that some businessmen don't think breaking the felony statutes is all in a day's work. The resentment by some at having been driven to make criminals out of themselves must have been ferocious. Others apparently wouldn't make illegal contributions even under coercion. Instead, choosing to make the legal, individual contribution, they went home and sold their wives' and families' stock to kick in money in excess of what they thought they could afford. By the time the McGovern menace had been defeated and corporate America had figured out how much it had cost and under what circumstances much of the payments had been extracted, Richard Nixon's credit must have been used up.

No holder of the modern presidency resented the limitations put around the office's formal powers and strove against them as Nixon did. Almost everybody who has written about the frog president of Watergate has made note of it. William Safire quotes Nixon's handwritten cry of despair in the margin of a memo: "govt. doesn't work."[16] Charles Colson tells this anecdote:

> One Friday afternoon early in 1970, Nixon flew into one of his angry tirades against the federal bureaucracy. For a year he had been asking for a simple executive order to create a commission to study ways to help Catholic schools. It was a campaign pledge. Several aides had been stalling on it. . . . "Chuck, I want a commission appointed now!" he told me. . . . "I ordered it a year ago and no one pays any attention. You do it. Break all the ——china in this building but have an order for me to sign on my desk Monday morning."
>
> I called the Department of Justice first; all executive orders are drafted and cleared there. But the assistant whose office

handles such things curtly told me that the department was closed for the weekend; he could not put anyone to work on it until Monday. No wonder, I thought, the president explodes in frustration. He probably thinks he's running the government.[17]

J. Anthony Lukas records some of those Nixonian explosions: "When a bureaucrat deliberately thumbs his nose, we're going to get him. . . . The little boys over in State particularly, that are against us, will do it. Defense, HEW—these three areas particularly. . . . There are many unpleasant places where civil service people can be sent. . . . When they don't produce in this administration, somebody's ass is kicked out. . . . Now, goddammit, those are the bad guys—the guys down in the woodwork."[18] Or this description of villainy baffled from Woodward and Bernstein's *The Final Days:*

> Dean complained that the IRS was not cooperating with him in his efforts to uncover damaging information about one of the contributors to the campaign of Democratic presidential candidate George McGovern. The President was outraged. "Well, goddam, they ought to give it to you," he told Dean. Nixon went on to plan how after the election he would make sure that the IRS became more cooperative. He would fire IRS Commissioner Johnnie Walters for his failure to cooperate.[19]

Actually Nixon went much further than firing the head of the IRS. He positioned himself to can every presidential appointee. It was a putsch against himself, a sort of administration-sponsored coup d'etat. It began on the morning of Wednesday, November 8, 1972, the day after Nixon's electoral Trafalgar, when the senior staff, still hung over from the victory celebrations, were marched into an 8:00 A.M. meeting where their newly elected leader told the people who were most responsible for helping him win his huge victory:

> I was reading Disraeli the other night and Disraeli spoke of how his administration of the British government lost its spark after being reelected. The campaign took too much out of them, he said. They became a "burned-out volcano" fresh out of ideas

and energy. Well ... I am not a burned-out volcano and the
second administration will not be one either. We are going to
inject new vigor and new energy into the government. . . .

With that, Nixon turned the meeting over to his Lord High
Executioner, H. R. Haldeman, who informed them,

> as the president indicated, some things are going to change
> around here. . . . The president and I are meeting with the cabi-
> net shortly. We are going to direct them to obtain written letters
> of resignation from all appointed subcabinet officers in the gov-
> ernment and submit them along with their own resignations.
> And the president has directed that everyone in this room also
> hand in a letter of resignation. . . . We just want to show we
> mean business.[20]

This act was followed up almost immediately by a number
of major changes in the cabinet that were perceived as perfidi-
ous ingratitude. In reality it was but another of a series of
attempts by Nixon and those around him to get a handle on
running the government. Four years previously RMN had
begun his troubled administration by appointing men he considered good managers. Some were also national politicians
with political power bases of their own, like former governors
Romney and Volpe of Michigan and Massachusetts. The un-
derlying assumption was that to straighten out the government,
you find good managers and then give them the authority to do
the job right. Thus Nixon, as President Carter was to do eight
years later, let his cabinet appointees pretty much pick their
subordinates.

The results were intensely unspectacular. Indeed the situation was no different than that under Lyndon Johnson as it was
described in a secret report prepared for the president by railroad executive Ben Heineman: "Top political executives—the
President and the Cabinet Secretaries—preside over agencies
which they never own and only rarely command. Their managerial authority is constantly challenged by powerful legislative
committees, well organized interest groups, entrenched bureau

chiefs with narrow program mandates, and the career civil service."[21] Under these circumstances it's hardly remarkable that cabinet secretaries tend to switch primary loyalties to their department and begin to conceive of the White House staff as the adversary.

The second try at running the government was Nixon's New Federalism. With it came revenue-sharing and other devices to take the decision-making for operational programs out of Washington and—where it wasn't possible to transfer the authority to state and local governments—at least to get "into the field," into the regional offices. While Congress was being pushed to get the feds out of local government in areas like city planning and education, it was also being invited to make some things like welfare a national responsibility. The feds would get out of every area where a lesser level of government could do the work better, and would concentrate on those things that were regarded as national by nature.

Revenue-sharing came into existence, but for the most part decentralization didn't work. The middle-level federal civil-service managers to whom authority was being moved proved to be more rigid, more rule-bound, and even less venturesomely creative than their sludgy counterparts dozing back on the seat of government. Nixon tried a third time. He proposed to Congress the reorganization of government into four super-cabinet agencies, Human Resources, Community Development, Rural Resources, and Economic Affairs. At the same time, Nixon began to move administratively in the opposite direction. A beefed-up White House staff—in which a profusion of task forces, committees, working groups, and councils flourished like germs in a dirty toilet—assumed the look of an antibureaucracy, a left-handed mirror-image bureaucracy on the other side of the black hole of government. As more of the routine nonsense of administration had to be cleared through the appropriate antibureaucrat in the White House, more time was left to civil-service underlings to develop and shape policy. By taking more control, the White House actually had less of it.

Come the end of his first term, Nixon and Ehrlichman, who was the President's closest collaborator in domestic matters, were ready for another try. If the Congress showed no interest in the super-cabinet idea, Nixon would go ahead and do it de facto. Secretary of Agriculture Earl Butz became the super-secretary for Natural Resources, likewise Caspar Weinberger of HEW for Human Resources, James Lynn of HUD for Community Development, and the Treasury's George Shultz for Economic Affairs. By impounding appropriated money and using the latent statutory authority vested in the executive branch, it seemed the federal machine might have an effective governor slipped onto it. All that was needed was to put loyal, trustworthy people who understood and sympathized with the White House into the higher subordinate positions of department and agency. Thus the demand for the resignations.

The wholesale collecting of all those slips of paper was one of those we-mean-business gestures that Nixon and his people used, causing more alarm in others than progress for themselves. Taken with other steps Nixon was pursuing, the threat of the personnel changes came near to causing a panic. Writing after the fall, a panel of the National Academy of Public Administration implied that it would have been curtains for democratic government had Nixon been able to carry out what he was trying to do:

> The U.S. government would be run like a corporation—or at least a popular view of the corporate model—with all powers concentrated at the top and exercised through appointees in the President's office and loyal followers placed in crucial positions in the various agencies of the Executive Branch. . . . No one can guess how close the American government would be to this hierarchical model had not Watergate exposures halted the advance towards it—at least temporarily.[22]

If the chief executive isn't to place his "loyal followers" in crucial positions, where does he place them? In insignificant jobs of no power and importance?

The hierarchical model that the National Academy warned against and Nixon strove for to the degree that he sought to place power in the president's hands isn't ipso facto unconstitutional. It would be a change, however, from the office as it is now, with its decidedly limited powers to run the branch of government over which it reigns but often doesn't rule. The American system is a highly centralized but not unified system. It is made up of isolated, centralized segments which are remarkably impervious to any attempt to integrate them into a larger plan of activities. The honeycomb of agencies, administrations, bureaus, and commissions, frequently presided over by officials the president hires but can't fire, was erected by men who understood how such structures confined the man in the White House. In this manner the government could provide a high degree of centralization to control an industry like railroading and yet be unable to use that centralized power for any purpose wider and beyond the industry.

Centralization of the parts without unity of the whole has served industry groups, unions, and others with narrowly particular interests well. So the consternation at what Nixon was trying extended to every organized group living in harmony with its own set of agencies and bureaucracies. From cattle grazers in happy symbiosis with the Bureau of Land Management to teachers' organizations resonating as one with the U.S. Commissioner of Education, this meant that the president was changing his role to policy maker and manager from his traditional one of mediator and umpire. That would be alarming in any president, because all of them, Nixon included, always claim to represent all the people—and therefore, with a very different and generalized constituency, they are liable to regard industry-agency relationships as wrong-headedly parochial.

Nixon couldn't live with a definition of the presidency which in some ways made the occupant of the office a Mikado, an all-glorious, omnipotent personage who in a technical sense has vast formal power, but in reality can't use it. To a degree, every modern president has been vexed by the contradiction of taking blame for the conduct of a huge bureaucracy over which he has been given slight and inexact control. Moreover, it's hard to accept the political actuality when you are being incessantly told that you are the most powerful man in the world. You are expected to figure out for yourself that most of the time the Omnipotent President, while not exactly reduced to the hollow ignominy of the Doges of Venice, resembles the chairman of the board in that he guides, cajoles, scowls, smiles, blesses, condemns, and casts the tie-breaking vote to resolve arguments between disputants of roughly equivalent power. Thus even a Lyndon Johnson, who comes down to us in memory as an arm-twisting power boy, was a consensus president who generated a feeling of exceptional power insofar as he was able to create coalitions to support him. In his minutes of maddest imperial delirium LBJ never did anything to alarm so many and win so few as Nixon did when he careened off in his final attempt to train the executive branch to bit and bridle.

In proceeding as he did, Nixon threatened nearly every organized interest, when in fact he had nothing so drastic in mind. He was already fighting on too many fronts with the liberals, the antiwar people, the win-the-war people, the Pentagon, and the resentful segment of corporate America when he stirred up the remaining animals in the forest. Even if he had been wise enough to take on government reorganization at a time when the part of the nation with no interest in the question was content, Nixon probably would have lost. The last attempt at a restructuring of similar magnitude and purpose was Franklin Roosevelt's. Nixon hoped to succeed with his reorganization on the strength of his huge 1972 victory. That's why he began trying to implement it just hours after the ballot-counting was done, but Nixon's political power in 1972 was as nothing next to Roosevelt's in 1937. True, Nixon had carried all but one state in the Union while FDR's opponent had managed to win two in 1936, but FDR had a Congress that was better than two-to-one Democratic. Moreover, loyalty to a president of the same party was greater then and, what is more important, the coattail effect was still in working order forty years ago. A number of the members of the Democratic majority owed their election to the Roosevelt landslide. FDR was stronger than Nixon in other ways, not the least of which was his superiority as a practitioner of the political arts.

Yet FDR, the Babe Ruth, or shall we say Hank Aaron, of American politics, lost his reorganization bill in the FDR-controlled House 204 to 196. At the time it was said that if FDR or his managers on the hill had done this or that, the bill might have been saved, but it's probably not so. Everybody was against it. The president of the AFL—there was no CIO yet—attacked one of its main provisions as giving "autocratic dictatorial authority." The goo-goo reformers were against it because they thought it weakened civil service. Groups like the New York Chamber of Commerce objected because it would give the president "such tremendous control over the economic and social activities of the people of this Nation that it would be only a short step to dictatorship, and a form of government similar to that prevailing under the Communist, fascist or Nazi systems." Father Coughlin, the Roman Catholic radio priest from Detroit whose national following in the early and middle thirties was probably exceeded only by Huey Long and FDR himself, said the spirit of the bill was "the spirit of centralization of power, the spirit of perpetuating a needless emergency, the spirit of defeatism."

The way to stop FDR was to have "modern Paul Reveres" get on their steeds and betake themselves to Washington. Several thousand middle-class souls from the Atlantic-coast cities took the adjuration literally and rode to Washington to exercise their right of protest. The group from Boston was led by Paul Revere's great-great-granddaughter. The sentiments of the protestors and many others who agreed but didn't make the trip were probably summed up by the marcher who said, "I see no reason why Congress should give the President powers of a Julius Caesar."[23] Reports to the contrary about the imperial presidency notwithstanding, no Congress ever has permitted it, and when one president at length was foolish enough to look like Caesar, he was promptly kicked out of office.

Roosevelt, who knew when to settle for what he could get, accepted a vastly adulterated bill and went on to other things. The final Roosevelt government reorganization left the presidency in pretty much the shape Jimmy Carter found it. Our traditional fear of a too-strong executive had worked its will and the United States was stuck with the governmental paraphernalia people have been railing against ever since. That hasn't led, however, to any shift in opinion. Present-day Congresses are no more likely to revamp and reorder the regulatory agencies than they were in Roosevelt's day. Instead we seek to see if we can do without regulation by relying on the hope that free-market competition can do what commissioners, boards, and hearing officers cannot.

With his drive to capture control of the executive, Nixon succeeded in alienating, if not frightening into deep hostility, almost all the groups in the country which are the substance and sustenance of our politics. With little more than a coterie of Hollywood stars to throw up the appearance of support, a friendless Nixon would have to rely solely on the formal, legal powers of his office to keep himself going. The English equivalent of what Nixon was attempting would be if a prime minister, after losing a vote of confidence in the House of Commons, tried to stay in office and govern. The analogy is inexact, but it suggests something of what it means to exercise the authority of an office with only the legalities.

Even the Pentagon, which in theory is under total presidential control in his role of commander-in-chief, rebelled. In his book *Nightmare: The Underside of the Nixon Years*, J. Anthony Lukas describes what happened:

> . . . as demonstrated by the public skepticism toward the October 1973 [Middle East] alert—the country might no longer trust the President if the time came when military force had to be used. Over at the Pentagon, this problem had already occurred to Defense Secretary Schlesinger. Determined to stay in Washington until the Presidential crisis had been resolved, he gave orders that the armed forces were to accept no commands from the White House without his countersignature. This would protect not only against the President's starting a war somewhere to distract attention from the events at home but against the use of any military unit in the domestic power struggle.[24]

So far as it's known, Schlesinger's subordinates in the Pentagon, civilian and military, acquiesed in this usurpation of the commander-in-chief's prerogative without demur. There was reason enough for the Pentagon to aid in any little way the bureaucracy could in greasing the chutes for Nixon. Despite his reputation as a mildly psychotic anti-Communist warrior, RMN had been niggardly in delivering new hardware. Melvin Laird, Nixon's first and longest-tenured Secretary of Defense, didn't do what most cabinet appointees do when taking office, which is to march off and become the principal spokesman for their bureaucracies. As John Ehrlichman said of the high-level appointees to the departments and agencies, "We only see them at the annual White House Christmas party; they go and marry the natives."[25] During a period when the proportion of the federal government's budget devoted to arms expenditures was going down,[26] Laird chose not to play the role of the protesting ambassador from the Pentagon to the White House. To the brass it must also have seemed that Nixon was thinking of taking over in an unprecedented operational sense when he jumped his creature, Alexander Haig, over 240 more senior men to make the one-time Kissinger protégé a four-star general and army vice chief of staff. Lower levels of expenditures are one thing—the military realizes as well as everybody else that its appropriations are contracyclical, to be held down in good times and kicked up in poor ones, as happened when Ford and the recession reached the White House about the same time—but promoting men to the top who owed more to the president than to the military bureaucracy was more serious, especially when coupled with the pursuit of policies the Pentagon and its supporters didn't believe were in the national interest. China, SALT, and detente may have seemed little better than word games to segments of the lib-lab left but it looked like national suicide to significant portions of the right.

Nixon's position was uniquely weak. Even the last couple of years of Herbert Hoover's administration weren't comparable. Unpopular as Hoover was in the country at large, the man retained the goodwill and the cooperation of many important political groups, including the Democratic leadership in the House of Representatives, almost till the day he took his bitter automobile ride up Pennsylvania Avenue with Franklin Roosevelt.

But Nixon's enemies still needed an instrument with which to attack him. That was Watergate, and that also explains why Watergate, generally accepted as the third-rate burglary attempt the White House said it was in June and July of 1972, became a thunderous source of scandal and shame eight months later in March, 1973. By March, Nixon had finished his work of surrounding himself with hostiles, and they, profoundly convinced this was a battle to maintain their own power and place in the society, were looking for a weapon.

As early as August, 1969, a *Washington Star* gossip columnist was speculating about where Nixon got the money he was conspicuously spending. "But," writes J. Anthony Lukas, "not until the summer of 1973 did the persistent reporters and congressional investigators begin asking seriously where Nixon got all that money while serving as President."[27] Since investigators rarely are able to learn anything by investigating they were helped by leaks on every imaginable subject detrimental to the president. The story of how the judge presiding over the Ellsberg trial, W. Matthew Byrne, Jr., was offered the directorship of the FBI got out with its implication that in return the judge was to suppress information about the Plumbers' burglary of Ellsberg's psychiatrist's office; more astounding was the leak to the *Providence Journal* by an IRS employee of data on Nixon's tax returns. Heretofore the blueprints for America's ICBMs were less closely held than a president's tax returns; the Government Services Administration, which knows how to be as dense as untreated sewage when it cares to be, began giving out quick and accurate answers to how much government money had been spent at San Clemente and for what. The bureaucracy was fighting back in the way it always does against insubordinate superiors. It was leaking, but everybody and everything in Washington was leaking on Nixon, whose spokesman, the comical Ron Ziegler, bewailed, lamented, and denounced what was happening to his presidential master. Under other circumstances this huge spillage of quasi-confidential information would have caused much consternation but now the rules were in suspension.

Civil libertarians who otherwise would have been shocked into presentations of amicus curiae briefs waited until after the fact to criticize Judge John Sirica's performance as a black-robed avenging angel, threatening long sentences on the indicted Waterburglars unless they squealed. One of them, James McCord, broke and wrote Sirica the letter implicating higher-ups. If that same letter had been written under other circumstances, nobody would have paid any attention to it. McCord had no personal knowledge of higher-ups ordering the Watergate job; he had hearsay. Sirica took this one seriously because, if it didn't mean much in law, it meant a great deal in politics. It was a quasi-confirmation that there were indeed goods to be gotten on Nixon, and it cleared the way for McCord's testimony before the Ervin Senate Watergate Committee, where hearsay was not only admissible but solicited for national television.

None of this goes to exculpate Richard Nixon. Nor is it so important to stop and wonder at the use of foul means to expose yet fouler deeds. What it does show is the process by which those with the motives unhorsed a president. Since they never concerted together, they never understood that their resistance to him would bring about his impeachment. The imperial, ascendent presidency is a basic axiom of our politics, and the men and women who shot Nixon down believed in it every bit as much as Nixon. As the defiance of individuals and groups signaled other individuals and groups that they could do the same, it slowly and then more rapidly became apparent that they could not only checkmate this president but remove him. Men began to talk about redressing the balance between the executive and legislative branches, about using Nixon's fall as a means to be sure no future president would be so ambitious. Congress, the home of the specialized constituency and the particularized interest group, would give political meaning to this struggle by ensuring its primacy.

If the presidency isn't quite the imperial office it's depicted, it's not without considerable power, some of which rests on the reverential respect so many Americans have for it. Only a rage could energize and embolden the people in the society, who have the greatest need in ordinary times to encourage this respect, to move personally against the office's occupant and drive him into exile. The Nixon tapes supplied the nutrition to feed the rage. Had the existence of these recordings come to light under another president, Johnson or Kennedy for example, it's inconceivable that either Congress or the other upper-stratum people demanding the public playing of the tapes would have done so. They might have tut-tutted, viewed with alarm, and pointed in dismay, but they would never have considered the publication of verbatim transcripts of Oval Office conversations. When, at length, the bowdlerized and misleadingly edited version was published, one of the responses was to demand more and better. Another was to express indignation at four-letter scatology in the Presidential Palace. From the scalded reaction you couldn't tell whether Richard Nixon had defiled the office of president or of pope. Whereas admirers of foul-mouthed chief executives from Jackson through Lincoln to Johnson had described them as warm, earthy masters of their native American vernacular, Nixon was conceived as a man who had done doo-doo on his oath of office by saying poo-poo inside the White House. The bonfires of self-righteousness were kindled. What was too derogatory or tasteless to be printed or put on the air was loudly spoken. The man was a drunk and a homosexual, and he was guilty of everything from disloyalty to the Republican Party to serving pickled baby toes as a canapé at cocktail parties.

As the attack mounted, Nixon hid and cringed. From time to time his people would try to counter allegations that he'd used agencies like the FBI for political purposes with the assertion he wasn't the first president to have done so, but brain fire had got hold of his growing number of detractors. In truth, peacetime surveillance of unorthodox political groups begins in 1920 with FBI infiltration of the American Civil Liberties Union.[28] The spying went on for fifty years during which time hundreds if not thousands of people who helped the organization had official smudges put on their reputations by being included in the bureau's records. This enemies list included everyone from Supreme Court Justice Felix Frankfurter, Jane Addams, and Clarence Darrow to Pearl Buck, John Dos Passos, and Theodore Dreiser.

Nor was the FBI spying secret. Nixon's attackers in Congress and the press took the position that invasions of civil rights by the FBI and other agencies were a shocking surprise, and that one of the unattended fruits of the Watergate scandals was the long-delayed revelations of these indefensible activities. As a political theatricale, the performance was well received, but like so much drama it was more fiction than fact. The victims knew what was happening to them, and from Roger Baldwin, the head of the ACLU, who began protesting in the 1920s right through the labor movement, the civil-rights movement, the anti–Vietnam war movement, and the women's movement, the complaints had been loud and the evidence to back them up had been persuasive. On March 8, 1971, antiwar people broke into the FBI office in Media, Pennsylvania, where they stole documentary proof that it was the policy of this federal agency to harass dissenters and break up their organizations. Xeroxes of this material were sent to newspapers and broadcasters, but there was no inclination to make a big thing out of the matter. Nor was this the first time in recent decades the mass media chose not to follow up on incontrovertible evidence that the government was violating people's civil liberties to destroy them politically. In the early 1960s, FBI agents, showing their official identification, contacted a number of news executives and offered them transcripts of what purported to be the conversation carried on by Dr. Martin Luther King, Jr., at a sex orgy. Nothing appeared in the public prints. At the time editors said it was to save Dr. King from embarrassment. Even so, you would think, if civil liberties were a matter of such concern, that

editors with a voluntary confession from the FBI would have
begun investigations of who else was being similarly victimized.
Nor was it just the media who understood that it was federal
policy to fudge on the Bill of Rights. A former assistant director
of the FBI, Quinn Tamm, has explained how J. Edgar Hoover
kept the appropriate committee of the House of Representatives
apprised of his bureau's illegal activities: "Every time that Mr.
Hoover went before the House Appropriations Committee on
off-the-record discussions, not on-the-record discussions, he
told the House Appropriations Committee, then headed by
Congressman Rooney—everything that the FBI was doing. He
was proud of his black bag jobs, wiretaps, the information that
he was getting. The Presidents knew about it. . . ."[29]

Thus some of the railing against Nixon must have been hy-
pocrisy; some of it, however, was more than likely out of the
mouths of people who had put aside all remembrance of their
complicity in similar acts. The newspaper editors, who were so
disturbed over revelations of attempts by Nixon to use the IRS
to get his opponents, probably really had forgotten the American press has been advocating the use of the IRS to catch
otherwise untouchable and unpopular persons since the late
1920s and the demands that Al Capone be put away. For fifty
years, when the government has been unable to get you any
other way, it's been able to get you with the IRS.

But that was different. That was gangsters or labor leaders
or Communists. And the people who said that was different
were perfectly correct. The difference, though, was that for the
first time in this century, at least, a president had not merely
lost the trust and confidence of the ruling classes, but was, if not
at war with them, something close to it. A president was threatening to use the huge powers of the executive branch against
them, not just against the social and political pariahs. Thus a
move was on, by White House inspiration, to take away the
license of a televison station owned by the *Washington Post,* a
newspaper whose owners and managers had, heretofore, always
been close supporters of each successive president and the government policies associated with them. What neither the *Post*

nor Nixon knew was that Nixon didn't have the power to lift the license. Dean Burch, Nixon's appointee as chairman of the Federal Communications Commission, doesn't serve at the president's pleasure. The position was created to make it difficult for the White House to control it, and Burch, though he remained a Nixon loyalist to the last hour, never allowed his agency to be used as an instrument of intimidation against the businesses it regulated. At that time, though, people imagined the White House's power as being next to infinite. It would have been inconceivable to most knowledgeable Washington people that an agency like the FBI was so bureaucratic, so independent, and so insubordinate that the president had to create his own amateur sleuth organization—the clownish Plumbers—to get his skullduggery done.

Some of the violence and near unanimity of the upper-class reaction to Nixon in his last year in office undoubtedly came from overestimating his power. That was natural enough. *He* certainly overestimated it, but beyond that, Americans are brought up to hate and fear Caesarism and to suspect it of every president. Nixon was doubly frightening because he was seen as the usurping despot, the tyrannical man on the horse which our political culture has terrified itself with for the better part of two centuries.

Neither side understood that the apparent power of the American presidency was a reflection of the power of the very groups and interests which broke with Nixon. A few political scientists could see how the office's occupants were dependent on a consensus for their ability to act. But our presidents had been so representative of and tied to the institutions and groups which provide their power that it had never occurred to anyone a Nixon would come along and so separate himself from his indispensible base.

Our upper circles of power and policy-making, as well as millions of lesser Americans, exalted the presidency because it exalted them. If he were the most powerful man on earth, then we were the most powerful people. With the military stalemate in South Vietnam, the term "imperial presidency" was coined and made to appear the perversion of the three men who lived in the White House during the 1960s. If there was any empire, we had nothing to do with it. That was the emperor violating American traditions and values.

Nixon has been seen as the last and the worst of this aberrant line, but a number of his immediate predecessors have had to suffer in reputation with him. Johnson's name was already in poor repute when Nixon was administered the oath of office, and John Kennedy is getting the business now with the revelations about his mistresses, his acquaintances with the gamier sort of Hollywood star, his manner of speech and mode of thought which we're now told wasn't so much different from Nixon's, not to mention assassination attempts against Castro and plots against other foreign leaders. But it needs something close to deliberate forgetfulness and the most distorted selection of the facts to picture Americans as sweet innocents tricked by the small band of the Best and the Brightest immediately around Kennedy. Not only was Kennedy's military adviser, Gen. Maxwell Taylor, a loud proponent of America using "counterinsurgency" to deal with "brushfire wars," i.e. Vietnam; he had even written a book attacking the more static Eisenhower approach to these matters. For the mass of people who don't read volumes like Taylor's *The Uncertain Trumpet*, there were movies and television programs aplenty justifying murder, assassination, intrigue, perfidy, and treachery as legitimate tools in furthering America's mission of freedom, to use the kind of expression so popular in the period. Specific acts of bloodshed had to remain hidden for reasons of state, but as the James Bond movies and scores and scores more attest, the fact that we did such things was known, approved, and praised.

The three presidents of the sixties did not act alone but in accordance with the political, though not necessarily with the formal, structure of their office, which does seem to permit enormous latitude of action. When the last of the three actually tried acting alone, he was decapitated. When things started to go bad, however, all of them came in for the retrospective blame of taking too much on themselves.

Every president has come in for his share of the blame and sometimes more, but presidents in the past had their defenders too. Even in a country which has regarded the city of Washington as suspect ever since the day Pierre L'Enfant laid it out, the universally low opinion of modern presidents is surprising. Harry Truman is the only man to live in the White House since 1933 who currently enjoys anything like popularity. Eisenhower is ignored while Franklin Roosevelt and his New Deal are perceived as what turned an equitable and serviceable government into a tyrannical bureaucracy, did mortal injury to the free-enterprise cornucopia, made budget deficits fashionable, caused inflation to be added to death and taxes, established the snooping, prying, regulating, rule-making, buttinsky system, that is to say, installed Big Brother in Washington and set 1984 as the year of extinction of American liberties.

Such a view fits well with the national belief that the American golden age is in the past. The present may be the zenith of American power, the time of the planet-embracing colossus, but the golden age of the individual, of the free-market Eden, of leafy streets and the squeak of screen door and creak of porch swing in the summer night—that America, so largely imaginary, is the one we want to return to.

In this tale of innocence lost, the president has played the serpent's role; he is the devil who made America un-American. The belief that evil ones walked about is an old one, going back, as it does, to the geographical remoteness of foreign enemies and the nineteenth-century suspicion of and hostility to the politics and culture of immigrant millions. What's novel is the transference of this feeling to the state. The government is the enemy, the governors are the traitors, not to favor a foreign power or ideology, but to foster the subversion and destruction of native American values for power and paranoia, for Big Brother and Franz Kafka.

As the personifications of government, presidents are made to bear the blame for the asphyxiating official intrusion into the once-enchanted garden. But presidents, be they devious or forthright, proud or humble, witty or dour, facile or thumb-tongued, feel the same way. Presidents are Americans too, and they think very much as most other Americans do about Big Brother, Big Government, and Big Bureaucracy. Franklin D. Roosevelt, whose name and whose administration have come to be thought of as the father of everything Americans despise and fear about their government, was as frustrated and defeated as a taxpayer unable to get a straight answer out of IRS. "The Treasury," Roosevelt said, trying to get action out of the inert structure which he theoretically administered,

> is so large and far-flung, and ingrained in its practices that I find it almost impossible to get the action and results I want—even with Henry [Morgenthau, Jr.] there. But the Treasury is not to be compared with the State Department. . . . But the Treasury and the State Department put together are nothing as compared with the Na-a-vy. The admirals are really something to cope with—and I should know. To change anything in the Na-a-vy is like punching a feather bed. You pound it with your right and you pound it with your left until you are finally exhausted and then you find the damn bed just as it was before you started punching.[30]

But this same man punched larger featherbeds than that. The Navy Department was as nothing compared to the National Recovery Administration of the early 1930s, which saw the government, at the behest and design of important elements in big business, try to take bureaucratic hold of the entire economy and administer it out of the Great Depression. FDR neither campaigned for nor wanted such a thing, but presidents, like the rest of us, mostly have to succumb.

In the past eighty years, a progression of them have had to look at a recurring set of similar problems; the attempted solutions for these problems never issued from the presidents themselves, seldom from the parties they represented, but mostly from an evolving consensus of ideas and outlooks in the society's major power configurations. Thus a glorious disaster like the National Recovery Administration wasn't a child of FDR's paternity, nor particularly that of the men closest around him, and certainly not of the Democratic Party's. That deformed brat of political economy reflected a plausible development in the stream of experiments, ad hoc attempts, logical solutions, and long-odds gambles by the nation's leadership groups to find a measure of stability and prosperity for our kind of technological, corporate capitalism. Outlandish efforts like the NRA come to be equated with the presidents in whose administrations they occur, but the growth and elaboration of the mega-institution pushed, drove, controlled, and guided presidents quite as much as it did lesser people.

Part 2

You know, the only trouble with capitalism is capitalists; they're too damn greedy.

Herbert Hoover

2

The NRA: Mobilizing America

The lead on the *New York Times*'s front page for September 1, 1933, would be read with a bit of irony today. Below a headline which told the world, ROOSEVELT SAILS PAST THE CITY AS HARBOR CRAFTS TOOT, the paper reported that "President Roosevelt sailed past most of Manhattan Island last evening aboard Vincent Astor's yacht, the *Nourmahal,* on his way to Washington to take charge of the national recovery campaign." Fashions in poverty-fighting change as they do in most else. In the early 1930s, consumption, spending money, even by paddling around on a millionaire's yacht, wasn't regarded as a tasteless indifference to the poor but as helping to spend our way out of the Great Depression.

In the fall of 1933 nobody knew it was the Great Depression yet, and that even after FDR had spent two full terms in the White House, millions would still be out of work. Nevertheless, it was the most serious bottom of the business cycle since the early 1890s, bad enough so that for the first time there was broad agreement across party lines that the federal government should do something to stop it. That something was the national recovery campaign that FDR was sailing off to take charge of. The country agreed with the new president who repudiated

the theory that the periodic slowing down of our economic machine is one of its inherent peculiarities—a peculiarity which we must grin, if we can, and bear because if we attempt to

tamper with it we shall cause even worse ailments. . . . This
attitude toward our economic machine requires not only greater
stoicism, but greater faith in immutable economic law and less
faith in the ability of man to control what he has created than
I, for one, have.[1]

People were of no mind to wait out the misery, not only
because by the fall of 1933 this recession was already longer and
more severe than most, but also because there was a new conviction that the nation, through the federal government, could
mobilize the society in a total way to accomplish almost anything. That idea was, as much as the League of Nations, the
legacy of the Great War. By the 1970s, only those of advanced
years were old enough to remember a federal government
which did not commandeer the nation when it was thought
necessary. Sixty years ago centralized power, coordination, and
planning were words coupled with the values of efficiency and
prosperity. The First World War—the Great War, as they
called it—confirmed what marvels the concentration of power
could perform. Looking back from the vantage point of the late
twenties or early thirties, it appeared that it was by these better
and more rational ways of organizing people, machines, and
markets that America had become the arsenal and the granary
for the Entente Powers and victory.

By today's standards of the near-totalitarian power Washington assumes in a crisis situation, the Wilson administration's centralization was flawed, spasmodic, and dependent on
volunteer cooperation to a degree unthinkably dangerous in
an emergency now. However, compared to the Civil or Spanish-
American wars, it was a new era which taught many to think
the lessons learned in war could be applied in peace. Lincoln
fought his war without a Department of Justice to codify,
classify, and control all manner of antiwar subversives; more
crippling, he had no central national bank by which the financial structure of the nation could be put to the service of
war as Wilson could later use the Federal Reserve Board. The
Wilsonians had put schools, agriculture, news, entertainment,

transportation, everything in service to the state, and it had worked.

The men who learned government in the Wilson administration came back to power in time to be confronted by an economic catastrophe which appeared to them as grave as the war they'd brought the country through a decade earlier. Herbert Hoover served under Wilson as the food czar, and next to the president himself emerged from the war the best-known and most-respected civilian hero. Franklin Roosevelt was assistant secretary of the Navy under Wilson and even more impressed by what the war had shown government might get done when it galvanized the country as it did in 1917. "It is important that we should again explore the possibilities of what William James called 'the moral equivalents' of war," wrote Rexford Tugwell, one of FDR's most pro–national-planning, anticapitalist economic advisors. "The ordeal of war brings out the magnificent resources of youth. . . . The ordeal of depression ought to try your mettle in similar ways. The feeling which shook humanity during the War and which after the War reshaped the entire civilization of mighty nations is called for again."[2]

By 1977 when Jimmy Carter got around to using the moral-equivalent-of-war phrase to sell his energy program, the thrill of crisis-created togetherness was not what it once was. Back then in the twenties and early thirties, the long, bureaucratic bad dream of the western world was just beginning; the new government in Russia could still look like a pretty good idea to non–Party members and nonfanatics; it was only a few years before that Kafka had written his books and fewer yet were the number of people who appreciated the fact that they were prophecy. Now we accept each new call to stifle our individuality in the mobilization for the common good with common misgivings and a dragging heart. There were those in the early 1930s who felt the same way about the antidepression mobilization, but not so many and not so loud. "What does a democracy do in a war?" asked Al Smith, the conservative 1928 Democratic presidential candidate. "It becomes a tyranny, a despot, a real monarch. In the World War we took our Constitution, wrapped it up and laid it on the shelf, and left it there until it was over."[3] Alf Landon, the man who would be the GOP candidate opposing FDR in 1936, was ready to enroll in the fight on Al Smith's terms: "If there is any way in which a member of that species, thought to be extinct, a Republican governor of a mid-western state, can aid in the fight, I now enlist for the duration."[4]

Barron's magazine, a conservative organ of business that would normally choke before it printed such words declared,

> Of course we all realize that dictatorships and even semi-dicta-
> torships are quite contrary to the spirit of American institutions
> and all that. And yet—well, a genial and light-hearted dictator
> might be a relief from the pompous futility of such a Congress
> as we have recently had. . . . So we return repeatedly to the
> thought that a mild species of dictatorship will help us over the
> roughest spots in the road ahead.[5]

Those almost insouciant words appeared in February, 1933, just a month before FDR took the oath of office. In him *Barron's* got their genial, light-hearted, indeed even jaunty dictator. Only such a predisposition to follow if somebody would lead can explain the invention and passage of the National Industrial Recovery Act, which in its own way was as wacky as prohibition. Prohibition is a lot wackier to us than it was to the Americans who regarded it as a way of fighting "the whiskey trust," a business whose product was considered as socially beneficent as we consider heroin. In like manner, the National Industrial Recovery Act appears insanely ambitious and the gravest, if craziest, menace to personal liberty, but both are but an elaboration on a theme of social and economic policy we still play.

The right and the duty of the government to supervise and direct the population's use of pleasure drugs, be they whiskey, tobacco, or LSD, was as unchallenged then as it is now. Prohibition against liquor has been dropped because it can't be enforced; prohibition against heroin is still believed to be enforceable. The debate in these matters is over tactics only. In the same way, the National Industrial Recovery Act represented the most dramatic and inclusive government intervention in the free market—World War I aside—America had ever attempted, but the principle wasn't new and has never been abandoned in practice. By the early 1930s, major groups in American capitalism had long been convinced the free market was too risky for large investors. FDR and the National Recovery Administration must be seen as but one of a series of attempts by business primarily, but by others as well, to rectify the misfires and misdirections of the free-enterprise system without damaging or impinging on the property and wealth of the system's largest stockholders.

In the 1890s William McKinley was proposing government intervention in the maritime industry with subsidies for shipbuilders. The idea that tax money should be given away in such manner was considered mildly outrageous, but what McKinley was looking at was what the heads of railroads, oil, steel, and other industries were recognizing throughout the whole pre–World War I era: the free market didn't work, at least not in their interest. These men had no particular love of government intervention, but what they were seeking was protection against the kind of unchecked competition that would put them out of business. Railroads, steel, and oil tried, as we will see, to save themselves by playing around with various forms of monopoly, but as these efforts failed, some sooner and some later, they came to the government for shelter against the storms and uncertainties of laissez faire. They still huddle in the lee of government power, clamoring for subsidies with McKinley and Carter and the shipping industry, and with McKinley and Carter and the steel industry; or they want to be saved by regulation or by tax incentives or by being allowed to operate as a legal monopoly or, all else failing, by public prayer conducted by the chaplain of the United States Senate.

The present edifice of state capitalism has come about through seven successive decades of experimentation, adjustment, and ad hoc jerry-building. By looking at some of these attempts, by seeing why they were mounted as they were and what was retained and what was abandoned, we can come to a better understanding of the workings and reasons for our own, contemporary political economy. The National Industrial Recovery Act is a good place to start because with its passage America passed, temporarily and uncertainly to be sure, into an economy planned and run by big business.

The legislation itself contained several disparate elements. A section of the bill mandated a countercyclical public-works program of the sort we still rely on when the business indicators commence to drop, but the memorable part of it gave the president the power to license any and every business in the country as a way of enforcing their adherence to the fair business practices which would bring us out of the depression. These business practices were called industrial codes, and in theory, at least, there was to be one for each industry; in fact there were hundreds, prescribing prices, wages, market shares, sales practices, the quality of products, and the quality of the working conditions under which they were made. "As one instance out of scores, the manufacturers of egg beaters and bird cages were not put under the Wire Code, but had separate codes of their own," wrote George Creel, who during World War I had served Wilson as chairman of the Committee on Public Information.[6] By the terms of the bill, America's entire industrial economy was put under federal control in an attempt to push prices up by regulation in very much the same way that, under other circumstances, Washington tries to prevent them from going up. The desired direction is opposite the one we're used to, but regardless of which way the arrows point, the problems are similar. You can have a black market under price minimums just as you can have under price maximums. Hence the major reason for codes was to eliminate *under*selling one's competitors by paying one's labor less, offering rebates, or doing anything that would lessen costs. It was hoped by these devices to keep profits and wages up, thereby keeping purchasing power up, and so end the Depression.

The means chosen for this endeavor—which far outstripped the administrative capacity of the federal government circa

1933 or even now—was the organizational apparatus used during World War I. The old War Industries Board, which attempted to plan, schedule, and coordinate the flow of material of every sort through industry committees, was reconstituted and set up again. World War I's dollar-a-year volunteer business executives were back to man the hundreds of committees and draw up the codes with a representative of labor and another from that amorphous body of humans known as the consumer, that trimember holy family of politics—management, labor, and the public—which has been the formula ever since.

The idea of the law, and the National Recovery Administration it spawned, wasn't FDR's, although it became the most important piece of legislation in those first hundred days. The basic idea for the National Industrial Recovery Act—that every industry be allowed immunity from the antitrust laws so it might write a set of rules to eliminate the free market, or "move from competition to cooperation," as they said in those days— came from business. Left-wingers like Tugwell embraced it as the enabling machinery for the planned economy, but the two men generally credited for the idea are Gerard Swope, then president of General Electric, and Henry I. Harriman, president of the United States Chamber of Commerce. Swope approached Hoover with his proposal for a way to end what many businessmen and economists felt was a ruinous free-market competition that was driving prices down and companies into bankruptcy. Nor was the Swope idea pure capitalist greed unadulterated by the milk of altruism. The industrial codes would also benefit workers by eliminating child labor—with adults out of work by the millions, kids belonged in school anyway— instituting the forty-hour week and other necessary health and safety regulations.

The Swope plan for ending the depression was first offered to Hoover, who, judged on his record as an interventionist president, and former secretary of commerce, might have been expected to approve of the idea. But no, Swope's idea of the planned economy looked too much to Hoover like the regimented economy. You have to draw the line of limits of federal action somewhere, and Hoover had his pencil out. The Swope plan was the corporate state, the legislation of an American version of a Mussolini-style economic fascism; as such it must have been uncongenial to Franklin Roosevelt who, regardless of what his detractors still say of him, wasn't a fascist. But he was a politician with a problem; he had no very clear program of his own. More often than not, incoming presidents are better off politically without dramatically new and different programs of any consequence, but 1933 was one of the rare moments when a little creative dictatorship, a la *Barron's,* was being demanded of the new president.

Unless he proposed a program to Congress, Congress would give him one. Senator (later Supreme Court Justice) Hugo Black of Alabama was pushing a share-the-jobs bill that aimed to increase employment by making the thirty-hour week mandatory. As the Black bill made its way through Congress it metamorphosed into such a piece of pro-union legislation that Roosevelt could support it only at the risk of pissing off too large a segment of big business. The administration had to have a bill of its own.

The man usually given credit for the means of transmitting Swope's and Harriman's ideas into law was one of the most delightfully colorful men ever to hold high office in modern Washington. Gen. Hugh Johnson was the protégé of Bernard Baruch, the Wall Street stock speculator who got out before the crash and thereby earned himself a reputation as an infallible sage. Baruch moved to Washington and for years would sun himself on a bench in Lafayette Park opposite the White House, where he dispensed little wisdoms to the newspaper reporters like the nearby nannies apportioning gumdrops to their small charges. Johnson had assisted Baruch on Wilson's War Industries Board and had seen firsthand how planning and coordination could eliminate the waste and other undesirable by-products of competition. Now America was going to whip the depression, and the National Recovery Administration, the most radical creation of the New Deal, would be the visible vehicle by which America went to war. And the deputy commander-in-chief of that war would be the stentorian, impolitic, but by no means unintelligent General Johnson, a West Point graduate, lawyer, a cavalry officer who rode with General Pershing in the insane Mexican Punitive Expedition of 1916–17, and a man newspaper reporters kindly referred to as "hard-drinking." During World War I Johnson had helped set up the first conscription since Lincoln's time before moving on to Baruch and the War Industries Board. After the war, he had been the head of an agricultural-implements company in the midwest, where the hard times for the farmer began a decade before the city people began hurting. Those years had convinced Johnson that government intervention in the free market of agriculture was a necessity.

The big-business parentage of this as well as other programs of the period was no secret at the time. It's only in the last generation that the idea of the New Deal as a coup d'etat of social workers, liberal bleeding hearts, and reforming eggheads has taken root. Roosevelt, who had the perfected schizophrenia of the finished politician and who knew more about consensus politics than many who have come after him, seems to have regarded the bill as a satisfactory mishmash in which all important elements would get what they needed. Indeed there was a clause in the bill (section 7a) that gave labor the right to organize and bargain collectively.

Although 7a scared the hell out of a number of businessmen just as it caused labor leaders a premature and groundless joy, there were a number of people on the left who thought the bill was a rotten idea. To Norman Thomas, the head of the Socialist party, it was "a complete denial of the bases of the old capitalism, but . . . set up instead a capitalist syndicalism still operated for profit, a scheme which is in essence fascist."[7] Huey Long, the kingfish political eclectic from Louisiana, told his fellow senators, "Every fault of socialism is found in this bill without one of its virtues. Every crime of monarchy is in here, without one of the things that would give it credit. . . . It is a combination of every evil that can possibly be imagined, worse than anything proposed under the Soviet, because in this thing we go into the realms of the imaginary and the unknown."[8] Long, who voted every which way on the bill, finally went for the public-works bait in it. Donald Richberg, a New Deal liberal lawyer who wound up as Johnson's second in command at the NRA, had insisted on having that section leading the bill because if "industrial control leads off, with public works as a secondary, incidental part of the program, it will be difficult to avoid violent opposition from those now clamoring for public works who might swallow a somewhat 'fascist' proposal to get their 'democratic' measure of relief."[9] The men in the Senate whom history designates "Progressives" weren't willing to swap Richberg's dash of fascism for public-works jobs. For the most part they voted against the NRA; but something is better than nothing, and America went to war against bad times.

With the signing of the bill into law, "the great summer offensive against unemployment," as FDR called it, began. We still have summer offensives, but in the last decade they've become trifling attacks on behalf of ghetto youth. When the Blue Eagle—the thunderbird emblem holding a cluster of lightning bolts in one talon and a gear, yes a gear, in the other—spread its wings a nation broke into motion. To organize and orchestrate the hysteria, General Johnson brought in the man who had conducted the prototype Liberty Loan drives during the Great War. Every medium of communication was pressed into service, for every citizen had to be impressed into signing to support the eagle. "In war, in the gloom of night attack, soldiers wear a bright badge on their shoulders to be sure that comrades do not fire on comrades," President Roosevelt said. "On that principle, those who cooperate in this program must know each other at a glance. That is why we have provided a badge of honor for this purpose, the Blue Eagle, a simple design with a legend, 'We do our part,' and I ask that all those who join with me shall display that badge prominently."[10] In the light of the flight of the Blue Eagle, Jerry Ford's 1975 WIN (Whip Inflation Now) campaign doesn't look as much like demented asininity as it did to many who refused to wear the WIN buttons on their lapels. The difference that forty-two years made wasn't that we were more sophisticated or less vulnerable to officially conceived and centrally directed hysterical nonsense; it's merely that the WIN campaign was the wrong vehicle at an impropitious time. For most people the economic conditions of 1975 weren't bad enough to propel them out to the streets to parade for better times. Rest assured we shall be marching and carrying on again, for this sort of thing seems to be as much a part of our culture as it is in Red China, but it remains to be seen whether we will provide ourselves with as much amusing idiocy as they did in 1933.

Since every agency and institution was enlisted to get the public to buy more and buy now and to get every business operation to sign an NRA code, the Post Office Department issued a stamp which set off one of those minor flurries that delight all lovers of Americana. "The new NRA stamp, which gave rise to a controversy two weeks ago when it was charged that the figure representing agriculture was 'Russian,' has aroused a second furore among stamp collectors and others," the *New York Times* reported.

> The latest contention is that the stamp constitutes an aspersion upon American business interests. H. L. Lindquist, publisher ... of the weekly magazine Stamps, said that letters received from all parts of the country ... complained that the NRA stamp depicted "capital out of step with every one else." Over the caption, "In a Common Determination," the design shows the farmer with his alleged Soviet scythe, a business man, an aproned laborer and a woman. The farmer, the laborer and the woman have their left feet forward. The business man's right foot is forward. ..."[11]

From Washington the chief of the Stamp Division explained that if somebody wasn't out of sync it would look as though the figures were "goose-stepping." The episode illustrates the ambiguity of Roosevelt's thinking. He had been given an enormous, if temporary, grant of power to plan and run the American economy, but he resolved to do it through volunteerism of one sort or another. During the entire life of the NRA he never used the licensing authority given him. Indeed the administration never used coercion to effect or enforce the quasi-fascist program it had embarked upon. Partly this was owing to something more than a suspicion that the law was unconstitutional and partly to a deeply held aversion to exercising this kind of authority. We forget that American presidents *are* Americans—power men, perhaps, megalomaniacal maybe, but existing in an American frame of reference, with the values, the hesitations, and the unresolved questions common to the milieu from which they come.

It was preposterous but not untypically American to believe that the goals of the NRA would be accomplished through voluntary regimentation or some other such contradiction in terms. In one form or another it's still the preferred method of trying to reach major economic objectives. We repeatedly resort to "voluntary wage-price guidelines" and have an absolute horror of governmental allocation of capital, preferring a complex and highly inefficient system of "tax incentives" that displeases us so much we then turn around and denounce them as "tax loopholes."

In 1933 the press and the air were full of reports of the most bizarre industry groups devising codes and signing them. The golf pros got themselves a code of "fair practice," as these rules to fight "economic cannibalism" were called; likewise everything from the dogfood industry to burlesque, which agreed to no more than four strips a show to spread the work around. Even the cemeteries wanted a code so they might fly the Blue Eagle, which was now being affixed on every product produced by a company which had pledged adherence to its particular industry's code. At the Congress Hotel, the Chicago Association of Dance Masters introduced a step called, what else, the Blue Eagle, "a fox trot done to music that resembles a march." There had to be a song to go with the dance, and "the NRA Prosperity March" is so bad it should not be forgotten:

Join the good old N.R.A., Boys, and we'll end this awful strife.
Join it with the spirit that will give the Eagle life.

Join it folks, then push and pull, many millions strong.
While we go marching to Prosperity.

How the nation shouted when they heard the joyful news!
We're going back to work again, and that means bread and shoes.
Folks begin to smile again. They are happy and at ease.
While we go marching to Prosperity.[12]

As events transpired they didn't march to prosperity, but up Fifth Avenue in New York City, a quarter of a million of them, to disperse in Central Park. The day was September 13; they commenced marching at one-thirty in the afternoon and didn't stop until the cigar-makers bringing up the rear closed out the parade around midnight. The stockbrokers passed the reviewing stand and booed the mayor as New Yorkers are wont to do; the refreshment and souvenir vendors complained that the million and a half reported sidewalk viewers were violating the Blue Eagle pledges by not buying, possibly because they were broke; nevertheless there was a Miss Statue of Liberty, torch and all, in the parade, bagpipers in Highland costume, the Roxyettes, and the corps de ballet from the Music Hall; Metro-Goldwyn-Mayer released basketsful of pigeons as its delegation marched by, but Paramount Pictures had a line of dancing girls in Blue Eagle getups. A more prosaic contingent trooped up the avenue carrying a sign which declared, "We will not buy Ford cars until Ford signs the NRA." Cantankerous Henry, failing to understand how profoundly standpattish Roosevelt's NRA administrators were, thought if he signed the pledge he would be letting a union in his place of work. After failing to charm the old-boy industrial genius into coming to the White House and signing the pledge, Roosevelt told a press conference, ". . . we have got to eliminate the purchase of Ford cars,"[13] but the government continued to buy Henry's motor cars even as the general went about the country saying things like, "When every American housewife understands that the Blue Eagle on everything that she permits to come into her home is a symbol of its restoration to security, may God have mercy on the man or group of men who attempt to trifle with this bird."[14] Newspapers reported that retail customers refused to buy merchandise lacking the Blue Eagle, as Johnson said no criminal law would be needed to deal with code violators. The same thing would happen to them

> as happened to Danny Deever, NRA will have to remove from him his badge of public faith and business honor and "takin of his buttons off an' cut his stripes away" break the bright sword of his commercial honor in the eyes of his neighbors—and throw the fragments—in scorn—in the dust at his feet. It is a sentence of economic death. It will never happen. The threat of it transcends any puny penal provision in this law[15]

Even acting as Roosevelt's economic viceroy, Johnson was less sure of his power, legal or moral, than his loud swagger made him seem. On the day of the march to prosperity, he remembered,

> I stood in the reviewing stand in that parade and there were hundreds of people I knew who waved as they went past. Down below were massed batteries of cameras and I knew if I raised my hand higher than my shoulders, it would seem and be publicized as a "Fascist salute." So I never did raise it higher, I just stuck my arm out straight and wiggled my hand around. But that didn't help me—*Time* came out saying I had constantly saluted *au* Mussolini and even had a photograph to prove it, *but it wasn't my arm* on that photograph. . . . I think it was the arm of Mayor O'Brien who stood beside me which had been faked onto my body. [italics are the General's][16]

It wasn't long before Congress and the media were after Johnson for more than Heil-Hitler salutes. Nobody but the manufacturers in certain industries were getting anything out of the NRA, which more and more people said stood for National Run Around. Blacks may have actually been made worse off by its operations. The way the law was structured and administered it not only failed to give protection to the broom pushers and menials, in some cases it provided the incentive to get rid of them. Langston Hughes, the black poet, composed "The Ballad of Roosevelt" to make the point:

> The pot was empty.
> The cupboard was bare.
> I said, Papa,
> What's the matter here?
> I'm waitin' on Roosevelt, son,
> Roosevelt, Roosevelt,
> Waitin' on Roosevelt, son.
>
> The rent was due,
> And the lights were out.
> I said, Tell me, Mama
> What's it all about?
> We're waitin' on Roosevelt, son,
> Roosevelt, Roosevelt,
> Just waitin' on Roosevelt. . . .
>
> And a lot o' other folks
> What's hungry and cold
> Done stopped believin'
> What they been told
> By Roosevelt,
> Roosevelt, Roosevelt—
>
> Cause the pot's still empty,
> And the cupboard's still bare,
> And you can't build a bungalow
> Out o' air—
> Mr. Roosevelt, listen!
> What's the matter here?[17]

There were others who were just as interested in what the matter here was. Leon Henderson of the Russell Sage Foundation led a delegation of consumers down to Washington to complain about the high prices the NRA seemed to be the cause of.

Johnson was soon pounding his desk and shouting about "unjustified complaints." Then, much to his surprise, Henderson began shouting back. He told the General in strong language that the consumer was being pushed around and that he had better do something about it. "If you're so goddamned smart," Johnson roared, "why don't you come down here and be my assistant on consumer problems?" Probably to the General's consternation, Henderson took the job.[18]

But cooptation couldn't save the situation. In a ploy that most administrators don't have the guts for, Johnson convoked a "Field Day of Criticism" for all who wanted to come and bitch. The Field Day turned into Four Field Days, and by now everyone was getting on Johnson's tail. While he talked and drank too much, labor, the liberals, the Federal Trade Commission, and the Senate went after him. The wounded old bear, who had predicted when he got the job, "It will be red fire at first and dead cats afterward," fell back on an old ploy and appointed a committee to investigate himself and his agency. In what he himself called "a moment of total aberration" he suggested Clarence Darrow, the radical, left-wing lawyer to chair it. The result was that Johnson was shot to pieces. Too loud, too drunk, too remorseful, and too pro-business and anti-labor. Roosevelt, who hated to fire people, waited for the general to get the signal and check out.

Subsequently a merciful Supreme Court declared the whole mess unconstitutional. Before that the general had lurched offstage to be considered, along with the NRA, aberrational moments in their turn. The general never even got his biography written, but neither the form nor the style of the NRA was especially deviant. A couple of generations later Ford tried many of the same techniques to deal with inflation; the fifties saw the same techniques used vis-à-vis domestic dissenters or subversives: patriotic parades, mass-media mobilization, oaths, and the eagle, no longer just blue, on every bumper sticker adjuring the populace to love America or depart instanter. By the 1950s, however, drives and mobilizations of this sort had become so much a part of the white noise in the social background that it seemed a thing of nature, rather than an artifact of policy. Liberal intellectuals delivered themselves of disquisitions on the spirit of conformity, the vogue word of the period, seldom pondering that if everyone was playing the same tune somebody must have been directing the band.

3

"Competition Is War and War Is Hell"

The form of the NRA's attempts at manipulating the economy were new for peacetime, but the fact of the government's doing it set no precedents. The credit or the blame for first trying to use public power to stop a recession or a panic, as they liked to call them back then, goes to Franklin's cousin, Teddy, whose secretary of the treasury put some $35 million at the disposal of the major New York banks in 1907 to try to save the situation of creditors demanding money from debtors, mostly banks, which couldn't cover their obligations.

Theodore, like Franklin, wasn't disposed to take the vicissitudes of the business cycle lying down. The federal intervention in 1907 was no more successful than the federal intervention in 1933, but it's inconceivable, given everything we know about Teddy, that he would have stood by and let the country suffer financial panic if he knew how to avoid it, any more than the leaders of free enterprise spurned the aid on Adam Smithian principles. The 1907 Panic was painful, severe, but short—particularly in comparison with the Great Depression. The institutional and legal tools for dealing with it were more varied and more far-ranging twenty-six years later, but the basic idea, namely that the unregulated free-market system was too mercurially unstable, was already a preoccupying conviction in the minds of many leading businessmen and politicians. "Competition is war and war is hell," said Arthur Eddy,[1] a leader in the movement to abolish both. In 1912 Eddy published a widely read book entitled *The New Competition* which argued that cooperation between competitors is better.

People back then equated economy and efficiency with large, uniform organizations even more than we do. Big business was to be protected, guarded, and encouraged. "Our aim is not to do away with corporations; on the contrary," said Teddy, "these big aggregations are an inevitable development of modern industrialism, and the effort to destroy them would be futile unless accomplished in ways that would work the utmost mischief to the entire body politic."[2] And he said it again:

> This is an age of combination, and any effort to prevent all combinations will be not only useless, but in the end vicious. . . . We should, moreover, recognize in cordial and ample fashion the immense good effected by corporate agencies in a country such as ours, and the wealth of intellect, energy and fidelity devoted to their service, and therefore normally to the service of the public, by their officers and directors.[3]

Most people today, just as most people then, probably would squint at TR's assertion of corporate "fidelity" and suchlike, but, except for the minuscule number who think small is beautiful in economics, most would still agree with him that the large corporation is inevitable and that it is to its productivity that the nation owes its wealth and high standard of living.

In fact, when Teddy uttered the sentiment, corporate America as we know it didn't exist. There were very few really large corporations and the monopolies that exercised people of that generation as much as people of this were almost nonexistent —though some industries like tobacco and oil were dominated by one or even a few companies. The dream must come before the reality; in these statements what Teddy was articulating was the path he and many others wanted America to follow and he therefore believed it was "inevitable" that America would follow. He was building the big-business America that he was telling everyone they must adjust to. It confused the more simple-minded and unimaginative of his Progressive following, as he understood when he said,

Half of them are really representative of a kind of rural toryism, which wishes to attempt the impossible task of returning to the economic conditions that obtained sixty years ago. The other half wishes to go forward along the proper lines, that is, to recognize the inevitableness and the necessity of combinations in business and to meet it by a corresponding increase in governmental power over big business; but at the same time these real progressives are hampered by being obliged continually to pay lip loyalty to their colleagues, who, at bottom, are not progressive at all, but retrogressive.[4]

Always there are the small-business free-enterprisers, and always there is Theodore Roosevelt or one of his successors in power. For regardless of party, and very often regardless of the strongly held values of some of those who came to live in the White House, all of them, save William Howard Taft, served and furthered the notion of the strong, centralized state in which the corporation played a special central role. Yet before 1912, before Taft had left the White House, a model of government finagling with an important segment of the economy was in place and accepted by all but perhaps the far, far left and the right, as is the case today. Nor was this abrogation of laissez faire an experiment in some small coldframe off in the corner of the garden of economy. Close regulation of the sort by which we moderns ensure that the market isn't too free was operating before the First World War with the railroads, the greatest of all the country's industries, employing 1.7 million men in 1907 with a payroll of over a billion a year. Great-great-grandma and -grandpa understood the significance of this government intervention, to use a word not current at the time. It's only in our own era that we imagine that regulation is of a later date and of liberal, humanitarian, and hemorrhaging-heart invention.

Woodrow Wilson, who bled for the small businessman, the independent professional, the family farmer, if only because that part of our America was so much part of his growing up in the post–Civil War south, was captured, excited, and drawn forward by the same view of his country as that which animated Teddy. Writing in the 1880s, Wilson prophesied and embraced what was to come:

> The copper threads of the telegraph run unbroken to every nook and corner of the great continent, like the nerves of a single body, transmitting thought and purpose with instant precision. Railways lie in every valley and stretch across every plain. Cheap newspapers make the news of every country-side the news of the nation. Industrial organization knows nothing of state lines, and commerce sweeps from state to state in currents which can hardly be traced for number and intricacy. Ideas, motives, standards of conduct, subtle items of interest, airs from out every region travel with the news, with the passenger on the express train, with the merchant's goods and the farmer's grain. Invisible shuttles of suggestion weave the thoughts and purposes of separate communities together, and a nation which will some day know itself a single community is a making in the warp and the woof of the fabric. The extraordinary way in which the powers of the federal government have been suffered to grow in recent years is evidence enough to the process.[5]

Between the time when Wilson wrote those words and Theodore Roosevelt's ascent to the presidency, similes like copper threads resembling nervous systems changed from being fresh language into clichés, and the powers of the federal government which Wilson thought so large in the 1880s were considered much too weak for the proper running of the country in the first decade of the new century. The nation was finding out it could not tolerate unfettered free enterprise, and nowhere could it tolerate it less than in its largest industry, the industry in which it took the most pride—its railroads. The "impossible doctrine of protection of the public by railway competition," to quote Balthasar H. Heyer, a Taft appointee to the Interstate Commerce Commission, was repudiated by much of the society.

It was repudiated as much by capitalists as by socialists, and it is that which makes the abandonment of competition in favor of regulation in the railroad industry so illustrative of the change in thinking about free-market economics. It was the capitalists, the owners as much as the workers or the shippers, who had to contemplate the disastrous fact that between 1893 and 1897, a sixth of the entire nation's trackage—41,000 miles —had gone into receivership. Before flying to the government for protection, the railroad managers had tried everything they could think of to save themselves from a competitive system which forced them to cut prices until profits turned to losses.

They had tried to limit competition through holding companies which owned and controlled separate but competing railroads. The Northern Securities Company was such an attempt to prevent competition between a number of midwestern railroads and was owned by tycoons like James J. Hill, Edward H. Harriman, and J. P. Morgan. But the holding company that killed transportation competition also offended shippers and others who complained of high rates and poor service. They pressed TR and Washington for antitrust action, and it was the Northern Securities case that was supposed to have been the occasion for the following oft-quoted discussion:

> "If we have done anything wrong," said Mr. Morgan, "send your man to my man and they can fix it up."
> "That can't be done," said the President.
> "We don't want to fix it up," added Mr. Knox [first name Philander; TR's attorney general], "we want to stop it."
> Then Mr. Morgan asked: "Are you going to attack my other interests, the Steel Trust and the others?"
> "Certainly not," replied the President, "unless we find out that in any case you have done something that we regard as wrong."[6]

Morgan also tried out monopolies as well as holding companies to get around the perils and disasters of competition. Having got hold of the prosperous New York, New Haven, and

Hartford Railroad, Morgan tried to use it as the means by which he would establish a complete monopoly of public transportation in New England. He wanted the whole thing: railroads, coastwise ship traffic, even the trolley-car systems. To buy all this he watered the New York, New Haven's stock. In 1903, the line had $93 million in stocks and bonds outstanding; ten years later it had $417 million. Tens of millions seemed to have vanished, never to be traced, in three hundred subsidiary corporations which were, according to the Interstate Commerce Commission, "seemingly planned, created and manipulated by lawyers expressly retained for the purpose of concealment or deception."[7] The monopoly was never established but the costs of trying may have ruined the New Haven and perhaps New England railroading forever.

A number of railroads were working out the question of their future prosperity by merging with their competing or complementary roads, but by 1905 too many people and too many diverse interests had given up on a purely private-sector approach to transportation. Farmers, manufacturers, railway workers, everybody who used a railroad—and that was everybody—wanted the rates regulated or the service improved, or *something.* To fit the tone of the times, Teddy made a speech in Harrisburg in which, like Nixon, he discovered an "inherent power" "outside of the enumerated powers" in the Constitution, the goal of which was "a constantly increasing supervision over and control of great fortunes used in business." Some railroads, like the Pennsy, backed regulation and saw it as the only practical way to run the industry. The Pennsylvania's lawyers had written the law prohibiting rebating, and in 1906, its president, Alexander J. Cassatt, said,

I have for several years believed that the national Government, through the Interstate Commerce Commission, ought to be in a position to fix railroad rates whenever the rates established by the railroads themselves are found, after complaint and hearing, to be unreasonable. . . . Let the Government regulate us. For my part and for my associates in the Pennsylvania Railroad Company, I am generally heartily in accord with the position taken by President Roosevelt, and we have been all along; I told the President himself when he made his first recommendation on this subject to Congress, more than four years ago, that I believed him to be in the right.[8]

Perhaps Cassatt had a premonition. A year later on July 27, 1907, Gov. R. B. Glenn of North Carolina ordered W. W. Finley, president of the Southern Railway, arrested for failing to observe the state's law limiting passenger fares to two and a quarter cents a mile. Federal regulation had to be better than that. But whether it's true, as a few have argued, that the railroad industry had gone for federal regulatory protection, the rest of the society had. Only one, lone academic economist, a man at the University of Chicago, published a professionally reputable book attacking regulation; it was so well received that he, poor fellow, emigrated to Australia not long afterward.[9]

The Interstate Commerce Commission, created in the 1880s and shorn of all power by the courts, was outfitted with another pair of fangs and incisors by new legislation giving the ICC the power to set maximum rates and control the industry in a number of other ways: The Hepburn Act of 1906 passed a Republican House by a score of 366 to 7; the Mann-Elkins Act of 1910, which further strengthened the ICC's power over the railroads by making it legal for the railroads to eliminate price competition under the commission's supervision, went through the Senate with only twelve dissenting votes. Thus when the first characteristically governmental bureaucracy was created, it was neither Democratic nor Republican, inspired exclusively neither by business nor liberal reformers. Everybody was for it because almost everybody thought they could use this new institution to serve their own purposes.

Maybe the railroad men who backed it were thinking as Charles Francis Adams, Jr., of the Union Pacific did back during the 1880s, the time of the original legislation: "What is desired, if I understand it . . . is something having a good sound, but quite harmless, which will impress the popular mind with the idea that a great deal is being done, when, in reality very little is intended to be done."[10] Only this time in reality a great deal was intended to be done. America was beginning on her first adventure with price control, and it wasn't long before all the parties in contention were acting in a painfully contemporary way.

Titanic battles began to be fought over ICC appointments and rate cases. As the railroad men came to see that they were being badly snookered by the shipping interests, they came to agree with Edward Payson Ripley of the Santa Fe, who told his peers at a dinner one night in 1909, "Our troubles are with this class of well-meaning men who have zeal without knowledge and enthusiasm without sanity; these we may not reach, but the great mass of the solid and substantial citizenship may perhaps be induced to stop and consider whether ... this greatest of all the country's industries is being fairly treated."[11]

At this early juncture the ICC had not yet fallen under the control of the railroads, which were unable to get themselves rate increases in a period of inflation. In fact the western roads were sued by Taft's attorney general for violating the Sherman Act merely for submitting a joint petition to the commission. Another phenomenon which we in the century's eighth decade are familiar with appeared as soon as the commission was armed with real power in 1906; both Roosevelt and Taft successfully prevailed upon it to hold up rate increases in order to win elections. Not that the president ran the commission. The ICC, like the infinite number of agencies later shaped in its image, was designed to be an arena of competing influences of which the White House would be one. A strong influence, without a doubt, but not an all-dominating one, as Wilson found out when he twice tried to get rate raises.

Commissions like the ICC—with legislative, judicial, and administrative functions, run by presidential appointees who don't serve at the pleasure of the president but for specific terms —have been successful at blocking the growth of effective White House power. When agency agendas and presidential agendas have coincided it has seemed a matter of luck as much as anything else. The luck ran against Wilson, who finally got Congress to suspend the ICC during World War I in the interests of efficiency while the government took over and ran the railroads.

By 1917 when the government acted, rail freight was in a state of such dangerous chaos there was fear the system would fly apart. Freight-car shortages were cutting coal and steel production; terminal congestion in New York was so bad shipments were being unloaded and left sitting between the tracks; wheat was marooned in the midwest. It was alleged then, and it's still maintained by some economic historians, that the transportation mess of 1917 was owing in considerable part to the railroads' inability to raise money for modernization and expansion of their tracks and rolling stock. That was blamed on ICC price controls.

Regardless of the argument's merits, there's no doubt you do strange, often unintended things when you put price controls on one industry while leaving those it must buy from and sell to free to charge what they want or what they can get. One effect is to push management and labor into an alliance. The unions know that if the bosses can't charge more, they can't get more out of the bosses. Management's distaste for the smell of labor unions circa 1915 was still too strong a tradition to see the kind of working relationships that government control in the auto industry has created between management and labor. Nevertheless the railroad brotherhoods, as the unions were called, did begin to support management demands for rate increases. "In times like this men go back to primal instincts," observed Mr. A. B. Garretson, chairman of the Railway Brotherhood Conference Committee in 1916. "Now the public is the carcass and we are all perhaps the vultures. . . . The country will pay."[12]

Under the ICC's price-control system a variety of groups, businesses, and locales got to play carcass or vulture. Freezing the rates as the ICC did meant that bulk shippers held an advantage over shippers of finished goods; long-haul shippers did better than short-haul shippers; certain commodities like soap and salt enjoyed preferential rates. This probably influenced the location of factories and plants and most certainly forced certain groups of consumers to subsidize others. None of this was done in accordance with any kind of overall plan; politics invented and bent structures of government to force a no longer quite so free market to play favorites, sometimes to help the poor and sometimes for less noble motives. With all its contradictions, the model for our present muddle was created and perfected in those ragtime days of bowlers, knickers, camisoles, and hard gold money.

4

Inspector
America

An economy such as turn-of-the-century America's needed more than the intervention of the ICC to help it. Thus it was during Teddy's administration that the national police power was created and applied to the first federal consumer-protection legislation—mandatory meat inspection. In this episode we have the textbook case of reformers and industrialists using each other to reach a common goal.

In our own time, we've seen how regulation of one sort or another by the states has begun to protect doctors from negligence suits. In much the same way the craftier big-time capitalists of Teddy's decade understood that supporting certain reforms would defuse radical, even socialist sentiment palpably growing across the country, as well as shield their enterprises from court-imposed liabilities. That seems to have been the reason that men like August Belmont bought the outlandish idea of workmen's compensation and proselytized for it. At the 1911 annual meeting of the National Civic Federation, an amalgam of reformist liberals, tycoons (like Andrew Carnegie), and safe idealists, a speaker on the subject explained, "We must make a move toward compensation soon. Otherwise we will continue, with ever-increasing impetus, down the broad way of the employer liability laws, which lead to social destruction."[1]

The Ralph Nader of the Progressive era—at least that's the part he's cast in by the writers of some of our history books—

was Upton Sinclair. Sinclair's book *The Jungle* is a novel that was supposed to stir people's sympathy for the workers enduring the wages and working conditions in the packing plants. Instead, the middle-class liberals who read it were revolted by the descriptions of the sanitary conditions surrounding the meat they ate. "I aimed at the public's heart," Sinclair wrote in a much-quoted sentence, "and by accident I hit it in the stomach." Sinclair, a socialist who enjoyed a reciprocally mistrustful and contemptuous relationship with the president, quite understood why the packing industry and the White House found him annoying but fundamentally useful:

> the federal inspection of meat was, historically, established at the packers' request; . . . it is maintained and paid for by the people of the United States for the benefit of the packers; . . . men wearing the blue uniforms and brass buttons of the United States service are employed for the purpose of certifying to the nations of the civilized world that all the diseased and tainted meat which happens to come into existence in the United States of America is carefully sifted out and consumed by the American people.[2]

The real problem was with exports.

In 1905 the English medical journal *The Lancet* ran a series of articles alleging filthy conditions in the Chicago meat-packing houses. Ever since the late 1870s and early 1880s, American meat had been intermittently attacked as unhealthy by medical authorities in countries that imported it. From time to time, Italy, Germany, and France had embargoed American meat. Hence, far from fighting inspection, the major packing houses had been lobbying for it. "This government inspection thus becomes an important adjunct of the packer's business from two viewpoints," quoth J. Ogden Armour of the Armour packing family the year after the *Lancet* article. "It puts the stamp of legitimacy and honesty upon the packer's product and so is to him a necessity. To the public it is insurance against the sale of diseased meats."

The problem wasn't with the Armours, the Swifts, and Cudahys, but with the small packers, and despite the widespread belief at the time that there was a "meat trust," it was the small packers who packed most of America's meat and were not interested in the burdens and additional expenses that government inspection would surely bring with it. That pattern has persisted to this day. Small industrial firms are usually the ones most injured and least able to take advantage of Washington's use of the police power, because adhering to a multiplicity of health and safety standards is expensive and they are least able to pass on their expenses to their customers. Not that biggies like to pay more either. Although freely conceding they wanted the toughest possible compulsory meat inspection system, the big packers used their considerable political influence to defeat legislation that would have charged the packers fees for this service. Sen. Albert Beveridge, Teddy's Progressive friend and supporter, who had been one of the main congressional movers for the legislation, told his colleagues that the government seal of inspection was worth millions as advertising and he couldn't for the life of him see why the beneficiaries shouldn't pay for it.

They didn't, but the law was no sooner passed than Teddy himself cabled the American ambassador to the Court of St. James's to tell English food buyers the act "can and will guarantee the fitness in all respects of . . . meat containing [the] Government stamp."[3] You can't ask for more than the president to push your pork chops for you. Subsequently industry only rarely got the White House to go door-to-door for it, but the use of government inspection and certification is used to sell everything today from stocks and bonds to baby rattles. The government, through the Federal Trade Commission, even inspects and by implication certifies advertising. Whether the public—whoever she is—gets most of the protection from the system or the manufacturers do is a question without a definitive answer. Obeying federal regulations may or may not make products safer but they unquestionably do confer a high level of immunity from damage suits on the products' makers.

The Socialists understood the game. Robert Rives LaMonte, writing in the *International Socialist Review*, predicted that regardless of which party won the 1912 election, "we shall get more workmen's compensation acts, more and more restriction upon child labor, more and more regulation of women in industry" because "too widespread joblessness and a wage too far below a decent subsistence level leads to agitations that threaten the whole fabric of capitalism."[4] Ultimately, the *Review* observed, the businessman would see "that he can carry on certain portions of the productive process more efficiently through his government than through private corporations."[5]

Not that every businessman saw it that way. Not only do similarly situated people and institutions calculate their self-interest differently, but individuals really do have values they will hold to even at considerable economic cost. So while those business interests taken with cults of efficiency, bigness, and concentration were liable to understand that they needed the government to make their dreams come true, others didn't. In 1905 the leaders of the Interstate Commerce Law Commission, a pro-railroad-regulation group of diversified shippers, hired armed guards to keep out antiregulation businessmen led by David Parry, president of the National Association of Manufacturers, an organization which went every which way on a number of these issues in this period.

Ideally, sophisticated businessmen would perhaps have preferred a world where they could go on their merry way, merging and monopolizing without hindrance from Washington, but the same conviction that free-market competition best served the interests of efficiency and the customers was at work then as now. They felt they had to choose between the vagaries and random legal violence of the Sherman Antitrust Act and some form of regulation. Regulation could not only protect them from the Justice Department but also permit security by stabilizing costs and markets. When you and your associates have hundreds of millions of dollars tied up in an enterprise, the thrills and chills of an upsy-downsy market may not have the allure they hold for the disinterested but convinced student of political economy who doesn't own a dime's worth of stock. Once a corporation has been allowed to grow to gargantuan dimensions, even politicians hostile to it grow antsy at what may be the consequences of mucking around with it. One factor —maybe not a major one—in the decision not to prosecute International Harvester during Teddy Roosevelt's administration was the 25,000 people who worked for the company. Large corporations that get into trouble hold their employees hostage against hostile government action or even government indifference. During the 1974 recession it was thought that several major manufacturing corporations were saved by the Federal Reserve Board, not out of solicitude for the management but horror at the thought of so many jobs vanishing. Real estate investment trusts, in which some banks had invested frightful sums of money, were allowed to flounder and gulp red ink unaided. Few jobs were at stake.

If the Progressives were tugging and demanding that primeval market conditions be restored by government action on the one side, on the other were the Socialists. Unlike the disordered, discombobulated, and often deranged American left of the latter sixties, the turn-of-the-century American Socialists had a coherent critique of emerging corporate capitalism, a program of their own, and a demonstrable ability to attract votes. By 1912 they had elected 1,200 people to public office and were particularly strong in western states like Oklahoma, Washington, California, Wisconsin, and Texas. By 1911 the first Socialist had been elected to Congress, and by 1912 they had elected the mayors of seventy-four American cities from Berkeley, California, to Schenectady, New York, and come close to electing mayors in Cleveland and Los Angeles.

There were also a number of free-lance radicals infecting the popular mind during the period. Samuel "Golden Rule" Jones got himself elected mayor of Toledo and proceeded to take clubs away from the police, kick up the minimum wage of municipal workers by a third, build a city golf course, and start free kindergartens for the toddlers and free lodging-houses for the bums. As almost invariably happened in the days when lefties were winning elections, all the newspapers and both political parties ganged up to try and beat Golden Rule, but the old boy got himself reelected four times and died in office. In Kansas they got so mad at Standard Oil they passed a law providing for the construction of a state-owned refinery. Everywhere cities were converting from private to publicly owned water and gas. Socialist ideas were spreading. In part the reason was that the more adept Socialists of the period presented a socialism of a very American sort. When Gene Debs, the leader and predominant personality, talked politics there were no alien syllables in his speech. The International Workers of the World, the Wobblies, are the better known and the romantic heroes of the time, but Debs talked Amahrican, and the folks listened:

> Jesus taught that the air and the sea and the sky and all the beauty and fullness thereof were for all the children of men; that they should all equally enjoy the riches of nature and dwell together in peace, and bear one another's burdens and love one another, and that is what socialism teaches and why the rich thieves who have laid hold of the earth and its bounties would crucify the Socialists as those robbers of the poor crucified Jesus two thousand years ago.[6]

When radicalism clothes itself in such language it's possible to see how the party could have 961 locals and 12,000 members in a place like Oklahoma. By 1905 Teddy was saying "that the growth of the Socialist party in this country" was "far more ominous than any populist or similar movement in the past."[7]

The observation was made against a background of industrial violence that those of us who lived through the racial violence of the 1960s should appreciate. While the members of the ruling circles are predisposed to see the chaotic torch of anarchism every time a black kid breaks a pawnshop window and loots the trinkets, the feeling that the country might fly apart was especially lively just then.

If Teddy fumbled, overdid it, and sometimes talked at cross purposes with himself, fashioning a new order for a new age isn't done with one smooth gesture of the sweeping hand. When the coal miners went on strike in 1902, Roosevelt decided the government should intervene in what had theretofore been regarded as a purely private matter. To justify the action, he invented for himself an "old common law doctrine under which any peasant could take wood that was not his, if necessary for the preservation of life and death in winter weather."[8] But first, before turning himself and the rest of the country into shivering peasants, Teddy attempted to jawbone the opposing sides into an agreement.

George F. Baer, who led the coal-mine operators, might have been sent over from Soviet Central Casting to play the capitalist boss. In response to being invited to the White House to meet the president of the union, Baer announced, "We object to being called here to meet a criminal, even by the president of the United States." Baer summed up the mine owners' position that the strike was no one's business but their own with one of the history books' most cherished quotes: "The rights and interests of the laboring man will be protected and cared for—not by the labor agitators, but the Christian men to whom God in his infinite wisdom has given the control of the property interests of this country."

Against this, Teddy ordered Maj. Gen. J. M. Schofield to make ready his troops to seize the coalfields. "I knew this would form an evil precedent," apologized Teddy. Actually it didn't, though more than thirty years passed before Congress limited the presidential—if not the governmental—power to settle labor disputes by creating the National Labor Relations Board.

Although the strike was settled without Teddy having to seize the coalfields, the possibility of effective governmental intervention grew as the Supreme Court began reversing its earlier decisions, which had all but reduced the Sherman Act to a nullity. As a consequence Teddy and his attorney general, but mostly Teddy, had wide discretionary power as to whom they would go after and who would be given a pass. Somebody had to be gone after, because the mobs on the streets were demanding a periodic corporate hanging, and nowhere were Debs's "rich thieves" more visible than in the giant monopolies.

Nor did it help to cool things down when executives often made no bones about preferring monopoly arrangements to trusting to the uncertainties of the unrigged market. An executive of the American Tobacco Company, a true monopoly, wrote,

Unrestricted competition has been tried out to a conclusion with the result that the industrial fabric of the nation was confronted with an almost tragic condition of impending bankruptcy. Unrestricted competition has proven a deceptive mirage, and its victims were struggling on every hand to find some means of escape from the perils of their environment. In this trying situation, it was perfectly natural that the idea of rational cooperation in lieu of cut-throat competition should suggest itself.[9]

That sounds horrendous, but between 1890, when American Tobacco was formed into a trust with over 90 percent of domestic cigarette sales, and 1907, when the corporate controversies may have reached their apex, sales slipped to 74 percent. Since it was so easy and required so little money to get into the cigarette business, a corporation could put together a monopoly but couldn't hold it. Nor could American Tobacco do what monopolies are supposed to do—raise prices—so that the objections to the corporation had to be in the area of size and concentration of power. These are good arguments but they've seldom been important ones in the decades of acrimony over antitrust. From Theodore Roosevelt forward, presidents have gone out of their way to assert there could be no licit objection to bigness per se.

As mentioned in the case of International Harvester, bigness can constitute a form of social fait accompli that almost forces the government to buoy up economically disadvantageous companies such as Lockheed, Chrysler, and Pan Am. Bigness, even the bigness of a distressed and limping corporate mastodon, does confer a questionable power, and bigness may create special problems without compensating convenience. For Americans at the beginning of the century the bigness question was

posed by the creation of U.S. Steel, the father whale of capitalism. The company was so big that Arthur T. Hadley, the president of Yale, declared that unless precautions were taken
against it, an emperor would be enthroned in Washington
within a generation. J. P. Morgan's whopper consisted of 213
different companies, 1,000 miles of railroad, the Mesabi iron
range or a large chunk of it, more than 100 ore ships, and more
than a third of the blast-furnace capacity of the country. In
Chicago, Mr. Dooley told his friends in amazement:

> Pierpont Morgan calls in wan iv his office boys, th' prisident
> iv a national bank, an' says he, "James," he says, "take some
> change out iv th' damper an' r-run out an buy Europe f'r me,"
> he says. "I intend to re-organize it an' put it in a paying basis,"
> he says. "Call up th' Czar and th' Pope an' th' Sultan an' th'
> Impror Willum, an' tell thim we won't need their savices afther
> nex' week," he says, "ye better put that r-red headed bookkeeper
> near th' dure in charge iv th' continent. He doesn't seem to be
> doin' much," he says.[10]

A number of the precursor companies making up U.S. Steel
had themselves been the children of various forms of corporate
marriage entered into in hopes that larger units would have a
better chance of steadying the market. That could not be as long
as Andrew Carnegie stayed out of the arrangement. Carnegie
could make steel cheaper and more efficiently than anyone else.
For a price, $226 million, Morgan got Carnegie's company,
around which the rest of U.S. Steel was formed. In theory this
monster should have been able to drive every competitor to the
wall by lowering prices; in actuality U.S. Steel never tried,
because to do so would mean lowering its own prices and
therefore diminishing the revenues it had to have to pay off
Carnegie and the others who were bought out to bring the
leviathan to life.

The early years of the great corporation's existence are a
record of dampening competition and attempting to freeze the
industry into changeless status quo. U.S. Steel's head, Judge
Elbert H. Gary—also the founder of Gary, Indiana—attempted

to arrange genteel price-fixing agreements through a series of dinners to which steel executives from other companies, and the press, were invited. It was Gary who heard the members of a House committee call his proposals "semisocialist" after he told them,

> I believe we must come to enforced publicity and governmental control . . . even as to prices, and so far as I am concerned. . . . I would be very glad if we knew exactly where we stand, if we could be freed from danger, trouble and criticism by the public, and if we had some place where we could go, to a responsible governmental authority, and say to them, "Here are our facts and figures . . . now you tell us what we have the right to do and what prices we have the right to charge."[11]

The place U.S. Steel went was to Teddy in the White House for permission and protection for J. P. Morgan's metallurgical leviathan. The most celebrated case of this sort was when Morgan, and his business associate George Perkins, either put the blocks to Teddy or hoodwinked him or in some other way gulled the old Bully Boy into giving them an antitrust pass on buying the Tennessee Coal and Iron Company. In an atmosphere of bank-panic hysteria, Morgan's men boarded a special midnight train in New York and highballed it for Washington. The next morning they were at the White House talking to Teddy, who had a notoriously poor head for business and a talent for not asking the most obvious questions when business topics arose. Unless they were allowed to pick up TC&I and feed it to U.S. Steel, they told Teddy, the brokerage house which currently possessed the controlling interest in TC&I's stock would fold and there would be a horrible run on the banks, which, of course, there was anyhow. As they talked, a line was held open between the White House and Morgan's famous, tapestried library in New York where George Perkins waited to hear the outcome of this bodacious bluff cum con game.

Word that TR had given Morgan an antitrust exemption got out during the Taft administration. It enhanced no reputations that Perkins had helped Roosevelt get the vice-presidential nomination in 1900 and was a campaign-fund conduit, to use a word they didn't use that way then, in 1904 and again when Teddy raised the call of the Bull Moose in 1912 to run as a third-party candidate. Whether that puts TR in Nixon's class with his dealings with ITT and the milk-fund contribution, or merits Theodore's being chiseled off Mount Rushmore, the twenty-sixth president made anarchy and confusion out of the enforcement of the Sherman Act. Sometimes there would be prosecutions and White House invective on the subject of "malefactors of great wealth," and sometimes it would be take-a-plutocrat-home-to-lunch week. Teddy explained it all by saying that his policy was to smite what he called the bad trusts and pass out scrolls to the good ones. To this day historians have been unable to figure out how Teddy assigned a corporation to one or the other slot in his good-bad dichotomy.

Deciphering the meaning in the bubbles in the Oyster Bay Roosevelt's ebullient head is less important than noting that, with or without immunity from antitrust prosecution, a number of major industries still lived a troubled and often near-disastrous existence. Merely being allowed to play monopoly if they could would not be enough for industries like steel and oil. Not only did the largest corporate units in these industries find it next to impossible to hold their near-monopoly positions without the aid of outside political power, but the industries as a whole have frequently been in such turmoil that their leaders could not conceive of survival, or at least profitability, without favorable intervention by the government.

J. P. Morgan saw his near-monopoly U.S. Steel Corporation drop from having 63 percent of ingot and casting production at the time of creation to 46 percent twenty years later. One of the company's own top executives, Charlie Schwab, who quit after a fight with the offensively teetotaling, obnoxiously religious Judge Gary, bought a small, almost bankrupt steel company and proceeded to beat the pants off his former employers. The company, Bethlehem Steel, did it by using technological innovation, by superior plant location, and by having the business foresight to cash in on the war in Europe. In 1916 Bethlehem paid a 30 percent stock dividend and in 1917, 200 percent. Charlie had proven being good and big did not necessarily mean maximum profitability. What Charlie didn't prove is the industry's ability to go it alone in a purely private-enterprise existence, as its incessant calls for special tax breaks and a return to McKinley tariff protectionism testify.

At the same time, the Rockefellers' Standard Oil, the epitome of TR's bad trust, as Morgan's U.S. Steel was Teddy's good trust, was learning that being big and bad doesn't always pay off as well as sin is supposed to. In 1880 Standard was producing about 90 percent of the nation's oil; by 1910, the year *before* the courts ruled that Standard must be broken up into smaller parts, the company's share was down to 60 percent and dropping. It was the luck of the draw that Teddy, a strong believer in the weaknesses of free enterprise, should have elected to force Standard Oil into competition by antitrust legislation. By all rights he should have applied his ideas of government-supervised enterprise to the oil industry. Most of the presidents and most of the oil executives who came after Roosevelt put little stock in unfettered and unregulated industry. In the last two or three years oil men have spoken of regulation as something unclean, not to say immoral, but for most of the last sixty years they have accepted it and frequently demanded it. In 1927 Walter Teagle, the president of Standard of New Jersey, explained, "The oil industry is faced with financial chaos unless the government can help to extricate it from overproduction."[12] The collapse of the Rockefeller monopoly saw one-corporation dominance replaced by what appeared to oilmen and nonoilmen as a competition that might drive prices ridiculously low, encourage profligate use and waste of oil, which would then bring on a shortage.

The year 1913 saw the passage of the oil-depletion allowance. The purpose of what was to become the most debated and most infamous of all tax loopholes was to encourage discovery and production. Even before the First World War this resource was understood to be particularly valuable, the management of which could not be left to the oil companies by themselves. In that light, far from being a departure, President Carter's conservation plan has ancient antecedents going back to Taft's time. It was the Wonderful White House Walrus—Taft looked exactly like a Daddy Walrus—who first set aside two large oil fields for the Navy's use against the possibility we'd run out of the stuff. Under Wilson, oil became so scarce or the price so high that his secretary of the navy ordered six destroyers to seize a quantity of fuel from the Associated Oil Company in San Francisco. Wilson added the Teapot Dome field to the naval reserve so that Albert Fall, Warren Harding's secretary of the interior, could take a bribe and lease it away.

Despite the Teapot Dome scandal, the government policy under the Republican Normalcy wasn't to allow oil to relapse into being a purely private enterprise. "The Allies floated to victory on a sea of oil," said Lord Curzon after the First World War,[13] and Harding understood full well the military importance of this commodity was too great to be laissez faire and indifferent to it. His policy was to conserve domestic oil supplies while fostering the capture and exploitation of foreign oil reserves. Or, as Secretary of Commerce Herbert Hoover explained it, his department was helping "oil producers to secure foreign holdings of oil lands and elsewhere with a view to enabling them to continue to supply oil to the United States in event of exhaustion of their oil holdings here."[14]

To do this Harding pressured Congress into not raising the tariffs on oil while it was busy raising import duties on practically everything else. Of most lasting significance were the State-Department–oil-company shenanigans. Secretary of State Charles Evans Hughes used the Open Door Policy to get Standard of New Jersey into what had theretofore been an Anglo-French oil concession monopoly in what was called Mesopotamia (Iraq and Iran and such). After the Open Door had admitted the Americans it was slammed shut, but behind its panels you could hear a dreadful row that went on for years until someone peeped through the keyhole shortly after World

War II and discovered a roomful of dead Englishmen. In the American colonies of the Philippines, Costa Rica, and Haiti, the Open Door remained locked, with restrictions slapped on outsiders' oil prospecting. In 1928, after years of wrangling and dickering, an Anglo-Dutch-American consortium got exclusive marketing rights for Russian oil. During the same decade, Standard of New Jersey, with State Department muscles, acting like a camel with a stainless steel nose, got under the Dutch oil tent in Indonesia and soon had almost 30 percent of the production. American ownership of the Mexican and South American fields was yet larger. Not a bad record for a bunch of midwestern boys who had been billed as yahoo isolationists.

Coolidge created the Federal Oil Conservation Board because of "the patent fact that the oil industrial welfare is so intimately linked with the industrial prosperity and safety of the whole people, that government and business can well join forces to work out . . . practical conservation."[15] Before those unobjectionable sentiments could be translated into anything very concrete the Great Depression hit the oil industry early. It was already in deep trouble brought on by overproduction when the rich Seminole fields in Oklahoma were discovered. The result was much agitation in the government and the industry to save the people in the oil business by asking Congress to grant an exception to the antitrust statutes. The Coolidge administration, however, was suffering from the same conflicted schizophrenia on this subject that every administration from Theodore Roosevelt's to Jimmy Carter's does. The same people bounced around on one side of the question and then the other. For example, Hoover, who favored antitrust exemption in 1926, was opposing it in the early 1930s when the price had literally gone to a dime a barrel.

Without the oil companies being allowed to collude, how was production to be lowered unless the government did it? To the men of the 1920s, it seemed Washington was already doing too much of that in agriculture, transportation, and the still new Federal Trade Commission. So the states would try regulating production. When the enormous East Texas fields were discov-

ered, they got grim about it. Alfalfa Bill Murray, the governor
of Oklahoma, declared martial law in August 1931 to stop the
pumping of what the *New York Times* called "the once precious
'black gold.' " America had moved so far from its laissez faire
ideal that soldiers would be used to try to do what the market
wouldn't.

The headlines spoke of troops in the oilfields, but the actuali-
ties were considerably less dramatic than those words suggest.
Instead of writing about combat-ready battalions, the *Daily
Oklahoman* described this application of military force to an
economic problem as follows:

> Where not so long ago a flock of milch cows chewed their
> meditative cuds in bovine peace, Oklahoma's army was biv-
> ouacked Tuesday night to enforce silence and unproductiveness
> in the Oklahoma City oil field. In command was the gaunt and
> determined Cicero Murray, cousin of a truculent governor bent
> on stopping the flush production of oil until the price of crude
> mounted [sic] to $1 a barrel. . . . Ordinarily when a hostile army
> invades a place the entire population runs for the storm cellar
> . . . but Colonel Murray came and saw and conquered in a state
> of high glee. Oil men waved and giggled when the army ap-
> proached. "Shut her down," they shouted, adding such little
> delicacies as "whoopie," "hell's bells," "meow," and "hot dog-
> gie."[16]

The hot-doggie-meow arrangement was superseded by the
NRA, which did get prices back up by holding down production, but when the Blue Eagle was winged and brought down
by the Supreme Court, something else was needed to take its
place. What the industry wanted, however, was noncompetitive
regulation without public supervision. It got what it wanted,
not by passing one law, but by erecting an edifice of impenetra-
ble complexity. Via what was called the Interstate Oil Compact,
the producing states set prorated production quotas. These
quotas were set on the basis of consumer demand forecast by
the Bureau of Mines; violators of production quotas were pro-
hibited from sending their contraband across state lines with

the passage of the fetchingly named Connally Hot Oil Act. On top of this, tariffs and informal agreements between the Department of Interior and the companies with foreign holdings limited imports. It was a system which defied the understanding of anyone outside the industry, and it was made more complicated by myriads of marketing agreements, pools, and other rigging devices which the government had no formal knowledge of but which it probably concurred in.

Then, after having midwifed this elaborate system of under-the-surface regulation (a system FDR personally approved of by turning down proposals that the industry be regulated like a federal public utility), after setting all of that up, in spring of 1936 the Justice Department convened a grand jury in Madison, Wisconsin, and several months later indicted twenty-three oil companies and fifty-eight people for criminal violations of the Sherman Act.

Loud and pained screams and shouts could be heard from the industry. The use of the FBI to sniff out evidence was angrily resented. The G-Men were supposed to stick to tracking Alvin "Creepy" Karpis or John Dillinger. The choice of Madison for the trial was considered proof that the Justice Department wanted a lynching, for the city had a reputation for Progressive antitrust sentiment. By the time the trial began in October, 1937, the defendants had been pared down to eighteen major oil companies, three trade publications, and forty-six individuals. Serving as chief counsel for the defense was Col. William J. "Wild Bill" Donovan, later to head up the wartime OSS, which became peacetime CIA. Oil-company executives will be oil-company executives, and when they hit Madison they turned public opinion against them with their high living. They took over the leading hotel, the country club, a number of the most opulent private homes, and an entire bank building whose occupant had gone to the big vault in the sky. The trial itself was an indecorous affair during which it was brought out that the big oil companies had made agreements with independent refiners, or their "dancing partners" as they called them, to keep oil off the market. The companies contended that such agreements had been condoned and encouraged by the government, to which Robert Jackson, the head of the Justice Department's antitrust division, replied, "There seems to have been an impression in the country that only a part of NRA was unconstitutional, that the part they did not like was unconstitutional, but they could still use those parts they did like;"[17] sixteen corporations and 30 oil executives were convicted of conspiracy.

This was followed by the Mother Hubbard suit, so named because of the breadth of the charges against twenty-two major oil-company defendants. The onset of World War II prompted the Justice Department to suspend it. The case enjoyed slight resuscitation afterward, but with the coming of the Cold War the department asked for its dismissal in 1951. Laissez faire, free-market competition, is incompatible with the coordination, planning, and allocation of resources and production required for mobilization and the quasi-permanent war alert of our own times. Conservatives, with their free-enterprise faith, seem unable to grasp that their military and militant foreign policy assures the continued existence of the centralized state they profess to abhor.

The Truman-Eisenhower approach was pretty much that of Harding. Domestically, the oil companies were to control prices but not be so gauche about it that the government would be embarrassed into going back to court; abroad, the oil companies were to control as much of the world supply as they could get their greasy little hands on. At this they were so successful they began to threaten the profitability of domestic oil production, which, in turn, led to the creation of yet another dizzying, complicated system for oil-import quotas.

The execution of these policies probably contributed to the execution of an unknown number of persons in faraway places as we, through instrumentalities like the CIA, connived and fought to maintain access to oil from Iran to Indonesia. By twentieth-century standards, the total who got offed in post–World War II conflicts in which oil figured was probably modest; a million would be the uppermost figure, and many of their survivors doubtless received CARE packages. On the bright side, the oil companies made money and the people of the United States got drunk and made air-conditioned and other energy-intensive forms of whoopee on lots and lots of cheap oil. From Taft to Carter no president has given serious thought to abandoning this strange admixture of government-supervised laissez faire monopoly that characterizes the way the industry is structured. The reason for that is, high profits or low, cartels or no, the oil companies were selling their product at what most of their customers have considered a reasonable price. In that sense they did split the profits with us, and we, as beneficiaries, haven't cared to ask too many threatening questions.

In the decades of evolving and oscillating oil policy, one of the constants is that there is no correlation between which way the policy may be moving and the party in power. It's impossible to say the Democrats stood for these approaches and the Republicans stood for those. The truth is that no meaningful division of opinion or principle has ever separated the two. Both have presumed that, depending on the exigencies of the moment, greater or less control may be necessary but that it must be done without disturbing the basic patterns of ownership and organization in the industry. In this respect FDR's administration is the most beguiling. Perhaps it was because it lasted so long, but at one time or another it tried out *all* the oil policies within the allowable limits just mentioned.

Although the second Roosevelt is used as the collectivist monster to scare college students demanding too many tax-financed social services, another constant is that our presidents enter office committed to bringing about the utopia of moderate-sized enterprises competing against each other in a gentle and ethical world so that the sum of all these competitions is the furtherance of the public good. Those who leave office alive have cause to depart with their views significantly moderated by their experiences. (The views aren't always moderated, though, even with cause. After he left office, Hoover acted as if it had been some other fellow who did all those New Dealish things, and, of course, the Democrats had no motive to set the record straight.)

Even in moments when the advantages of the free market are considered so much cant, the belief in it may break out. Just when the NRA and the new noncompetition type of competition was most in favor, Congress and the Roosevelt administration decided the system of government subsidies and favoritism to a few companies in the nascent airlines industry was unpardonably wrong. The government, through the medium of airmail contracts, had been helping three big companies and excluding the independents. This was done by negotiating contracts at meetings called "spoils conferences." This so scandalized everyone that FDR announced the army would fly the mail —we didn't have an air force then—pending the establishment of some bona fide free-enterprise competition. This form of socialism didn't work either. In just a few weeks the army mail planes cracked up no fewer than sixty-six times, killing twelve pilots.

5

When Big Brother
Was a Baby

The habit of lurching one way and then another in accordance with the dictates of whim or public clatter dates from the first Roosevelt's incumbency. Teddy's New Nationalism envisioned a central government that would guide and regulate the economy to serve a variety of goals. At Osawatomie, Kansas, in 1910, Teddy sketched an America that was disturbing to many propertied people who read the speech but which we can recognize as a partial outline of the nation we presently live in:

The state must be made efficient for the work which concerns only the people of the state; and the nation for that which concerns all the people. There must remain no neutral ground to serve as a refuge for lawbreakers of great wealth, who can hire the vulpine legal cunning which will teach them how to avoid both jurisdictions. The betterment which we seek must be accomplished, I believe, mainly through the national government. The New Nationalism puts the national need before section and personal advantage. The New Nationalism regards the executive power as the steward of the public welfare. . . . The man who wrongly holds that every human right is secondary to his profit must now give way to the advocate of human welfare, who rightly maintains that every man holds his property subject to the general right of the community to regulate its use to whatever degree the public welfare may require it.[1]

Teddy, who had declined to run again in 1908 but would in 1912, envisioned the president in his own person deciding what the public welfare might be. For the most part that meant helping emergent corporate America as best he could. One of the consequences was that the Trust-Buster busted precious few trusts. Only the bad ones—and only Teddy knew which they were. It was an eccentric, uncertain, and personalized modus operandi, but it worked. It pleased most big tycoons and it pleased the public who in their beloved Theodore had a president who was popular the way presidents just can't be any more.

His walrus-shaped protégé and successor was another matter. Willie Taft was a true conservative and a literal-minded one. Later on he developed sympathies for the working classes, but he still thought of Herbert Hoover as a Progressive and it worried him. In the end, Taft was too much of a conservative for big business, for he carried out the antitrust campaign Teddy was always talking about. Indeed, Taft filed almost twice as many suits under the Sherman Act as Teddy, and he didn't play favorites. Under Taft, "entente," as Roosevelt's special understandings with potential targets of litigation were called, vanished. While TR described what he was doing as using "Hamiltonian means for Jeffersonian ends,"[2] Willie disdained such self-deceptions. He stuffed his cabinet with corporation lawyers on the theory that government should have "at least as good legal services as any private corporation and . . . lawyers who thoroughly understood corporation methods could best advise me how to compel them to obey the law."[3] Taft wasn't quite as one-dimensional as that. He did espouse a measure like federal licensing of corporations, as does Ralph Nader, but in their hearts both would rather rely on competition than regulation, which is why William Howard and his corporate-lawyer associates sued everything that moved in the tall tiger grass of 1910 capitalism. For Teddy all this litigiousness to enforce Adam Smithian principles was just that, an almost quixotic effort "to put business of the country back into the middle of the 18th Century,"[4] which, of course, is just when the famous Edinburgh professor of political economy lived.

All of this is by way of prelude to the 1912 presidential election, which retrospectively looks like one of the few in which voters were offered something approaching a clear policy choice. The background was this. Teddy, who had served almost the full four years of the assassinated McKinley's second term, won election in his own right in 1904, triumphing over a conservative, Democratic nonentity. In 1908, using the power and the patronage of the presidency, which was far greater then than now, Roosevelt forced the Republicans to nominate his three-hundred-pound secretary of war, the conservative Ohio lawyer Taft. Besides being a person of endearing charm and lovability, Willie was a conspicuously able judge and administrator, but not an especially good politician.

Eventually Teddy and Willie probably would have had a falling out anyhow—most men come to despise their successors—but Taft's obdurate fidelity to the gentlemanly code caused him to make mistakes that those less encumbered with scruples might not have made. In the end, these two fallen-out friends who had worked together so well so long discovered that they didn't believe in the same things. Roosevelt was right about Taft: he was the spokesman for the past, just as Teddy and the man who won the 1912 election, Woodrow Wilson, were the foremost spokesmen and builders of our own contemporary political economy.

What helps to obscure the importance of 1912 is that every president has expressed his belief in the Taftian scheme of society at one moment or another. Some, like the supremely articulate Wilson, could say what Taft meant more clearly than Taft. Every working man, Wilson said in 1912, should be able to "hope and believe that if he were dependable and faithful and got a little bit ahead he could himself begin to look forward to independence in business and to employing somebody else, adding his energy to the growth of the business of the country. . . . What I am fighting for personally now is to see the average man is not kept down and denied that opportunity."[5]

Sixty-five years after the fact, we can see 1912 as a choice between less government with more laissez faire and more government with less laissez faire, but it's doubtful the voters then

looked at it that way. This was a period when the words liberal
and progressive, which had a good sound to many American
ears, were applied to a man like Roosevelt, not only because he
was regarded somewhat inaccurately as a trust-buster, but because he was associated with reform. Appointed to the U.S.
Civil Service Commission in 1889 by President Harrison, he
made a loud name for himself in that cause; next as a New York
police commissioner he made an even bigger reputation as a
fighter against corruption, political patronage, and any number
of bad things.

"Reform" is the word used to rationalize a redistribution of
money or power. The turn-of-the-century reform Teddy was
associated with saw the upper middle class increase its power
under the slogan of making municipal government "nonpolitical." Typically, the introduction of civil service was the device
used to lessen the ability of immigrant-based political machines
to control patronage; the less patronage, the less able they were
to win elections and rake off contracts just at the time when the
money in municipal government was growing because the size
of the cities was growing and the services they were offering
were expanding. The commission form of government or vari-
ants thereof based on citywide, as opposed to ward, representation wiped out minority chances. In Dayton, Ohio, before
reform, the Socialists with 25 percent of the vote elected five
public officials; after reform in 1913 with 35 percent of the vote
they elected zip and in 1917 with 44 percent of the vote they
elected zilch.

The effect of reform on the struggle for adequate representation among ethnic- and racial-minority groups was just as inju-
rious, but the Progressives of that period entertained opinions
on those subjects not well known anymore. Teddy, who was
broad-minded enough, to use an idiom of those times, to invite
a black man to lunch at the White House, habitually referred
to the inhabitants of places like Central America as dagos and
jackrabbits. William Allen White, the famous Progressive
newspaper editor from Emporia, Kansas, thanked his Maker
that "We are separated by two oceans from the inferior races

and by an instinctive race revulsion to cross breeding that marks the American wherever he is found."[6]

Wilson wasn't so sure the oceans were really wide enough to keep the undesirables out of the neighborhood:

> . . . now there came multitudes of men of the lowest class from the south of Italy and men of the meaner sort out of Hungary and Poland, men out of the ranks where there was neither skill nor energy nor any initiative of quick intelligence; and they came in numbers which increased from year to year, as if the countries of the south of Europe were disburdening themselves of the more sordid and hapless elements of their population, the men whose standards of life and of work were such as American workmen had never dreamed of hitherto . . . yet the Chinese were more to be desired, as workmen if not citizens, than most of the coarse crew that came crowding in every year at the eastern ports.[7]

These words of Wilson's were written in his *History of the American People* some years before he thought of running for president, and he tried to wiggle around them when they were thrown back at him in 1912. The "hyphenates"—Italo-Americans, German-Americans, etc.—never entirely lost their suspicion of Wilson, who also confirmed the blacks' fears of what a southerner would do if he got into the White House. Under the administration of the Virginia-born and southern-reared Wilson, the Treasury and Post Office Departments, the two places in the government with a noticeable number of black employees at the time, had their work areas, toilets, and lunchrooms segregated. Blacks were demoted and some pains were taken to make sure that no mistake was made that would permit a black person to supervise whites.

Even in the context of the times, this was a trifle retrogressive, but aside from that it would be an error to associate the reformism of the era with the notions we encapsulate in contemporary expressions like "social change." It's often to the advantage of the upper-middle-class reformer, however, to give the impression that his cause is connected in some metaphysical way with that of a great social movement. John Gardner's Common Cause, a modern mugwump organization started with money from the likes of the Rockefellers, had the feeling of crusade about it when in fact the kind of electoral reforms it espoused and which Jimmy Carter later embraced are those which will help certain middle-class trade, professional, and union organizations, but which are so tepid in their implications that they serve only to make a once-strong word like "reform" weak. The Republican party mugwumps of the 1880s espoused such things as the Australian or secret ballot, and did so with an astonishing zeal considering the mechanical and minor nature of these changes. The Carter proposal to permit election-day registration at the polls isn't the significant enlargement of democracy his administration has called it, but the wimpiest mugwumpery, a minor change in the rules.

At the same time, both Roosevelt and Wilson hinted at a new kind of egalitarianism which asserted it should be the duty of the national government to make sure that life's race was fairly run. Wilson's New Freedom insisted that

> There has come over the land that un-American set of conditions which enables a small number of men who control the government to get favors from the government; by those favors to exclude their fellows from equal business opportunity; by those favors to extend a network of control that will presently dominate every industry in the country, and so make men forget the ancient time when . . . eager men were everywhere captains of industry, not employees; not looking to a distant city to find out what they might do, but looking among their neighbors, finding credit according to their character, not according to their connections. . . . In order to start an enterprise now, you have to be authenticated, in a perfectly impersonal way, not according to yourself, but according to what you own that somebody else approves of your owning. You cannot begin such an enterprise as those that made America until you are so authenticated, until you have succeeded in obtaining the goodwill of large allied capitalists. Is that freedom? That is dependence, not freedom.[8]

Here is Wilson, such a convinced believer in corporate power, corporate centralism, and corporate progress, equating free-market freedom with freedom-freedom. The new mega-organizations may manufacture the wealth to make us rich, but laissez faire—even that contradiction in terms, government-administered laissez faire—makes us free. This was the foundation upon which was founded the civil-rights movement, the women's movement, the War on Poverty, and the whole notion of a society as a regulated meritocracy that gives according to how you score on your multiple-choice tests. Wilson said it: " . . . service rendered the people by the national government must be of a more extended sort and of a kind not only to protect it against monopoly, but also to facilitate its life. . . . we are just upon the threshold of a time when the systematic life of this country will be sustained, or at least supplemented at every point by governmental activity."[9]

These sentiments in no way distinguished Wilson from Roosevelt, a fact Wilson understood when he remarked, "When I sit down and compare my views with those of a Progressive Republican, I can't see what the difference is, except that he has a sort of pious feeling about the doctrine of protection, which I have never felt."

The kind of egalitarian intervention that both men preached in 1912 and which successive decades would realize in practice may be liberal in our eyes, but it has never been threatening to corporate America. Just as some people can't be in favor of something if they know the Communists are also in favor of it, others can't agree with anything if they know big business agrees with them too. It's become a psychological necessity for many to think of the women's movement or the civil-rights movement as being against the Establishment—i.e., the collective mentality, if there is one, of big business.

But below the executive level, the modern big business organization is inherently egalitarian in the best and the most dismal sense. To the extent that people are made into personnel, each worker cut from a universal template and the clone of every other worker, planning the flow of work can be made exact. For millions of employees in the private sector, the incentive system has been as completely abandoned as it has in the civil service. It's simply too inefficient and costly—as the corporations are presently designed—to recognize merit, distinguished achievement, or anything else which emphasizes the differences between human units. Even in research laboratories where industry does its R&D work, it's been decided that rewarding exceptional accomplishment is disruptive.

If you think back over the history of the civil-rights movement or the modern women's movement, you'll see that resistance to its goals didn't come from the corporate board rooms. It came from anachronistic and faintly colorful has-beens of history in the rural south and in the blue-collar lower-middle-class population in the north which correctly apprehended that its members would be the ones to make the greatest sacrifice and adjustment.

The big businessmen of 1912 didn't foresee all that, but it's probably fair to say that the tendencies and directions of Wilson and Roosevelt were perfectly clear and didn't bother them. Forgetting such unspeakables as the Socialists, the candidate that Wall Street and corporate America was resolute in not supporting was William Howard Taft. The Taft campaign starved for funds, as the money rolled in from Wall Street on the Bull Moose candidate, the Great Trust-Buster, who had had the antimonopoly plank in the Progressive party platform crossed out by George Perkins.

Wilson teased Teddy about his "missing plank," not that he was exactly scaring his rich backers by saying things like "Nobody can fail to see that modern business is going to be done by corporations. The old time of individual competition is probably gone by. It may come back; I don't know; it will not come back within our time."[10]

At the same time the Taft people were throwing up a memo written to Teddy when he was president by his commissioner of corporations suggesting that the Morgan-dominated International Harvester not be sued under the Sherman Act. The damaging sentence read, "While the administration has never hesitated to grapple with any financial interest, no matter how great, when it is believed that a substantial wrong is being committed, nevertheless, it is a very practical question whether it is well to throw away now the great influence of the so-called Morgan interests, which up to this time have supported the advanced policy of the administration."[11] The support adverted to here included large campaign contributions.

Nor was this a case of standards being markedly different then from now. Teddy's money connections smelled so bad that his pal, Senator Beveridge warned, "If we're not careful, we'll be labeled a Wall Street promotion."

Unhappily for the Wondrous Walrus, it was he who got the Wall Street tag, then and now, but not Wall Street's money. He inveighed against Roosevelt's backers and against the tycoons putting money into his opponent's campaign:

> The businessmen are fools, like some of the voters. For a time they don't see their real interest; they don't have the power of discrimination. That man, T. Coleman du Pont, is one such man. I have no use for him whatever. They don't see beyond their noses. They only think of their particular interest and don't take a broader view. They are in favor of special privilege in the sense of having themselves favored and everybody else prosecuted. That is the attitude of Gary and Perkins and du Pont and the others.[12]

With Teddy accusing Taft of trying to restore competition to the economic system, the orotund president suffered the humiliation of finishing behind both Roosevelt and Wilson. But the choice that was made that autumn was far, far less clear to the voters than it appears to us. Wilson only came on as a big-stick, New Nationalism heir to TR from time to time. The other Wilson was saying things like

> Nothing could be a greater departure from original Americanism, from faith in the ability of a confident, resourceful, and independent people than the discouraging doctrine that somebody has got to provide prosperity for the rest of us. And yet

that is exactly the doctrine on which the government of the United States has been conducted lately. . . . I don't want a smug lot of experts to sit down behind closed doors in Washington and play Providence to me.[13]

Has Ronald Reagan or George Wallace said it more clearly?

Wilson gorged himself on moral force. "Remember that God ordained that I should be president of the United States," he is accused of saying by a politician with whom he broke, but you can believe he said something very much like it. He had the kind of ruthlessness which goes with being anointed. "A man of high ideals but no principles," Lindley Garrison, his first secretary of war, called him. This president didn't want for the healthy, normal, and necessary forked tongue of the working politician. He knew how to mislead by giving literal answers to questions that were posed with fuller meaning, a la Nixon. He could also flat-out lie to press and public and think he was right to do it, as this excerpt from the diary of Col. Edward House, his close confidant, attests: "When we reached the apartment and were munching our sandwiches before retiring we fell to talking about various matters. The Governor [this conversation took place shortly before Wilson was sworn in as president] said he thought that lying was justified in some instances, particularly when it involved the honor of a woman. I agreed to this. He thought it was also justified when it related to matters of public policy."[14]

It fell to this imperious, although not imperial, southern, Democratic decentralist to perfect and make permanent the work begun by Teddy Roosevelt and the cohorts of new-age progressivism who surrounded and supported him. At home the Democratic Wilson was to take the ideas of his Republican predecessor and extend them through peace and war until the modern unitary state could be seen on the national skyline. Abroad, Wilson didn't talk softly, and not only did he carry Teddy's big stick, he used it—not once, not twice, but repeatedly. By the time he'd stopped beating various parts of the globe over the head, the United States was on its way to being the kind of power it is now.

For most of his life Wilson wasn't a liberal by the standards of his own time or ours. In 1908, just four years before he ran for president as a liberal, he was being openly critical of William Jennings Bryan, three-time Democratic candidate—the beloved and revered voice of the agricultural masses of the south and west, or a dangerous radical if you belonged to the group that first backed Wilson in politics. "Would that we could do something," he wrote of the Great Commoner, "at once dignified and effective, to knock Mr. Bryan, once and for all, into a cocked hat." In 1910, Wilson ran for the only other public office he ever held, governor of New Jersey, picked for the nomination by a cabal of right-wing Democratic millionaires and George Harvey, the conservative editor of *Harper's Weekly.* Moreover, his election was accomplished in part because of the votes delivered for him by the tackiest political machines in funky places like Jersey City.

Nevertheless, to more and more people, he seemed to be the liberal hope of the Democratic party. At least he had William Jennings Bryan conned. Climbing out of the cocked hat whither Wilson had wished to dispatch him, the Boy Orator, never one to hold grudges, gave the New Jersey governor help indispensable for him to win the Democratic nomination on the 46th ballot.

Wilson's record as governor was modern, that is it conformed to the advanced but not too advanced best thinking of the more cosmopolitan ruling circles. Had there been a *Time* magazine he would have made the cover, although Man of the Year would have eluded him. The same fashionable cycles in politics exist today. Governors like Brown of California, Dukakis of Massachusetts, Carter of Georgia, and Dan Walker of Illinois all bloom about the same time and all emit the same scent—one of budgetary toughness but mildness on civil rights and liberties. Prior to that were the urban-crisis politicians and before them builders and big-vision boys who built the schools, the highways, and the urban-renewal projects of the Eisenhower-Kennedy period.

Ordinarily what's fashionable in one party is fashionable in the other. A case in point would be the remarkably long career of former Vice-President Nelson Rockefeller, who managed to stay current decade after decade, while less supple souls yielded to arteriosclerosis or exhaustion. It was in this sense that Governor Wilson of New Jersey was fashionable. Indeed, the good-government, reform, regulatory administration he provided his state was close to identical to the one afforded New York by its governor, Charles Evans Hughes, the Republican whom Wilson closely defeated in 1916 when reelected for a second term.

This isn't to assert that there were no differences between the men or the parties. There were, but the vision of the role and responsibility of government was a shared one. A Wilson might not see eye to eye with a Roosevelt or a Hughes on every question and every measure, but in contesting for the presidency against both of them Wilson wasn't the representative of a separate power base or of a conflicting set of doctrines. However emotionally committed he may have been as a little-government man, he soon was using the power of the central government as Teddy did, to attempt to prevent another economic bust. A hundred million dollars was rushed to New York to prevent a run on the city's financial institutions, emergency banking legislation was rushed through Congress, and other steps were taken to prevent the recurrence of the cyclical disaster of American capitalism. Beside these efforts, Congress provided low-cost insurance against ships sunk or captured by the Germans in order to get business moving again.

The great Wilsonian accomplishment in the general area of stabilization was the creation of the Federal Reserve System, the primary purpose of which was to protect the banks, their depositors, and their borrowers against these harrowing and recurrent money shortfalls. In the end the first permanent governmental institution erected for the purpose of sparing us from cyclical panics failed the test of the early 1930s, when the banks collapsed by the hundreds, taking people's savings with them. A minor irony was that the legislation as first proposed contained a depositors'-insurance provision, which could have protected the savings even if the Federal Reserve System itself couldn't rescue the banks in which they were housed. Depositor insurance would have to wait, though, until the banking legislation of the 1930s, and it would not be until even later that the managers of the Federal Reserve gave evidence of having learned how to conduct their business so as not to bring the banking system down by inadvertence and ignorance of what they were about.

For years politicians of both parties, bankers, and businessmen, had agreed that some kind of mechanism was needed to anticipate economic disaster and forestall it. There had been bills introduced and countless committees and commissions formed. The bankers themselves, however, couldn't unite on any given set of proposals. One rural banker described a meeting conducted by the big-city bankers dominating the American Bankers' Association by explaining, "That committee was stacked; that was the coldest deal I ever went against in my life. We were invited there simply and solely to set the stage, to have a crowd, to carry a spear and sing a song and dance around, so that the stage would be full while the bigwigs could have the spotlight placed on them."[15]

Cacophony of this sort was made to order for presidential leadership, and Woodrow Wilson believed a president should lead. Taft had also been in favor of some similar kind of banking law that would ensure banks could meet the cash-withdrawal demands of their depositors during runs or panics, but the old dumpling just didn't have Thomas Woodrow's whoosh and pizazz. The law itself institutionalized what Teddy had done in 1907 and what Wilson himself did in 1914. (The Federal Reserve Act was passed before the 1914 crisis but didn't go into effect until it was over.) Like the ICC legislation, it enhanced federal power and created a national financial instrument, but it by no means left the office of the president stronger.

In future crises it would be more difficult for a president to deal with Wall Street as Teddy had dealt with Morgan and his people. The time for that kind of free wheeling was passing. The economy was getting too big even for men like Morgan to be able to do much to affect it even if they cared to. When Hoover asked his own secretary of the treasury, Andrew Mellon, a man of staggering wealth, to kick in a paltry million to a pool to help save the secretary's hometown Bank of Pittsburgh, Andy told the president to go suck an egg.

Wilson wanted a true national bank a la Bank of England instead of the hodgepodge Federal Reserve System which presidents might influence but not control. The members of the Federal Reserve Board, like those of the ICC, were appointed by the chief executive but served not at his pleasure but for stated terms. At first these were ten years, but later, under the New Deal, they were lengthened to fourteen years so that the appointing power was much vitiated. In the decades following its creation, the board's powers have been strengthened, thereby making it somewhat easier to finance wars and war production. At the same time it has also worked to shield the banking industry from a certain amount of competition, but whether it has ever been able to provide the society with the economic equipoise it was created for is highly debatable. In the aftermath of the Great Depression, some economists have marshalled convincing arguments to show that the board's dunderheaded ignorance worsened the bank panic of the early 1930s, contributed richly to the second crash of 1937–38, and was one of the major contributing causes to the inflation and ensuing bust of the early 1970s because it foolishly printed too much money.

That it may not have worked very well is less important for our purposes than recognizing the importance of its creation in the building of the system which so irritates, enrages, and baffles us. When the next bad business recession hit in 1920–21, the Harding administration found that the levers and handles of economic manipulation bequeathed it by the Wilsonians were insufficient and added several new antidepressants. One was the Budget Bureau, which gave the executive branch some managerial control over itself in the effort to cut government expenses. The proposition behind lowering government expenditures was that if more money was left in the private sector, it would be

invested in employment-generating enterprises. The same reasoning was applied to the Harding tax cut—the first time the
tax rates were adjusted as an economic stimulus—but then the
income tax was barely eight years old. Cutting taxes in a recession is now nearly an axiomatic response, but the much-
sneered-at Harding did it first.

Neither Harding nor the other leading politicians of the
1920s were ever all that far to the right. When Harding made
up that neologism, "normalcy," he explained, "By 'normalcy'
I don't mean the old order, but a regular steady order of things.
I mean normal procedures, the natural way, without excess."[16]
Given the fandango Wilson had gotten the country to dance,
the vile and violent fight over the League of Nations, and given
a president too sick to see the members of his cabinet, a president so stricken he could do nothing but watch movies in the
White House and go for rides in his touring car, normalcy
sounded like sanity to the voters of the 1920s.

When Herbert Clark Hoover left the White House, in his
bitterness at FDR for beating him and at the electorate for
throwing him out, he exaggerated the differences between himself and his successor. The differences were there, all right, but
the coming of Roosevelt II was by no means the historic break
with our past that both Democrats and Republicans would
dwell on and magnify over the decades. Hoover was Harding's
secretary of commerce, a major figure in the eight years before
he actually moved into the White House, an instant success as
a bureaucrat who had no trouble adding three thousand people
to his department's payroll during his time there. It was Hoover
who pushed Harding into calling a Washington conference on
the 1920–21 recession; it was Hoover who advocated the first
government contracyclical spending program. He wanted to lay
away funds in good times to be spent on job creation in bad
ones, and when bad times came it was Hoover who signed a
nationally financed relief law under which the Federal Employment Stabilization Board came into existence.

He didn't sign the bill happily, because Hoover was a divided
man. He didn't believe in laissez faire, at least not at this point

in his long life, but he was much troubled by government action in what he viewed as the private sector. His answer to the problem was what was called "associationalism" in that era. He thought that through the building up and use of trade associations—what we'd call quasi-cartelization—the worst consequences of the free market could be mitigated and the government kept out of the matter. This was to be done voluntarily by businessmen, animated by economic togetherness. If Hoover alone had been possessed of these ideas, they could be disregarded as a harmless voluntarist fantasy, but they were held by a great variety of ruling-circle types in that period, including Franklin Roosevelt. In fact, the voluntarist ideal, far from dying with Hoover, was so much part of our political culture that even a centralizing, authoritarian president like John Kennedy could use it in setting up the Peace Corps. Under Johnson's ill-named War on Poverty, a multiplicity of efforts were undertaken to facilitate voluntarist activities among low-income people. Few of them were successful in establishing self-sustaining, private, low-income organizations and institutions, and the Nixon administration was fierce in its cutbacks on such programs; but what's worth noting is that the voluntarist ideal wasn't abandoned. New, equally unsuccessful programs such as Nixon's attempts to stimulate black capitalism were tried. Under the Carter administration we find people at work pushing the hybrid of government-paid-for volunteer organizations among lower-income people.

In 1927, in response to a damaging Mississippi River flood, Hoover organized a successful voluntary rescue effort. He raised $17 million in private contributions which were matched by $10 million in federal funds, and the endeavor seems to have gone off far better than the recent incompetent HUD disaster-aid projects, which supply the victims with bureaucrats but no emergency housing. "We rescued Main Street with Main Street,"[17] Hoover said, but he couldn't accept the idea that even a flood on the Mississippi was small potatoes compared to the Great Depression, and that the voluntary institutions he had worked so hard to put together throughout the whole decade weren't able to make an impression against such social disaster.

The nub of the Blue Eagle plan, brought to Hoover and rejected by him as fascism or the next thing to it, was to make his own "associational" idea compulsory. Far from being an exotically weird bird, the strangely colored eagle was a reasonable development from the best establishmentarian thinking of the 1920s. It represented no right-angle departure from the past but was part of the binding continuity of ideas and perceptions which dominated both parties and the leading figures in them. It was an idea that came a cropper, but so did every other idea that was tried to pump, lift, haul, or explode the United States out of the depression.

Part of the difficulty was that the range of thinkable thoughts was relatively narrow. Nothing could be proposed that might question the integrity or even the rationality of the major components of the American system. At the same time, the more astute members of the upper classes had that bad feeling that what was wrong would not surrender to tinkering. They were perplexed in much the same way as was Congressman James Mead when he made his Fourth of July speech:

> What a strange situation confronts us today. Will not our grandchildren regard it as quite incomprehensible that in 1930 millions of Americans went hungry because they produced too much food; that millions of men, women, and children were cold because they produced too much clothing, that they suffered from the chilly blasts of winter because they produced too much coal? I am not speaking in parables. This is the literal truth. To-day we are suffering want in the midst of unprecedented plenty. Our workers are without wages because they have learned to work too well. . . . President Hoover recently stated that the warehouses are bursting with a surplus of supplies and still people are denied them."[18]

6

To Market, to Market, to Sell a Small Pig

The Great Depression did not bring on the first inkling that the United States might have a chronic overcapacity problem. In 1912 Wilson was explaining, "We have a surplus of manufactured goods of which we must get rid or else do an unprofitable business." Our industries, he said, "have expanded to such a point that they will burst their jackets if they cannot find a free outlet to the markets of the world."[1]

The markets of the world did not take enough of the American surplus to prevent 1929 and all that. Although big business swung around to a low-tariff position and away from its historic protectionism, too many other elements in the society, smaller manufacturers and farmers particularly, wanted the noncompetition of high import duties, so the government's policy from Harding's time until the Second World War was to force the Open Door abroad while keeping it locked at home. That didn't produce much trade, although Harding, bless his soul, broke his back trying to do things like get subsidies for the merchant marine, and the exporting manufacturers tried to get Secretary of Commerce Hoover to buy the idea that private loans by American banks to foreign countries should stipulate that a certain percentage of the money had to be spent here. Proposals like that were just too contrary to the make-it-on-your-own attitude of the time, but good ideas never die; they keep worming their way into the political fruitwood. This one did, and we see it reborn after World War II as a condition of government loans and what Americans called foreign aid and foreigners called American aid.

Neither Hoover nor Franklin Roosevelt put much hope in resuscitating a gasping America through foreign trade. Nor, as the panic deepened, did they differ about using federal money to save engulfed and struggling banks and railroads. With Hoover's recommendation, Congress set up the Reconstruction Finance Corporation to make loans to faltering businesses. Like so many of the ideas put forward to fight the depression, the RFC was based on an invention of Wilson's administration for accelerating war production, the War Finance Corporation. Used to finance industrial expansion during the war, it was revived in 1919 to help American capital during the economic difficulties of the early 1920s. Not only did the War Finance Corporation serve as the model for the RFC; the same man, Eugene Meyer, headed them both.

But what seems to us slight differences in presidents and programs was not seen that way at the time. "This campaign is more than a contest between two men," Hoover said in his race against Roosevelt. "It is more than a contest between two parties. It is a contest between two philosophies of government. . . . You cannot extend the mastery of government over the daily life of a people without somewhere making it master of people's souls and thoughts."[2]

In the fall of 1932 those were not thoughts people particularly cared to listen to. Millions doubtless agreed with them, but their tummies were empty and tomorrow looked more frightening than today. Something had to be done, yet at the same time, structural change or radical change was politically unimaginable; the scaffolding of society must be held constant. So Hoover, who would never countenance any form of public ownership of enterprises traditionally thought of as private, sanctioned a government corporation making loans which amounted to subsidies to save the banks.

The trick was to keep all as it was—banks, railroads, factories, farms—while devising ways to overcome the intolerable inadequacies of uncontrolled entrepreneurial activity. The mess this may entail is nowhere better illustrated than in agriculture. By Hoover's time the debate had ceased to be over whether there should be government intervention but over what form it ought to take. The problem was that Mother Nature hadn't read Adam Smith.

In late winter, the farmer has to guess what he thinks market conditions may be like five or six months later. Given the vagaries of weather and the appetites of nematodes, the chances of guessing right one year are only fair. To do it two or three years in a row is chancy; it's one of the elements which makes farming an altogether too exciting business. Given the huge number of people in farming—as late as 1930, 22 percent of the labor force was in agriculture—and the fecundity of American farms, this enormous sector of our economy was almost always producing a surplus, that is it was producing more food than Americans could consume and keep the prices up. The farmer had to cope with awesome transportation and marketing problems as well as a perennial shortage of credit to buy new machinery, to provide him with working capital to get him from planting to marketing time, and to keep him going through the bad years. When farmers had their good years, a long chain of things had to break right for them, beginning with the weather and the weevil and ending with economic and political conditions everywhere on the globe that American agricultural products were being pushed in and sold.

Our contemporary view of the nineteenth century puts the emphasis on slavery and other questions that interest us now, but a great deal of the noise and controversy then actually revolved around the politics of farmers and farmers' demands for credit, for access to foreign markets, for low railroad rates and lower tariffs. Nor were the debates carried on in the tepid-temperature, problem-solving language of the modern manager. Then it was the sons of horny-handed toil against the money interest, and out of that was born a bipartisan group in Congress known as the farm bloc. From 1913 onward there is a stream of agricultural legislation for easier credit, for roads to bring produce to market, for programs to disseminate technical information, for grading and marketing, and for regulating various phases of the economic parts of the food chain. Despite the legislation passed under Wilson, Harding, and Coolidge, the 1920s were all downhill and lower prices for American farmers. Things were so bad that in '27 and '28, Congress passed huge agricultural-subsidy bills, both of which were vetoed by Coolidge at Hoover's advice.

The farm bloc didn't have the votes to override the vetos, but the next year, as president, Hoover signed the Agricultural Marketing Act of 1929, which created the Federal Farm Board and began an enormous effort to save commodity prices. Almost $350 million, a gigantic sum in those days, was lost just in the effort to save the price of cotton. It didn't work; prices dropped so low, under a nickel a pound, that it was selling for less than it cost to grow it. What had been the disaster of farm economics in the 1920s turned into a catastrophe during Hoover's administration in the early thirties. The poverty of the Okies and the southern sharecroppers has been celebrated, but even in Iowa, where the corn is always green and the cattle are fat, matters had reached a point beyond believing. These snatches from the 1932 diary of an Iowa farmer convey the times and their bafflement:

Our grain shock up well. The shocks are taller than last year. . . . But the price is all wrong. Nature has done her part well. Just men in their management are blundering. This harvest has been one of the most satisfactory we have ever had. . . . Our daily paper has stopped and we are not renewing it promptly. As a matter of economy I am resharpening old razor blades and when I shave I use any kind of soap instead of shaving cream. . . . I suppose some one will start the idea of growing beards. The oats market is a cent lower today . . . the Farmer's Holiday or "strike" was called for next Monday morning . . . the local news of the Holiday is that two truck loads of cream were dumped yesterday. Approximately three hundred dollars worth. A station is opened in town where striking farmers may leave their milk and cream to be given away. . . . Many folks

intend to use some corn for fuel, others would not think of
burning it.[3]

At length the Farm Board gave up trying to support agricultural prices. There didn't seem to be enough money in the world
to do it. Our inflation has made the expenditures of the Hoover
period look puny when calculated in our mini-dollars, but in
fact total government expenditures on federal, state, and local
levels for economic revival were higher in 1931 than in any year
under FDR. Federal expenditures under Hoover in 1931 were
exceeded by the New Deal only in 1934, '35, and '36. In the long
and sour years of Hoover's post-presidential life, he didn't put
it this way, but he could have said with some accuracy that he
tried spending our way out of the Great Depression but it didn't
work. "We cannot squander ourselves into prosperity," he
said,[4] but even by our standards it might have seemed that
Hoover had tried. Hoover's deficit in 1932 was $2,735,000,000
in a year when the federal budget was $4,659,000,000. By com-
parison, our deficit in 1976 was $66,461,000,000 on a budget of
$366,466,000,000, so the gap between what the federal govern-
ment was taking in and what Hoover was spending would be
frightening even to us moderns who are more accustomed if not
happier with large deficits.[5]

Although Roosevelt would emulate Hoover and go him one,
two, and three better in a number of areas, during the 1932
campaign he didn't put any pressure on the president to spend
yet more to save the farmer. Roosevelt's economic ideas, although not necessarily his social and political ones, were too
close to Hoover's. To him, deficit spending was one of the
"illusions of economic magic." In the 1932 campaign, he
proposed to spend without incurring a deficit by a formula that
Jimmy Carter would try out on the voters forty-four years later:

> We face a condition which, at first, seems to involve either an
> unbalanced budget and an unsound currency or else failure of
> the Government to assume its just duties. . . . This dilemma can
> be met by saving in one place what we would spend in others,

or by acquiring the necessary revenue through taxation. Revenues must cover expenditures by one means or another. Any government, like any family, can for a year spend a little more than it earns. But you and I know that a continuation of that habit means the poorhouse.[6]

Nor was such talk fluff for the voters. FDR's second message to Congress was a request for $400 million cut in veterans' payments and $100 million cut in federal government employees' salaries. Congress didn't like to vote against GI benefits then either, but the administration was able to push the bill through.

Many years later, one of FDR's original Brain Trusters, Tugwell, was quoted as saying, "We didn't admit it at the time, but practically the whole New Deal was extrapolated from programs that Hoover started." It would be more accurate to say that Roosevelt developed from Hoover as Hoover had from Harding and Wilson, and as Wilson has to be viewed as an extender and fulfiller of Teddy. As a young man, Franklin much admired his cousin Teddy and agreed with many of the things the foremost member of the Republican branch of the family did. The difference between them was the difference in time, circumstance, and evolution in upper-class thinking in a generation and a half. With a couple of exceptions like Taft and Nixon, that could be said of any two of our twentieth-century presidents. What sets them apart is better described as evolutionary sequence than disagreement.

Looked at from a distance, it seems each picks up where his predecessor leaves off. Hoover, who perfected welfare to ailing big businesses, wouldn't take the federal government further into debt to pay for similar aid for individuals. Roosevelt could recognize an untenable political distinction when he saw one, so that at the same time he was arm in arm with Hoover for the balanced budget, he could also say in the 1932 campaign, "If starvation or dire need on the part of any of our citizens make necessary the appropriation of additional funds which would keep the budget out of balance, I shall not hesitate to tell the American people the full truth and ask them to authorize the expenditure of that additional amount."[7]

So when the Farm Board's attempt to save commodity prices collapsed, the Hoover administration could think of going no further than advising farmers to destroy their crops in order to raise prices by creating scarcity. For such an undertaking to be successful, voluntarism had to give way to some form of government action. The New Deal took it. In yet one more attempt to get farm revenues up before every homestead in America was foreclosed on, the New Deal literally paid farmers to destroy crops and livestock.

For Iowa farm diarist Elmer Powers and many other Americans, farmers and nonfarmers alike, the destruction of food and fiber was terribly wrong, and nothing seemed worse than the mass killing of the piglets:

> This afternoon we were finally able to get the pigs delivered in town and by this evening they are well on the way to Chicago. Four hundred head of pigs went out of the village today. Our pigs weighed sixty pounds each. . . . Many farmers were around the truck while they were loading and they all regretted taking these fine pigs out of the lot at this time. Also many of these same farmers agreed that something must be done. In quite a few cases farmers were entirely out of money and will welcome the opportunity to cash in on this.[8]

By the middle of August 1933 pigs were coming into the country's principal stockyards faster than they could be killed. The *Chicago Tribune* reported,

> They came in all sizes. There were big pigs and little pigs—some of them so small that they slipped between the slats and ran squealing from one pen to another with hog buyers and government agents shooing them all over the lot. . . . Despite the fact that Sec. [of Agriculture Henry A.] Wallace's pig killing farm relief plan established a 25 pound minimum there were some piglets weighing as little as 5 pounds. . . . Eligible sows, and pigs weighing from 80 to 100 pounds are painted with a green stripe

down their backs, slaughtered and the meat set aside for distribution to the poor. Pigs weighing from 25 to 80 pounds are given a red stripe of paint and destroyed for fertilizer. . . . In two days Uncle Sam had become the world's largest buyer and painter of hogs. . . .[9]

A *New York Times* dispatch from Omaha two days later remarked,

> What makes it all so puzzling is that it goes against the tradition that past generations of agriculture have handed down to the present as to what constitutes a good husbandry, the teaching of the agricultural colleges, the work of the experiment stations, the two blades of grass idea, and even Mr. Wallace's own astounding experiments with hybrid corn to increase yields. What, one asks, is the value of the 4-H pig clubs and the big litter contests, if it only results in the production of pigs which are to be wasted? . . . how can a country waste its way back to prosperity?[10]

Those readers who could get through the *Times* that Sunday must have felt mildly suicidal when they put it down. The same paper also carried an article by Charles McD. Puckette of Greenville, South Carolina, describing the destruction of a quarter of the cotton crop:

> Just when it was "lay-by" time, when the cotton is worked no more until picking, the plow and the mule were taken out again to turn under the rows of plants already in boll and blossom. . . . As one drives through the Cotton Belt the scene is impressive. In every field a part lies bare earth. Through the dirt here and there, protrude a few withered down stalks; occasionally a boll has broken open showing dirty, unmatured cotton. . . . For all his years the mule has been trained to walk between the rows and not tread on the cotton plants. Recently the Brain Trust asked this conservative to change his ways, to trample on the rows as he dragged the destroying plow. Many a mule's hide, through which he receives his education, has suffered in learning the strange lesson of the New Deal. . . .

Henry Wallace and many of the other members of the Roosevelt administration were as depressed and as appalled as everyone else. They were driven to a program of destruction because they came into office too late in 1933 to institute production controls, and they could think of no other way to avoid a total agricultural wipe-out. The next year saw the beginning of the implementation of the labyrinthine systems of allotment, subsidies, marketing rules, and the rest of the machinery that has dominated American agriculture ever since. It did not save the family farm or the way of life that expression evokes, although family-run, or owner-operated, farms still dominate the production end of the food industry.

Nevertheless, if the New Deal did anything, it accelerated the rural depopulation which was already under way. Black sharecroppers were the first hit. Under the rules of the new government subsidy program, white owners had an incentive to kick black sharecroppers off their land and/or convert them into paid—miserably paid—workers. A different administration, not one that was of the cautious continuum of our historical succession, might have seized on the minute to give black farmers the forty acres and the mules they'd been promised seventy years before. You could find visionaries in the Department of Agriculture who may have had such thoughts, but nobody in power ever gave serious consideration to using the Great Depression as the occasion for changing the structure of things. If we look at some of the other Rooseveltian innovations, we see that the major ones were intended to make the extant economic machinery perform as it was supposed to.

Certainly that was the case with the Securities and Exchange Commission, one of the New Deal agencies that contributed to turning so many businessmen hostile to FDR. The SEC and some of the parallel banking legislation were to make the stock market function better by policing the swindlers and the speculators out of it. In the minds of Hoover, Roosevelt, and many, many others there was a connection between speculation, the stock market bust, and the depression. Hoover didn't move on that matter because, being more conservative than

FDR, he believed the federal government had no jurisdiction over a stock market located in New York State, but he thought that Roosevelt, as the governor of New York, should have moved to regulate Wall Street or curb its excesses. In any event, the resultant federal Securities and Exchange Commission, whose first chairman was the multimillionaire father of President John Kennedy, teed off businessmen but was in the mainstream of thinking then, and still is now. In the first forty-odd years of its existence it has had no demonstrable ability to prevent fraud or speculation of the wilder sort. Like many another regulatory agency, consciously or unconsciously, its rules for many years favored the large, already established brokerage houses and discouraged new companies from coming into the industry.

In recent years that's changed, but as a consumer-protection agency for the small minority of Americans who buy stocks and bonds, it has been somewhat of a bust. It has nonetheless forced companies selling securities to the general public to disclose a great deal of information about themselves which might otherwise not be available. Whether that public good outweighs the public bad arising from the burden this puts on small companies just starting out in the world is endlessly debatable. William Howard Taft wanted federal chartering of corporations for the same purpose of making large corporations publish the pertinent facts about their operations.

It fell on Franklin Roosevelt to be the president in the White House when it came time to institutionalize and enlarge what had already begun, as well as to try out a number of ideas that had been kicking around the most respectable circles for a generation or more. Roosevelt had the smarts and the sympathy for people to see that the time had indeed come—so that, where Hoover may have lagged and dragged, FDR led. It's hard not to believe, however, that many, perhaps most, of the more important pieces of New Deal legislation would have become law no matter which of the most important Democrats or Republicans of the time had been president. One wonders

not that they passed the Fair Labor Standards Act which out-
lawed child labor in 1938 but that it took them so long to get
around to it. By 1914, forty-seven states and the District of
Columbia already had laws prohibiting child labor. It was 1916
when the eight-hour day was made mandatory for railroad
workers; in 1923 Herbert Hoover led a public campaign in the
newspapers to embarrass steel executives into starting the eight-
hour day in their industry. That such should become federal
law fifteen years later ought to be a tipoff as to the conservative
nature of the bill, which was, incidentally, either opposed outright or given only the most pro forma support by major labor
leaders like William Green, the head of the AF of L, and John
L. Lewis, who held the same position with the CIO.

Traditionally union opinion on federal legislation of labor
standards—or even compensation for workmen injured on the
job—had run from iffy to hostile. Union leaders feared government control as much as management; they also believed they
could make a better deal for themselves than they would be
forced to accept from the business-influenced magistrates and
bureaucrats in Washington. As for laws bearing directly on
labor unions, John L. Lewis was quoted as saying, "The United
Mine Workers and the CIO [both of which he headed] have
paid cash on the barrel head for every piece of legislation that
we have gotten. . . . Is anyone fool enough to believe for one
instant that we gave this money to Roosevelt because we were
spellbound by his voice?"[11] At the same time, legislation like
the Wagner Labor Relations Act, which would take the sprawl-
ing disputes between industrial workers and managers off the
bricks and into decorous negotiating rooms, was the next thing
to inevitable. The disorder and violence were frightening, and
leaving matters for the president to settle through emergency
conferences called in the Oval Office, a la Teddy Roosevelt's
good works during the 1902 coal strike, couldn't go on indefi-
nitely.

The question is, How startling and how divisive were even
the labor laws which brought most of the right-wing hatred
down on FDR? Not very, in fact; there have been successful

attempts to "balance" them—i.e., make things somewhat more favorable to management—but since FDR's time no significant faction in either party has advocated pulling down the legal procedures and relationships that have taken the place of the brickbats and combats between the strikers and the scabs and Pinkertons. Since the Second World War, worker productivity in most of the industries susceptible to union organization has been so great that the workers they employ constitute a declining fraction of the labor force. Labor "power" has changed from a real possibility into the dreamy memories of old labor skates. Increasingly, labor unions are becoming labor contractors or brokers who first strike a bargain with management and then police their own members to make sure the deal is kept.

FDR and his collaborators did the most they could do, but it was also the least that could be done. Viewed from the perspective of the late seventies, the battles over something like the passage of Social Security seem absurd. The United States was the last major industrial nation to offer something to the old and sick, many of whom had been made indigent public charges by the forced reorganization of the family in a high-technology, corporate society. When Social Security was passed, more than forty state legislatures had already voted through one form of old-age pension or another, and England's had been functioning for a quarter of a century. Business opposition to pensions was loud, long, and fierce, but, other than doing nothing, it's hard to see how Roosevelt and Congress could have done less. True, Social Security was a departure, and an historic one; nevertheless, it could not have been more conservatively financed than through what became an increasingly retrogressive payroll tax. At the time the program was started up, a number of economists thought the sudden imposition of the new taxes took so much money out of circulation that it contributed to the second crash of 1937–38.

In all these endeavors, the power and arena of the federal government increased. Every group that was able to mobilize itself to make a political impression did so and got a little something going in Washington. It wasn't just that some got a subsidy and others a board or regulatory commission; it's that so many also got a government office and at least a petite, starter bureaucracy to dandle them, inform them, lobby for them, and represent them. In addition to undertaking chores that were never performed before, government became a partial administrative substitute for what had previously been done through various free-market mechanisms. Now virtually every activity in the society has some small place in this asymmetrical triumph of eclecticism encouraging it, cheering it on, planning, coordinating, propagandizing, and predicting great things for it.

If even the teachers of ancient Greek and Hebrew have their waning interests represented in some cubicle in the Office of Education or the National Foundation on the Arts and the Humanities, the power of the presidency has not matched the growth of government. The one tool the White House has to control this mass of activity, the Office of Management and Budget, is unable, let alone legally permitted, to run the government in the same careful sense that a company as large as General Motors is run by its central executive cadres. Back in the 1930s Congress made sure that no central planning office remotely commensurate in size with enlarged government was permitted to exist. Jimmy Carter, who has pronounced technocratic leanings, may try to get that kind of capacity in the executive branch, but even if he is given it, the contradictions and anomalies in the structure and action of government defy planning and coordination.

That is a Rooseveltian legacy. FDR was almost as mistrustful of tight central government as those who accused him of trying to force it on the country. He was a powerful president because he was a superb spokesman for the spirit of his times, because he was a seldom-rivaled master of the art of presidential pulpitry, because he was a politician of great skill, who loved to be loved, and loved to charm, inspire, connive, and trick. Such a president would not be too taken up with the institutional deficiencies of his office, because the immediate circumstances, as well as his own virtuosity at the job, made them relatively unimportant. Far from developing an internally consistent program, Roosevelt's two peacetime administrations of the 1930s included such diverse approaches that some historians say there were really two New Deals, the early collectivist New Deal of the NRA and the later, Second New Deal, which took up laissez faire again with renewed faith. The end of the decade saw the most energetic antitrust activity since the Taft administration. Thurman Arnold, the assistant attorney general in charge of the Antitrust Division, went at the task with high volume, much fury, and witty dedication but with a sense of the futility and incompleteness that comes to those in government service who can't avoid noticing that means and ends aren't often joined by reason. "As this is being written," Arnold wrote in 1937,

> a crusade against the Aluminum Company of America is in the first stages of its long struggle through the courts. . . . The reason why these attacks [against monopoly] always ended with a ceremony of atonement, but few practical results, lay in the fact that there were no new organizations growing up to take over the functions of those under attack. The opposition was never able to build up its own commissary and its service of supply. It was well supplied with orators and economists, but it lacked practical organizers. A great cooperative movement in America might have changed the power of the industrial empire. Preaching against it, however, simply resulted in counterpreaching.[12]

"Ceremonies of atonement" sufficed in the 1930s when, like now, there was no general agreement on what ailed the economy, nor any clearcut debate over alternative policies. FDR was no more enamored of budgetary deficits and welfare programs for individuals than the presidents who came after him and acquiesced in what none of them knew how to avoid. Like Wilson, like Hoover, and like his successors, Roosevelt first moved to support existing structures, especially business enterprise, and then, when that failed to trickle down to enough individuals, he supported the dole. From our perspective, he is the chef who cooked the great hodgepodge, the pudding which made permanent the thirty previous years of experimentation in making the political economy of the liberal corporate state. More than most guys, FDR has a right to plead that it seemed like a good idea at the time.

Part 3

American factories are making more than the American people can use; American soil is producing more than they can consume. Fate has written our policy for us; the trade of the world must and shall be ours. And we shall get it as our mother [England] has told us how. We will establish trading posts throughout the world. . . . We will cover the ocean with our merchant marine. We will build a navy to the measure of our greatness. Great colonies governing themselves, flying our flag and trading with us will grow about our posts of trade. Our institutions will follow our flag on the wings of our commerce. And American law, American order, American civilization, and the American flag will plant themselves on shores hitherto bloody and benighted, but by those agencies of God henceforth to be made beautiful and bright.

Sen. Albert J. Beveridge, 1897

"The Pacific Ocean . . . is in our hands now. Practically we own more than half the coast on this side, dominate the rest, and have midway stations in the Sandwich and Aleutian Islands. To extend now the authority of the United States over the great Philippine Archipelago is to fence in the China Sea and secure an almost equally commanding position on the other side of the Pacific—doubling our control of it and of the fabulous trade the Twentieth Century will see it bear. Rightly used, it enables the United States to convert the Pacific Ocean into an American lake."

Whitelaw Reid, 1900, Member of the Spanish-American War Peace Commission

7

"Do Not Make Peace Until We Get Porto Rico..."

Whether or not those who're ignorant of their history are doomed to repeat it, those who know it are less likely to be surprised by it. Vietnam wasn't a unique deviation. We had fought a nasty, take-no-prisoners guerrilla war in Southeast Asia before. Those who think of the 1964–75 conflict as a special betrayal haven't been told how long American leaders schemed to keep a toehold on the western rim of the Pacific and realize Whitelaw Reid's hope of making that body of water an American lake.

Our century began with the army waist-deep in the big muddy of what might be called Vietnam I—the Philippines. "The opposition tells us we ought not to rule a people without their consent," cried Teddy's friend Senator Beveridge, the Indiana Cicero. "I answer, the rule of liberty, that all just governments derive their authority from the consent of the governed, applies only to those who are capable of self-government."[1] Whether or not the Tagalog or Filipino people knew how to govern themselves, they knew how to fight, and they were unable to see any particular difference between their royal Spanish masters and the republican Americans who came to replace them.

The resulting guerrilla war was barely distinguishable from the one the United States would fight directly across the South China Sea from the Philippines sixty-five years later. A war

correspondent for the *Boston Transcript* filed this story for the
April 14, 1899, edition of his paper:

> "Just watch our smoke!" is what the Minnesota and Oregon
> regiments have adopted for a motto since their experiences of
> the last few days. Their trail was eight miles long; and the smoke
> of burning buildings and rice heaps rose into the heaven the
> entire distance, and obscured the face of the landscape for many
> hours. They started at daylight this morning, driving the rebels
> before them and setting the torch to everything burnable in their
> course.[2]

Three years later the same paper printed an interview with a
Congressman who had visited the island and quoted him as
saying, "You never hear of any disturbance in Northern Luzon;
and the secret of its pacification is, in my opinion, the secret of
the pacification of the archipelago. They never rebel in Northern Luzon because there isn't anybody there to rebel."[3]
Excerpts from our boys' letters home are almost as vivid as
the nightly appearance of the Vietnam War in our living rooms.
So we have L. F. Adams of Ozark, Missouri, writing, "In the
path of the Washington Regiment and Battery D of the Sixth
Artillery, there were 1,008 dead niggers, and a great many
wounded. We burned all their houses. I don't know how many
men, women and children the Tennessee boys did kill. They
would not take any prisoners." Sgt. Howard McFarland, Company B, 43rd Infantry, told the *Fairfield* (Maine) *Journal,* "I
am now stationed in a small town in charge of twenty-five men,
and have a territory of twenty miles to patrol. . . . At the best,
this is a very rich country; and we want it. . . . On Thursday,
March 29, eighteen of my company killed seventy five nigger
bolomen and ten of the nigger gunners. . . . When we find one
that is not dead, we have bayonets."[4] And A. A. Barnes, Battery G, Third U.S. Artillery, told his brother in a letter, "I am
probably grown hard-hearted for I am in my glory when I can
sight my gun on some dark skin and pull the trigger."[5]
Without benefit of napalm or carpet bombing, American
efforts at laying waste to the Philippine infrastructure, to use a

term of the military art that would not be coined for another half century, was so successful that General James M. Bell told the *New York Times,* "One sixth of the natives of Luzon have either been killed or died of the dengue fever in the last two years."[6] In round numbers that works out to about 600,000 human beings.

With a policy of forced deportation of villages and torture of natives thought to be especially unfriendly, the Filipino struggle produced its My Lai and its Lt. William L. Calley, Jr. The place was Samar and the man court-martialed was Marine Major Littleton W. Waller. He was acquitted, but the *New York Times* reported, "There has never, apparently, been any doubt that the marine officer did kill Filipinos, but he has contended he did so under orders from General Jacob H. Smith. His acquittal therefore is said by his friends to shift the responsibility from the Marine Corps to the army. . . ."[7]

Contrary to the notion that our great-grandparents murdered squaws and papooses without compunction while we at least agonize over our mass murders, there was enough consternation to have General Smith court-martialed. At the trial, Howling Jake's defense counsel conceded, "General Smith did give instructions to Major Waller to 'kill and burn' 'and make Samar a howling wilderness' and he admits that he wanted everybody killed capable of bearing arms, and that he did specify all over ten years of age, as the Samar boys of that age were equally as dangerous as their elders."

Since superpowers cannot admit they are ever under the necessity of shooting ten-year-old children, the general was duly convicted of "conduct to the prejudice of good order and military discipline." His punishment: admonishment. If being bawled out isn't condign to what he was convicted of, it may have been because his civilian superiors knew he had not really exceeded his orders. The sentiments of many responsible for the conflict are nicely reflected in Teddy Roosevelt's closing salutation in a letter to his good friend, Henry Cabot Lodge: "Give my best love to Nannie, and do not make peace until we get Porto Rico, while Cuba is made independent, and the Philippines at any rate taken from the Spaniards."[8]

It's impossible to say if the Spanish-American War was the last of our nineteenth-century struggles or the first of our ceaseless twentieth-century passages at arms. The talk about the strategic and commercial advantages of possessing the Philippines is much like our modern rationalizations; the absence of efforts toward total mobilization of the society is in the last century's mode. The Spanish-American War did not entail the centralization and coordination which later wars would bring; nor did the war's opponents run the risk of having the federal eagle drop its guano on their civil liberties.

By no means was the whole country swept away in gusts of jingoism at fighting Spain, much less at enduring a protracted campaign to suppress guerrilla warfare in the Philippine jungles. Large numbers agreed with antiwar leader Moorfield Storey when he told the Massachusetts Reform Club,

> Some represented in high Federal office think that war will improve business and increase the gains of the rich. I can't refrain from quoting the reply which was made to one of these last week by a Middlesex Yankee of pure blood. He was a manufacturer of woolen goods and a dealer in wool said to him, "We want war. Just think how it will raise the price of wool, and how it will serve to send your goods up." "Yes," was the answer, "but think how much more the dye stuff will cost. I can't afford to dye my goods in American blood."[9]

A dispatch from Manila printed in the *Boston Evening Transcript* said, "A majority of the United States volunteers are eager to return home. . . . 'we did not enlist to fight niggers' is a remark that is constantly heard." The relatives and friends of soldiers in regiments from such diverse states as Oregon, Tennessee, South Dakota, and Pennsylvania joined with the men in the clamor to come home. The governor of Minnesota made public a telegram from his state's soldiers demanding to be sent home; the parents of several hundred members of the First Nebraska Regiment insisted that "the government send back home those who have not contributed their precious fever-stricken or bullet-torn bodies to enrich the soil of Luzon."

As the years put distance between that time and ours, the war, the tales of torture and blood, disappeared; where some memory of the treatment accorded the American Indians was permitted to stain children's history books, the Philippine campaign vanished and the war itself was depicted as but an exuberant moment during America's Age of Innocence, a fling promoted by William Randolph Hearst to build Teddy Roosevelt's character and provide the yet infant American Republic with a tinge of international glory.

What it was actually providing was more than a tinge of international trade. The pursuit of riches in the Far East through the Open Door policy was enunciated by McKinley's secretary of state, John Hay. The door for trade and investment in China particularly, but in Pacific Asia in general, was to remain ajar and not to be slammed on the acquisitive American toes and fingers by the English, French, Germans, Russians, Japanese, and whoever else was at work ripping off hunks of the then-moribund imperial Chinese dragon. We would fight for our tenderloin of dragon meat because, as President Taft told us,

> In the international controversies that are likely to arise in the Orient growing out of the question of the open door and other issues the United States can maintain her interests intact and can secure respect for her just demands. She will not be able to do so, however, if it is understood that she never intends to back up her assertion of right and her defense of her interest by anything but mere verbal protest and diplomatic notes.[10]

On December 7, 1941, the United States again had occasion to substitute arms for mere verbal protest. The riches of Cathay, however, are mostly a capitalist fable. It persists today in the minds of those who would risk the solid and respectably profitable trading relationship with the Taiwan of Chiang Kai-shek, Junior, in order to lunge at the largely nonexistent business to be done with mainland China. It is an ancient delirium. As far back as 1939 the historian Charles A. Beard was warning against letting it draw the United States into a Japanese war:

> For years Western merchants and their intellectual retainers, including consular agents, filled the air with a great noise about how much money could be made in China as soon as four hundred million customers got round to buying automobiles, bathtubs, typewriters, radios, refrigerators, and sewing machines. Probably a few of these myth makers were honest. But many of them must have realized that this swarm of customers had neither the money nor the goods with which to pay for Western gadgets.[11]

At the outset of these attacks of giddy-mindedness, there was an organized opposition to such adventuring within the formal, electoral political process. The yen for dragon chops was debated and voted against by large minorities in Congress. President McKinley may have only decided to "put the Philippines on the map of the United States" after, as he related, he spent several nights on his knees communing with his Maker in the style Nixon and Kissinger would later make fashionable, but the ratification of the decision to ingest that enormous former Spanish colony got through the Senate by only one vote.

The celestial transmission to McKinley was garbled in transit. The Philippines were to be America's only pass at European-style empire-building. The advantages of a colony—the access to raw materials and the captive markets for manufactured goods—have to be balanced against the costs of administering the place, the problems of keeping garrisons there to overawe the inhabitants, and the damage to one's own self-esteem that comes from doing something one thinks is wrong. Americans think colonial imperialism is wrong and they always have, just as they can't face the fact of their own war crimes. The savagery of the Philippines vanished from our national memory because we couldn't stand to think about it.

Instead, the anti-imperialist values in American society sought for a way of maintaining dominance without appearing to destroy the other fellow's independent existence. We wanted a formula that would allow us to rule without appearing to. It's old hat now, but it was first tried in the Caribbean, especially in Cuba.

The American military occupation of Havana could and did cancel the victory celebration the Cubans had planned to mark the deposition of their colonial masters. "For years we have suffered," complained Perfecto Lacoste, chairman of what would now undoubtedly be named the Havana Liberation Front, "only to see, at this hour, our emotions changed from pleasure at the departure of the Spaniards to apprehension at the arrival of the Americans."[12] Nevertheless, while the executive branch was forbidding the Cubans to light a few firecrackers in delight at escaping four centuries of hildalgo peonage, the policy of putting another nation under a de facto protectorate was being disputed and fought over in the Senate.

The Platt Amendment, as they called the decree of the U.S. Congress specifying that the new Cuban government must cede the United States the right to intervene in the island's internal affairs, didn't dance to passage like the Gulf of Tonkin Resolution. The ability the authorities later acquired to silence any demurral on foreign policy did not then exist. The formal institutions of politics were able to reflect divisions of opinion, so that those on the losing side didn't have to feel voiceless. They may have been short on the final vote, but there were senators and congressmen and lesser politicians aplenty to state their sides of the question. In 1964 when the declaration of war against North Vietnam—for that's what the Gulf of Tonkin Resolution came to—passed, only two members of the Senate and not one soul in the House voted no. Shut out of representation, it's not surprising the antiwar elements took to the streets as soon as they were strong enough.

In the Dollar Diplomacy era before the First World War, the Democrats were the anti-imperial, antiwar party. Although some Republicans joined with them, it was chiefly Democrats who complained about the incessant landing of marines throughout the Caribbean and Central America to seize the customs offices and collect import duties to satisfy the debts owing to American and European businessmen. William Jennings Bryan, newly installed as secretary of state under Wilson, expressed democratic objections when he wrote his boss to say,

> ... it is pathetic to see Nicaragua struggling in the grip of an oppressive financial agreement. ... we see in these transactions a perfect picture of dollar diplomacy. The financiers charge excessive rates on the ground that they must be *paid* for the risk that they take and as soon as they collect their pay for the risk, they then proceed to demand of the respective governments that the *risk* shall be eliminated by governmental coercion. No wonder the people of these little republics are aroused to revolution by what they regard as a sacrifice of their interests.[13]

Bryan was to learn it's easier to denounce the policy of the government from the outside than to change it from within. Not too long after he'd unloaded his thoughts on the inequities of the Dollar Diplomacy usually linked to William Howard Taft's name, Wilson's Democratic administration was landing troops in the Dominican Republic, while Secretary of State Bryan was writing American representatives there to instruct them to tell the Dominicans that "no more revolutions will be permitted." The Dollar Diplomacy loans made to what we'd now call less-developed countries frequently contained provisos that the money extended had to be spent in the United States. Thus it was more than just the officers of the National City Bank—which dabbled in the Dollar Diplomacy business on a rather grand scale—who were getting cut in on the deal; this precursor of the forms of financial activity that would some day be called foreign aid also benefited manufacturers, shippers, and workers.

America's armed interventions in the Caribbean and Central America were so frequent they might almost be funny if the marines didn't discharge their weapons from time to time, as happened in Haiti, where two thousand or more people perished in the suppression of a long-forgotten rebellion. The policy of military intervention rested on more than the simple motive of making the Latinos pay their debts to American banks. We also wished to ensure that friendly governments would control all sites of potential coaling stations and naval bases which might threaten the Panama Canal. Even though the American-sponsored revolution in Colombia which gave us the right of way to dig the thing was of a CIA sort, we were new at the game of fomenting revolts without appearing to do so and often had to intervene directly. With years of experience and a multibillion-dollar CIA, we still sometimes fail, and then the government has to resort once more to William Howard Taft tactics, as Lyndon Johnson did in 1965 when he sent American troops into the Dominican Republic for the umpteenth time in the twentieth century.[14]

The thirst for profits and naval bases had to be disguised as service to a higher cause. Even the muggers of old ladies have taught themselves to believe that when they torture someone of advanced years to find out which mattress the life savings have been stitched into, they aren't preying on the helpless; they're striking back at an unjust society. In like manner, the least rationalization for such maraudings is the sort of brutal missionaryism which proclaims, "Barbarism has no rights which civilization is bound to respect," to quote Lyman Abbott, a turn-of-the-century imperialist and clergyman.

But Theodore Roosevelt could do better than that, and his statement of what's come to be called the Roosevelt Corollary to the Monroe Doctrine carries with it moral and political themes Americans were to hear and sometimes believe for many decades to come:

> If a nation shows that it knows how to act with reasonable efficiency and decency in social and political matters, if it keeps order and pays its obligations, it need fear no interference from the United States. Chronic wrongdoing, or an impotence which results in a general loosening of the ties of civilized society, may in America, as elsewhere, ultimately require intervention by some civilized nation, and in the Western Hemisphere the adherence of the United States to the Monroe Doctrine may force

the United States, however reluctantly, in flagrant cases of such
wrongdoing and impotence, to exercise an international police
power.[15]

The Roosevelt Corollary is the inverse of "If you're so smart,
why aren't you rich?" Americans like TR thought, If we're so
rich, we must be smart—smart enough to be the lawgiver to the
rest of the hemisphere in the early days of the century when our
most important foreign interests extended little further than
Puerto Rico and, later, lawgiver and policeman to the world.
FDR used that very phrase, which would become so odious in
the late 1960s, "arguing that in the immediate postwar period
the United States, the Soviet Union, Great Britain and China
would have to act not as 'trustees' but as 'sheriffs' or 'policemen'
for the rest of the world."[16] The notion that our world copship
is the result of megalomania infecting the central nervous systems of latter-day presidents is erroneous. The infection, sometimes dormant and sometimes virulently obvious, found a
congenial host in the American body politic before John Kennedy, to pick a modern name, was born.

Ex post facto, when this scheme or that went awry, the
ensuing mess has been blamed on presidents going off half-
cocked. In fact, the detonation of conflicts involving the United
States came only after the presidents were fully primed by
Congress and the decisive power groups. Certainly this was true
of Theodore Roosevelt and William Howard Taft in their
Caribbean buccaneering. Nevertheless, Americans have long
been suspicious that a president, endowed with apparently unlimited war powers in his capacity of commander-in-chief, will
"drag," "pull," "trap," or otherwise get us into a war without
our foreknowledge or consent. These old fears seemed to have
come true in the case of Vietnam, Lyndon Johnson's personal
war, which he and his despicable coterie of Ivy League Kennedy holdovers waged against the good sense and humanity of
an otherwise girlishly virtuous Republic.

But those groups in the United States that worry over events
thousands of miles away were ready to go to war in Southeast

Asia ten years before Johnson did. In April of 1954, then-Vice-President Richard Nixon told the American Society of Newspaper Editors, "If, to avoid further Communist expansion in Asia and Indochina, we must take the risk now by putting our boys in, I think the Executive has to take the politically unpopular decision and do it." With the Korean war but two years in the past and an estimate by the Army that it would take a million men to chase Ho Chi Minh out of his palm-treed hiding places, Ike played the coward and did the politically popular thing: he sat the dance out. But by every manner of subversion and subterfuge, the American government made it clear it would not accept the settlement agreed upon at the 1954 Geneva Conference on Indochina.

Lyndon Johnson, who need give way to no other man in the arts of political deceit, can't be fairly accused of tricking the country into war or manipulating a naïve Congress into voting for the Gulf of Tonkin Resolution. Such an interpretation substitutes the doctrine of personal blame—as with Nixon and Watergate—for events that are more plausibly explained by the tendencies and necessities of our system.

Johnson assuredly lied about certain aspects of the war, particularly about what it would cost and how long it could reasonably be expected to last, because getting shot in the head twelve thousand miles from home hadn't become politically any more popular than it was in Eisenhower's time. The incident that provoked America's first major military operation of the war and the resolution ratifying the war was about as convincing as Hitler's allegations of a Polish attack in 1939. Even if the North Vietnamese did do what Washington accused them of—inflict minuscule damage, if any, on American ships o' war which were poking their noses into a belligerent zone—only a nation which intended to go to war would use this flea bite as a casus belli. A few years later, when the North Koreans seized the U.S.S. *Pueblo,* capturing the vessel and its crew—a far graver act than the skirmish in the Gulf of Tonkin—the United States did not retaliate because, whether justly or unjustly provoked, it did not wish to go to war. On the other hand, if the Gulf of

Tonkin incident—it amounted to little more than a couple of guys in canoes puffing up their cheeks and discharging pea-shooters at two very large and very powerful destroyers—had not taken place, another incident would have been found. America's foreign-policy-makers had determined to use our military to resolve the dispute in Vietnam, and any pretext would have done.

The proposition that Congress and the rest of the innocent people of the United States were hoodwinked doesn't stand up when you read the *New York Times* editorial on the morning that the Gulf of Tonkin Resolution was passed:

> The United States had become a direct combatant on a signifi-cant scale, even if only briefly. The sword, once drawn in anger, will tend to be unsheathed more easily in the future. Congres-sional authority for future military action will, in effect, be delegated to the President by the joint resolution scheduled to be voted today. The President has rightly asked that the resolu-tion express a determination that "all necessary measures" be taken.[17] (The remainder of this editorial appears in the foot-note.)

A whole generation has had the Vietnamese debacle ex-plained by the theory that several omnipotent presidents abused their power. Yet two days after the editorial cited above, the *Times,* while asking the administration to "demonstrate that it is as resolute in seeking a peaceful settlement as it is in prosecut-ing the war" showed it understood exactly what was coming off:

> The Congressional resolution on Southeast Asia imposes the heaviest responsibilities on the President. As drafted by the White House and approved almost unanimously by Congress, the resolution is a declaration of national unity and a vote of confidence in the Tonkin Gulf decision. But it is much more than that. *It is virtually a blank check* [emphasis added] of "approval and support" for "all necessary steps, including the use of armed force," that the President may take not only to repel attack against American forces but "to prevent further

aggression" and "to assist any member [of the SEATO alliance] requesting assistance in defense."

It is doubtful that the resolution—despite Senator [Wayne] Morse's charge that it conveys "blanket authority to wage war" —literally delegates to the President any powers he could not already exercise. True, only Congress can "declare war" under the Constitution. But many Presidents have exercised the prerogatives of commander in chief of the armed forces to engage in hostilities without consulting Congress. President Truman even took the nation into a three-year war in Korea without direct Congressional sanction at any point.

In fact, the practice of Congressional resolutions—inaugurated by President Eisenhower in the 1955 Formosa crisis— derived from Republican criticism of the Korean procedure. But it is not clear, paradoxically, that this legislative restraint upon the Executive only operates before the resolution is voted. Once advance approval has been granted for unknown measures in unforeseen situations, the result must be reduced possibility for Congressional scrutiny and criticism.[18]

Of course, it has always been thus when a democracy resorts to arms; the ordinary checks on the executive power are weakened, but in the light of this editorial in the country's most influential newspaper, it strains reason to categorize the war as a presidential usurpation. Nor was the *Times*'s reaction deviant. The *Washington Post* cheered Johnson and the resolution, saying, "The paramount need was to show the North Vietnamese aggressors their self-defeating folly in ignoring an unequivocal American warning. . . ." And in Los Angeles, that city's *Times* told its readers, "Communists, by their attack on American vessels in international waters, have themselves escalated the hostilities—an escalation we must meet. Thus the struggle in Southeast Asia inevitably will become deadlier. At least now the cause is clear and we know what we are doing and why we do it."

Three weeks before the North Vietnamese BB gun sniped at our ships in the Gulf of Tonkin, the Republican presidential candidate Barry Goldwater told the country what was what in his nomination acceptance speech in San Francisco: "Yesterday it was Korea; tonight it is Vietnam. Make no bones of this.

Don't try to sweep this under the rug. We are at war in Vietnam." Then as though demanding that war be declared, Goldwater went on to say, "And yet the President, who is the Commander in Chief of our forces, refuses to say, refuses to say mind you, whether or not the objective over there is victory and his Secretary of Defense continues to mislead and misinform the American people. . . ."

The Gulf of Tonkin Resolution should have cleared up any ambiguities at the time, and it did. It was almost universally received as a declaration of a short, triumphant war by which the Red aggressors would be vaporized out of the jungle like so much monsoon rain. When the war lasted and lasted and lasted, the number of men willing to acknowledge their share of the responsibility for what had become a slaughter past all prevoyance dropped off rapidly, and the idea of the imperial presidency was taken up by liberals with a need to hide their pasts and exculpate themselves.

In the face of warehouses and microfilm libraries stuffed with the evidence showing that Congress, the intellectual professoriat, the international-minded segments of big business, big labor, the mass media, and virtually every other influential group in the country supported the war if they didn't actually clamor for it, this is what you can now read in the history books:

> Lincoln had said that the view that one man had the power of bringing the nation into war placed our Presidents where Kings had always stood. If Johnson construed the high prerogative more in the eighteenth century style of the British monarch than of the republican executive envisioned by the Constitution, his successor carried the inflation of presidential authority even further. For President Nixon stripped away the fig leaves which his predecessor had draped over his assertion of unilateral presidential power.[19]

America does not go to war by presidential caprice. Nor can a weaker case for the imperial presidency be found than the Vietnam War. John Kennedy, who sent the advance guard into

South Vietnam, prepared the way for the wider war with virtually unanimous support; Lyndon Johnson, a man who characteristically lined up broad backing from all power elements in the society before making a major move, converted minor strife into major conflict with every conceivable approbation, formal and informal. And Nixon, far from stripping away the last fig leaf concealing the genitalia of presidential absolutism, was forced out of the war by waning support and growing opposition at home.

More than an abuse of power, the Cambodian invasion—or "incursion" as a Nixon administration fearful of its political consequences minimized it—is an illustration of the danger for the man in the White House when he tries to go it alone. As the years of war succeeded each other, those who had welcomed the Gulf of Tonkin, thinking Vietnam would be no more than splatting a fly, began to backpedal. Where debate over war and peace had earlier been excluded from the political process, Sen. Eugene McCarthy of Minnesota entered the 1968 Democratic presidential primary in New Hampshire and found the topic had been restored to the list of permissible subjects. To be against the war was no longer tantamount to indulging in un-American activities. Sen. Robert Kennedy, a man with an uncanny ability to flare his nostrils and smell a trend, jumped from asking President Johnson to send him to Vietnam to take command of winning the war to being an antiwar candidate.

Richard Nixon, schooled in the proposition that diplomacy requires that other nations believe you have the means and the will to make war on them, strove to close down Vietnam on terms that would preserve that belief in Russian and Chinese stomachs. But as more and more elements in American society calculated that winning would cost too much in a variety of coin, Vietnam did indeed begin to become a president's war. The president, Kissinger, and others who were going to have to conduct foreign relations after it would be obvious to the major Communist powers that the United States had "bugged out," as the prowar party referred to a possible cessation of hostilities, ordered the fighting continued in hopes of finding a less ignominious end to the American role in the killing. But political time at home had run out, and Congress began using or threatening to use the power of the purse, as well as the legislative power, to yank the president backward and force an end to the war. It had to be done in a way that didn't betray those who had died and those who were still over there fighting. In this respect Watergate was a godsend for Congress, since if there was anyone to be convicted of betrayal of public trust, it could be Nixon.

At some point toward the end of 1972, Nixon seems to have given up trying to carry on the war long enough to negotiate an armistice that would at least look like a Korean-style stalemate. By televising the return of the POWs and making it a military spectacular, the administration used this, the only real concession they got from the North Vietnamese, as a substitute for victory. While it may have satisfied an unknown number of Americans, it couldn't have misled anyone else. The Russians must have understood that Nixon was forced to sign a disadvantageous cease-fire, not because the American army had been beaten on the battlefield but because so little support for the Southeast Asian endeavor remained that the President was unable to go on.

Insofar as Vietnam turned into a presidential war, it didn't happen out of willfulness or imperial whim; for the White House, continuing the war was necessary for the conduct of diplomacy, for making it possible to reach future peace agreements with the Red adversaries in Moscow and Peking. That's what Nixon kept saying in those years, and nothing has yet come to light to contradict his sincerity, although his reasoning was and is refutable.

Nixon and Johnson weren't the first presidents to be accused of using royal wiles to get us into war. The accusation was also made against FDR. His right-wing enemies even accused him of conniving in the Pearl Harbor attack—an unthinkable proposition for any president, but especially for Roosevelt, who not only had a particular affection for the navy but who also did all in his power to reduce American casualties when war did come.

If the charge of treason against FDR is ridiculous, a case can be made that he and his top people provoked the Japanese. No less a person than the American ambassador to Japan from 1932 until Pearl Harbor was tempted to think so. After FDR's 1937 speech suggesting that Japan be quarantined as an aggressor, along with Germany and Italy, Joseph C. Grew wrote in his diary in Tokyo:

> I have no right as a representative of the Government to criticize the Government's policy and actions, but that doesn't make me feel any less sorry about the way things have turned. An architect who has spent five years slowly building what he hoped was going to be a solid and permanent edifice and has seen that edifice suddenly crumble about his ears might feel similarly. Or a doctor who has worked hard over a patient and then has lost his case. Our country came to a fork in the road, and, paradoxical as it may seem to a peace-loving nation, chose the road which leads not to peace but potentially to war. Our primary and fundamental concept was to avoid involvement in the Far Eastern mess; we have chosen the road which might lead directly to involvement.[20]

In fact America came to a number of forks in the Pacific road and took the war turn repeatedly. After the United States had swallowed the Spanish Empire and was lying about belching like a boa constrictor digesting a two-hundred-pound boar, the Hoover administration raised a rumpus when the Japanese slurped up Manchukuo (Manchuria) in 1930. The Japanese continued to chomp away at bits and hunks of China in the 1930s, to the consternation and disapproval of the United States. The Tokyo view of these tut-tuttings was probably summed up by a Japanese delegate to an international conference who said, "Just as Japan was getting really skillful at the game of grab, the other powers, most of whom had all they wanted anyway, suddenly had an excess of virtue and called the game off."[21] In addition to quarreling over the largely nonexistent Chinese markets, Japan, a nation bereft of all natural resources but brains and labor, had to face new discriminatory tariffs raised against selling its manufactures in India and the rest of the British Empire. At the same time, the Hawley-Smoot tariff, enacted under Hoover, made sure there was no open door for Japanese trade in the United States; American action also excluded Japanese goods from such imperial appendages as the Philippines and Cuba. As early as the Versailles Conference, Fumimaro Konoye had warned the Americans: "If Great Britain closes her colonies to foreign countries, how can Japan maintain her existence with her limited territory, slender resources and poorly equipped factories? Under such circumstances Japan will be obliged to assume the same attitude as Germany before the war and destroy the status quo."[22] By Pearl Harbor the situation vis-à-vis the blocking of Japanese exports had reached such a point that Harry C. Hawkins, the head of the State Department's Trade Agreements Section, declared, "Most countries which negotiate commercial agreements involving reductions on tariffs and other trade barriers have either discriminated overtly against Japan by not extending the reductions to Japanese products or covertly by thinly disguised discriminations in the form of highly specialized tariff classifications."[23]

One way remained for the United States to put yet more pressure on Japan to back off from China and generally conform to the points of international etiquette listed for it by Cordell Hull, FDR's secretary of state. After letting the commerical treaty with Japan lapse, America began to embargo raw-material shipments to the Nipponese isles. Scrap iron and oil were cut off; then, when all Japanese assets were frozen in the United States, it was a matter of sitting back and waiting for the attack to come. On November 26, the secretary of war sent out the much-quoted message to commanders in the Pacific: "Negotiations with Japan have been terminated without an agreement on disputed points. Japanese future action unpredictable but action possible any moment. If hostilities cannot, repeat cannot, be avoided the United States desires that Japan commit the first overt act."[24]

Such is the case for the 1941 Pacific War being a presidential usurpation on behalf of those few American bankers and businessmen with a substantial stake in China, but it's a weak case. The Japanese were as much aggressing as aggressed against, and the militarists who had come to power in Tokyo, albeit partly as a reaction to American unfriendliness, were anything but Nice Nelly Plums. Nor were the Roosevelt administration's measures against Japan taken in stealth or without broad support. Even "isolationist" newspapers like the *New York Daily News* cheered the program of economic strangulation of the sons of the rising sun: "This country has a golden opportunity to put the squeeze on the Japanese military caste now, the proper object being to squeeze the Japanese out of China with economic pincers. If we let the chance slide for the sake of a few dollars for a few people, we'll be inviting a Japanese onslaught on us after Japan has conquered and reorganized huge, rich and industrious China."[25] The China Lobby, as the group of missionaries, businessmen, and believers in a special Sino-American destiny would come to be called in the 1950s, was already active in pushing for military and economic aid for China and against Japan.

Japanese-American relations had long been poisoned by fear on this side of the Pacific of the Yellow Peril. Racist acts by white men constantly embittered and angered the Japanese so that there was serious talk of war in 1906 when the San Francisco school board decided to segregate Oriental kids. The Japanese government said this humiliation violated the 1894 treaty providing equality of treatment for each country's nationals. Theodore Roosevelt, who could play the part of racist with our South American cousins, could also enunciate somewhat different values:

> I wish to see the United States treat the Japanese in a spirit of all possible courtesy, and with generosity and justice. At the same time I wish to see our navy constantly built up and each ship kept at the highest point of efficiency as a fighting unit. But if we bluster; if we behave rather badly to other nations; if we show that we regard the Japanese as an inferior and alien race,

and try to treat them as we have treated the Chinese, and if at the same time we fail to keep our navy at the highest point of efficiency and size—then we shall invite disaster.[26]

Teddy chose to integrate rather than fight, so a deal of sorts, one that would be illegal under present-day court rulings, was fixed up with the San Francisco board of education, and Wee Willie Taft was hoisted on board a steamship and ordered to Japan. One result of the trip was the Gentlemen's Agreement, an agreement that coolies weren't cool and the Imperial government would see that they didn't migrate to the United States. Gentlemen—i.e. businessmen, students, and similar nonthreatening types—would still be welcome.

That by no means ended the problems created for our diplomacy by domestic American racism. In 1913 the California legislature passed a law to prevent Japanese from owning land in the state. A Democratic party leader wrote Wilson to explain that the problem "is this: a non-assimilable people, clever and industrious agriculturists working for themselves as owners and lessees, take farms from [the] hands of white men in destructive competition. The tide must be checked, otherwise California will become a Japanese plantation and republican institutions [will] perish."[27] Japanese protests about the treatment of immigrant countrymen again reached the point that war talk was in the air, in part because Wilson, himself a racist, was singularly lethargic and graceless in dealing with the situation.[28]

Eleven years later, in 1924, the Japanese Exclusion Act was passed. The foundations had been laid for enmity, distrust and hatred. Japan was a very popular enemy. It was anti-Japanese sentiment of the vilest sort, especially in the west, which created the political preconditions for the internment of Japanese-Americans in the "relocation" camps during the war. But it wasn't just in California that race hatred thrived. The Japs, as they were invariably called, were depicted as humanoid rats or monkey-faces. *Time* magazine ran articles explaining how, by noting their sinister and inferior characteristics, you could tell a Jap from a Chinese; at another time it explained to its readers that "The ordinary unreasoning Jap is ignorant. Perhaps he is a human being. Nothing . . . indicates it." Or there was Admiral William F. "Bull" Halsey telling newsreel audiences and others, "We are drowning and burning the bestial apes all over the Pacific, and it is just as much a pleasure to burn them as to drown them. . . . I hate Japs. I'm telling you men that if I met a pregnant Japanese woman, I'd kick her in the belly."[29] In retrospect, the struggle in the Pacific between 1941 and 1945 ending with the flash french fry of the occupants of two entire Japanese cities, almost none of whom were soldiers, makes it look less like a war than a protracted race riot, but such enthusiasm for even those of the yellow-skinned enemy who were in utero serves to emphasize what a mistake it is to dump the blame on Franklin Roosevelt alone.

Where FDR assuredly did play Emperor President was in helping the English and the French in their war against the Nazis from September, 1939, to December, 1941, when the Germans declared war on the United States. White House hanky-panky was discovered when a new-model Douglas attack bomber on a test flight cracked up in a parking lot near the Los Angeles Municipal airport, and who should be pulled out of the wreckage but a representative of the French Air Ministry.[30] This led to the publication of an agreement to sell warplanes to the Allied Powers and prompted a large rumpus in Washington. Sen. Gerald P. Nye, who had headed an investigation into the connection between American arms sales and our eventual entry into World War I, led the demands that all aspects of the arrangement be made public:

> I have been one of those who have many times wished that we might have known in 1917 what we have come to learn about 1917 since that time. I only know I should never forgive myself were I, a few months or a year or two years from now, to have to say that I was in any way responsible for the lack of knowledge of what seems to be in the making in 1939.[31]

But there wasn't much lack of knowledge. Anybody who cared to know what was coming off could have guessed it, and men like Sen. Hiram W. Johnson of California, the old Roosevelt Progressive, asked on the floor of the Senate,

> Good God, do you not, gentlemen, think the American people have a right to know if they are going down the road to war? Do you not think the American people, with their experience of the past twenty years, should be informed if their rulers are going to take them even to the brink of war? Why should they not be informed? They are our masters, and the only master I recognize. Why should they not be informed if such is the course to be pursued by their government?[32]

The rhetoric, while a trifle grand, befitting a man brought up in a more formally elegant epoch, would not have been out of place in the early 1970s. But if a Nixon and a Roosevelt concealed specific acts and lied about them, as in one way or another they assuredly did, they could not conceal the general direction of events or their policies. Hiram Johnson knew the answers to the questions he posed that day; yes, America would be "going down the road to war." That fact sickened unto physical illness the men who'd been through it once before in 1917, particularly many of the old Progressives who had been such jingoes they regarded Wilson as something close to a slacker until the happy day of bloodshed came and he asked for a declaration of war. These men constituted the respectable center of the isolationist groupings of the late 1930s. Horrified and remorseful for the part they had played in sending young Americans to die for no readily visible good, they had come to hold that the only war America had any reason to fight should commence when the enemy landed on Cape Cod or Malibu.

It's not so certain that Hiram Johnson, however sympathetic he may seem to our eyes now, was speaking for the majority of people with organized political power. As Roosevelt, a World War I man with misgivings himself, moved sometimes deceitfully, sometimes ambiguously toward war, he made his intent clear. For the cosmopolitan segment of the population that concerned itself with foreign affairs, he was moving too slowly;

and for millions more, war—or at least war production—meant jobs. When, a few days before Johnson's speech in the Senate, FDR talked to the press about the bomber episode, one of the things he said was, " . . . for the last two years we have been encouraging foreign governments to buy planes over here; first, to put people to work in these idle factories, and secondly, to go through what might be called the experimental period of mass production that we don't know much about."[33]

It may have frightened and depressed the left-over leaders of the teens and twenties, but to many Americans the coming of war was a time of renewed hope and prosperity. We are not the first generation of Americans to figure out there are megabucks to be made in making guns and selling them. Back in 1910, William Howard Taft was puffing up the fact that the government had gotten Argentina to buy a couple of battleships costing $23 million. He got an order for another from Greece. Six years later, from those small beginnings, the vision of the military-industrial complex had formed itself in the brains of such as Howard E. Coffin, vice-president of the Hudson Motor Car Company and a member of Woodrow Wilson's Council of National Defense. "It is our hope," the good man exuberated to the du Pont family, "that we may lay the foundation for that closely knit structure, industrial, civil and military, which every thinking American has come to realize is vital to the future life of this country, in peace and in commerce, no less than in possible war."[34]

Thus, while no credible evidence exists that business got us into World War II or that business alone without other factors working can move a nation like this one into any war, by 1939 Americans had long associated somebody's war with good times. If the world wanted to fight, we were willing to sell the weapons. Indeed, while there is much inaccurate remembrance about sacrifice and unity during "the good war," in truth the sacrificing was done almost entirely by those sent off to fight.

The degree to which World War II brought prosperity to America is suggested by the fact that from 1940 to 1944, the last full war year, civilian goods and services increased; people

who couldn't afford decent food in the thirties were eating
again; with every extra nail and every board foot of lumber
going to beat the enemy, the number of supermarkets in the
United States grew from 4,900 in 1939 to more than 16,000 in
1944; on December 7, 1944, Macy's set an all-time sales record;
a final wartime sacrifice for victory was the law forgiving payments on three-quarters of the 1942 income tax.[35] As the country shifted to a war economy, times got better for huge numbers
of people. The folk wisdom of the blue-collar class is that war
means jobs, and though it can't be ascertained whether that
proposition lent support to the direction Roosevelt was taking
or whether other considerations influenced people, it is clear
that a great many people went along with him. " 'Help Wanted'
signs looked good, even if the job was carrying nitroglycerin,"
as someone has said of the period.[36]

Each step toward war was taken with loud assertions that
peace would be kept as far as America was concerned. The
Frenchman-in-the-plane incident, which made a huge, although relatively brief, noise, elicited soothing and pacific
words from the jaunty gentleman in the White House. Although rarely permitting himself to be quoted verbatim, he did
on this occasion when he said, "The [foreign] policy has not
changed and it is not going to change. . . . We are against any
entangling alliances, obviously. . . . We are in complete sympathy with any and every effort made to reduce or limit armaments. [He had just been caught doing the exact opposite.] . . .
As a nation—as American people—we are sympathetic with
the peaceful maintenance of political, economic and social independence of all nations in the world."[37]

Not much later the United States would be deeply entangled
with Great Britain in the Lend Lease program to ship war
matériel abroad, yet the most Roosevelt can be fairly accused
of was being a few months ahead of the majority of organized
sentiment. That qualifier, "organized," must be stressed because there were millions who, whatever their opinions may
have been, played no meaningful role in the lurch and stumble
toward war.

Roosevelt had what was not yet called the eastern media establishment behind him, the cosmopolitan millionaire class, some genuine antifascists, and a corporals' guard of persons who were shocked even to the point of going to war at Hitler's treatment of Jews and other helpless and hated people. (Not only did public-opinion polls show that few Americans—less than 10 percent—were agreeable to admitting Jewish refugees into the country, but it was well into the war before the American government lifted a finger or stamped a visa to help those Jews who still could be gotten to and saved.)

But until the bombing of Pearl Harbor, when all of the rules of public conduct were changed, there was continuing opposition to America's entering World War II. It wasn't centered in one political party and it was often incoherent because it was often self-contradictory. It included not only the Communists, beginning the day after the Hitler-Stalin agreement to divide Poland and nibble on the bones, but also a certain number of domestic antisemites, fascists, and other odoriferous types. Though the prowar groups were not above suggesting that he who was against the war or Bundles for Britain was automatically a junior storm trooper, there was also a respectable antiwar group. The fact that many of its members had little in common politically, except opposition to the war, made it less effective, but no less noisy.

It's impossible to conclude that Roosevelt was pulling the wool over anybody's eyes, that he was exceeding the tacit permission given him to nudge and nuzzle toward war, when you read the speeches of the antiwar people and realize they were not sustained. One of the most famous was given by Sen. Burton K. Wheeler, himself a Democrat of the progressive Wilsonian stripe, not unlike FDR. Speaking in January, 1941, Wheeler evoked the disaster of the Agricultural Adjustment Administration and the destruction of the cotton in denouncing Lend Lease:

> . . . it definitely stamps the President as war-minded. The lend-lease-give program is the New Deal's triple A foreign policy; it

will plow under every fourth American boy. Never before have
the American people been asked or compelled to give so bounte-
ously and so completely of their tax dollars to any foreign
nation. Never before has the Congress of the United States been
asked by any president to violate international law. Never before
has this Nation resorted to duplicity in the conduct of its foreign
affairs. . . . Approval of this legislation means war, open and
complete warfare. . . . Was the last World War worth while? . . .
Our boys will be returned—returned in caskets, maybe; returned with bodies maimed; returned with minds warped and
twisted by sights of horrors and the scream and shriek of high
powered shells. . . .[38]

FDR called Wheeler's speech "the rottenest thing that has
been said in public life in my generation," but that didn't end
it. That summer Wheeler sent out a million postcards, postage-
free on his Congressional franking privilege, some of which
reached men in the armed services. Every antiwar statement on
the cards was taken from the *Congressional Record,* but what
doubtless riled the administration the most was putting FDR's
own, already famous statement of the previous October on
them: "And while I am talking to you, fathers and mothers, I
give you one more assurance. I have said this before, but I shall
say it again, and again and again, your boys are not going to
be sent into any foreign war."[39] This so rankled Henry L.
Stimson, Roosevelt's secretary of war—who, in the seamless
continuity of American government, had been Hoover's secretary of state—that the old boy read a statement to the press
containing this sentence: "Without expressing legal opinions, I
will simply say that I think that [the postcards] comes very near
the line of subversive activities against the United States, if not
treason." But Burton Wheeler was no undergraduate peace
demonstrator in raggedy clothes with a smelly moustache. Dissent was still a part of our formal political processes so the next
day Stimson apologized.

And America went to war, although with misgivings, as
reflected at the time of the passage of the Lend Lease Act in the
diary of Sen. Arthur Vandenberg, an isolationist who would

later join the eastern Establishment to help command our forces in the Cold War: "I had the feeling as the result of the ballot was announced, that I was witnessing the suicide of the Republic. ... The proponents of this bill say it is the way to *peace* [italics Vandenberg's]. I pray to God that they are right. I pray to God that I am wholly in the wrong. Heaven has always protected us from our mistakes before; perhaps heaven will do so again."[40]

8

"America First, Let It Cost What It May"

Support, even reluctant support, is necessary for a president to wage war and that fact is nowhere better illustrated than in Woodrow Wilson's forays into Mexico. The seizure of the Mexican port of Veracruz in 1914 at the cost of 126 Mexican and 19 American lives took Wilson on a path quixotic, bellicose, and suspect domestically by many of the very elements a president must have to sustain a war.

Wilson's messiah complex wasn't something only his enemies could discern. The man really did say things like "I am going to teach the South American Republics to elect good men." Unhappily for the United States and the southern part of the hemisphere, T. Woodrow, who was a pluperfect, ethnocentric Anglo-Saxon of enormous knowledge about the history, customs, and institutions of the blond people, knew nothing about Mexico.

At that time the country, though in the midst of civil war, was newly dominated by a not especially amiable dictator named Victoriano Huerta. Not one to confine his human-rights campaign to diplomatic grumblings, Woodrow declared through the Department of State, in a circular note to most of the embassies of the world,

. . . The present policy of the Government of the United States is to isolate General Huerta entirely; to cut him off from foreign sympathy and aid and from domestic credit, whether moral or material, and so to force him out. . . . If General Huerta does not retire by force of circumstances, it will become the duty of the United States to use less peaceful means to put him out. It will give other governments notice in advance of each affirmative or aggressive [it wasn't such a no-no word back then] step it has in contemplation, should it unhappily become necessary to move actively against the usurpers. . . .[1]

It was while this was going on in the pinnacles of power that a Navy paymaster from the U.S.S. *Dolphin* patrolling off Tampico got arrested with his whale boat crew while going ashore to get gasoline. The bunch of them were released with mucho apologies as soon as the Huertista general in the vicinity found out. That ought to have been the end of it, but the idiot in command of the American squadron, Admiral Henry T. Mayo, refused to accept the apology and sent a message to the Mexicans telling them,

> I must require that you send me, by suitable members of your staff, formal disavowal of and apology for the act, together with your assurance that the officer responsible for it will receive severe punishment. Also that you publicly hoist the American flag in a prominent position on shore and salute it with twenty-one guns, which salute will be duly returned by this ship. Your answer to this communication should reach me and the called-for salute be fired within twenty-four hours from 6 P.M. of this date.[2]

Not only was this absurdity the formal cause of the death of 145 human beings and the wounding of another 266, but Wilson addressed a joint session of Congress on the matter and was ready to go to war when he looked over his shoulder and saw that nobody was marching behind him. The country agreed with Andrew Carnegie, who wrote Wilson that such a war "will in after days be held akin to the fabled war of the two kings to decide which end of the egg should first be broken."[3]

Presidents can use their commander-in-chief powers to stage raids a la Veracruz in 1914 or as Dwight Eisenhower did the Lebanon in 1957, but if a major coalition in the country doesn't

want it and won't support it, the purely formal authority to
order soldiers around the globe will not suffice to ignite a satisfactory international conflagration. A sustained effort, one that
demands blood and money, cannot be called forth by White
House whim. When a president assembles an insufficient coalition for war and still wages it against ferocious opposition, the
consequences may be far-reaching and damaging. That is what
happened with Wilson and World War I.

There's no agreement as to what started the First World War
or why the United States took part in it. Wilson himself said
he didn't know how the damn thing began: "Have you ever
heard what started the present war? If you have, I wish you
would publish it, because nobody else has, so far as I can gather.
Nothing in particular started it, but everything in general."[4]
That is also the best explanation for America's taking part—
nothing in particular, everything in general. Some wanted the
war because of genuine opposition to the German Empire's
Junker militarism; some felt a sentimental affinity toward the
English, whose empire was mostly resented by its still-mute
millions of nonwhite subjugatees; some were outraged that
Americans lost their lives when the munitions ships on which
they were passengers were sunk by Kaiser Bill's dastardly U-
boats; there were the hundreds of millions of dollars the Entente powers had borrowed from American banks so that an
Anglo-French defeat would be a catastrophe to J. P. Morgan
and other lesser but still mighty names on Wall Street; American manufacturers and farmers were making money, lots of it,
selling foodstuffs and war matériel to the Allies, although taking part in the war wasn't necessary to make money from it;
lastly, some thought a Europe dominated by Germany would
be a long-run threat to the United States and many for a brief
time came to think, as Woodrow Wilson certainly did, that this
was the war to save democracy, the war to end war.

In the sixty years since the April day that Wilson asked
Congress for a declaration of war, historians have switched
their judgment on the matter in accordance with prevailing

upper-middle-class foreign-policy opinions. In the early 1930s, there was much sentiment blaming World War I on Wilson's catering to the merchants of death; during World War II and the Cold War, Wilson and our reasons for participating were seen as more idealistic or ideological; and now, since Vietnam, Woody has begun to take his lumps again.

Whatever the causes, the more important consideration is what the war did to America. It is popular to think of 1917 as the moment America lost her innocence, the shattering time when an idealistic young people, still unaware of their world-straddling destiny, lost their young men and their illusions, first at Belleau Wood and Château-Thierry, and then at the wicked gaming tables of Versailles, where old-world viciousness cheated us out of a perpetual peace where every nation on the globe would be a replica of the North American republic. It is a theme ceaselessly repeated and elaborated on to explain everything from Warren Gamaliel Harding and the flappers to the modern novel and the decline of the family.

It is largely untrue. The truth is that there were millions who despised the war, had no illusion about it, never forgave Wilson for it, and gave it no more outward support than they were compelled to. If there was a loss of innocence, it arose because World War I taught Americans to fear their government; World War I showed ruling institutions and elite groups how to control and manipulate the society.

If World War I is used as the standard of conduct for wartime presidents and wartime departments of justice, then Richard Nixon's fling at violating people's civil liberties was quite modest. That may have less to do with Mr. Nixon's respect for the Bill of Rights than the nature of the opposition to his war as compared to what Wilson had to deal with. Wilson had to coerce a nation that thought it was free, and to do it he had to knowingly set loose an ugliness that hasn't been evacuated from our system yet. "Once lead this people into war," he said in a paragraph historians have felt compelled to quote repeatedly, "and they'll forget there ever was such a thing as tolerance. To fight you must be brutal and ruthless and the spirit of ruthless

brutality will enter into the very fibre of our national life, infecting Congress, the courts, the policemen on the beat, the man
in the street."[5]

Wilson's progression toward war was slow and often contra-
dictory for many reasons, not the least of which is that he
understood that "a war . . . required an illiberalism at home to
reinforce the men at the front." Politically he was pushed by a
prowar Republican party as well as by much Progressive sentiment, but he also had to confront massive antiwar sentiment,
which began with his own secretary of state, William Jennings
Bryan, who resigned because he thought Wilson was moving in
a direction that would make war inescapable.

There was a respectable amount of antiwar feeling among the
upper class, though as the danger of war grew, the efforts of
such men as former president Taft and Harvard president A.
Lawrence Lowell grew more feeble. These types clustered
around the League to Enforce Peace. The word "enforce" on
the league's letterhead was in red to show they weren't kidding,
but the organization "avoided all discussion of proposals for
ending the present war and adjusted its policy on military pre-
paredness and American intervention to a point midway between that of the Wilson administration and that of its more
belligerent backers. By the fall of 1916 it was including on its
letterhead the explicit statement, 'The League to Enforce Peace
does *not* seek to end the present war.' "[6] There will always be
cookie-pushers, but these were so ineffectual they're almost
endearing. They even had a convention under the slogan of
"Win the War for Permanent Peace."

Elsewhere in the society the opposition was not so thin. In
the House of Representatives an astonishing fifty congressmen
voted against the declaration of war. Unless politicians were
more heroic then than they are now, this vote indicates that
there was considerable antiwar sentiment around the country;
the available evidence suggests there was. The mail coming into
the office of Majority Leader Claude Kitchin of North Carolina,
who voted against the war, ran 90 percent in favor of his antiwar stand. Sen. Robert La Follette of Wisconsin, where nine
out of the state's eleven congressmen voted nay, reported that

his mail was ten to one against war. Mississippi's James K. Vardaman told the Senate, ". . . if the issue of war or peace should be submitted to the people who must fight the war, the voice of the people would be heard in thunderous tones directing the president to find some other way. . . ."[7] George Norris, one of the few Republican progressives unable to appreciate the glory of war, told the other senators, "We are about to do the bidding of wealth's terrible mandate and make millions of our countrymen suffer. . . ."[8] Borah of Idaho, who coined the phrase "America first, let it cost what it may," demanding that Wilson go to war, found out it was going to cost plenty, including freedom of speech. As the bills were introduced to Congress curtailing the First Amendment, the senator, who was beginning to have doubts about his prowar vote, wrote to a friend, "I am unwilling to Prussianize this country in order to de-Prussianize Germany."

Around the country there was a patriotic uproar of bands and bunting and enlistment that perhaps 60 percent of the population sympathized with and supported, and a concomitant degree of bitterness and refusal of cooperation by the rest. The Selective Service System identified 337,649 draft-dodgers, of whom 163,738 were apprehended or whose cases were otherwise taken care of before the conscription law lapsed,[9] but even these figures seriously understate the number of men and women opposed to what they considered Rockefeller's and Morgan's war. Better than numbers, the reality of the time is best conveyed by this front page story appearing in the August 1, 1917, *New York Times:*

STOP RUSH TO WED TO AVOID DRAFT

FEDERAL MARSHAL FORBIDS ISSUING OF LICENSES
UNLESS REGISTRATION CARDS ARE PRODUCED

Marriage Record Broken

. . . The little marriage chapel on the third floor of the Municipal Building . . . was the scene yesterday of 164 weddings, the greatest number by 14 ever performed in a single day in the history of the City Clerk's office. Of these 164 couples, the male members were, in at least 95 per cent of the cases, persons of draft age, a fact which in the opinion of both federal and city officials, was responsible for the rush.

A box accompanying the story informed the *Times*'s readers,

WOMEN WHO WED SLACKERS MAY BE SENT TO JAIL—
Washington, July 31. Women who marry men who have been drafted with the idea of aiding them to escape military service are as liable as their slacker husbands to be sent to jail. . . ."

Forty percent of the draft registrants in Donora, Pennsylvania, gave fictitious addresses; in Indianapolis, the draft board lists for the whole county were stolen; and so on.

Before 1917, the federal government was probably held in no higher repute than it was when Jimmy Carter campaigned on a rash promise to do something about controlling it. What World War I did was to teach people to fear their government and serve it. It is from that period that the belief was born that if the feds wanted you, they would invincibly nail you. Until Wilson and the Great War, Americans had the most minimal contact with Washington. There was no income tax and virtually no federal activity that might touch them. In 1917, the American population had not yet been taught to submit to the bridle and it was inconceivable that the federal government had the power to pick them off the streets, throw them in the army, and send them to their deaths overseas.

Yet that is what happened with the so-called Slacker Raids. Songs like "I'm a Yankee Doodle Dandy" and "Over There" may have roused the hyperthyroid, prowar faction of the population, but for thousands of others, America became a police state. Just as the Nixon administration had to create the Plumbers, the Wilson administration believed the official police apparatus under its command was insufficient. It sponsored the American Protective League, which ultimately enrolled 250,000 members in six hundred cities and towns to act as spies, auxilliary police, and quasi-deputized lynch mobs. The league was accused of burglary, or whatever you want to call entering without a warrant, not hundreds of times but thousands. To get to be an APL member, all you had to do was send a dollar to the Department of Justice, which sent you back a card saying you were a junior Secret Service operative. The APL's performance was so outrageous, and so many complaints were made that Wilson, perhaps out of a premonition of the uproar which did follow, wrote his Attorney General Thomas Gregory, "It seems to me it would be very dangerous to have such an organization operating in the United States." Gregory, whom historians consider something of a civil libertarian in the Wilson administration, said, no, the Justice Department needed this gang of mother's little marauders. Wilson let the matter drop, as he would virtually every other plea that the White House show some concern for the Bill of Rights during a war to make the world safe for democracy. His apologists have always maintained that Wilson was too busy in the struggle for world peace to devote the requisite attention to the struggle for liberty; the record suggests that this enormously gifted but vindictive man had found a rationalization in his Presbyterian conscience for his subordinates' jailing his political opponents—at least those who were unorganized or without power. Unlike Nixon, Wilson did not mess with the rights, privileges, and prerogatives of the upper classes. In the early seventies, senators began to worry about what kind of games the secret eyes of the executive branch might be playing with them. In 1917 Senator Hiram Johnson, yet another Republican progressive to become irreconcilably estranged from Wilson over whether the Bill of Rights is charter law or stuff to be recited on patriotic holidays, declared "the only place left in all this land where liberty finally may have its fight made for it, and where freedom may be protected, is right here in this body."[10]

The American Protective League/Chamber of Commerce bozos—for their membership seems to have been made up heavily of small-business ruffians—were needed to carry out the Slacker Raids. In Minneapolis, Detroit, Chicago, New York, and Cleveland, thousands of draft-age men were stopped by soldiers, police, and APLers. Men without suitable draft cards were jailed or handed over to the military for induction more or less on the spot. The *New York Times* reported 20,000 men were caught in that city's dragnet. Some say the real figure was closer to 60,000, and the attorney general himself said that in a three-day period 11,652 men were apprehended in Manhattan and the Bronx alone. Senator Joseph Frelinghuysen of New Jersey left us this description of the goings-on:

> I stood on a street corner and saw soldiers armed with rifles, with bayonets fixed, hold up citizens, compel them to stand waiting while there were crowds jeering at them, and when they failed to produce their registration cards . . . [men] were put in motor trucks and driven through the streets amid the jeers and scoffs of the crowd; they were sent to armories and there held for hours without food, practically without opportunity of communicating with their relatives and friends in order to procure the evidence demanded by the authorities.[11]

Everywhere throughout the country there were violent encounters between prowar mobs and war resisters. The situation was much worse than the hippie-hardhat encounters of a decade ago. There were hundreds of beatings, tarring-and-featherings, and dozens of other acts of violence, including the lynching of Robert Paul Prager, a young baker of German birth and possible socialist convictions who was captured by a drunken mob in Collinsville, Illinois, and lynched. Before they hung the man they let him write a last note: "Dear Parents: I must this day the fourth of April, 1918, die. Please, dear parents, pray for me. This is my last letter or testament. Robert Paul."[12] With a band playing patriotic songs in the courthouse, it took a jury less than half an hour to acquit Robert Paul's executioners of what the defense attorney called a "patriotic murder." The *Washington Post,* not under the same ownership it is now, excused the lynching with an editorial which explained, "In the East the public mind toward the war was much earlier divested of errors. . . . In spite of excesses such as lynching, it is a healthful and wholesome awakening in the interior of the country."[13]

Many prowar people were aghast. Teddy Roosevelt, almost maniacally in favor of intervention and conflict, was one of them and said so. Wilson said nothing. In the same speech in which T. Woodrow uttered the famous words, "The world must be made safe for democracy," the most un-namby-pamby of presidents also stuck it to the opposition when he warned, "If there should be disloyalty, it will be dealt with with a firm hand of stern repression."[14] Nor was that an uncharacteristic remark. It is part of the Wilsonian theme. "For us there is but one choice," he said two months later on Flag Day. "We have made it. Woe be to the man or group of men that seeks to stand in our way in this day of high resolution. . . ."[15]

Woody was a big-league woe-giver, but the situation which confronted him as president and leader of the war majority was dissimilar to and more dangerous than what Presidents Johnson and Nixon had to deal with. Outside the leadership of the civil-rights movement and the frailest of frail left-radical groups, no opposition to the war in Vietnam existed. None would have ever come into existence had the Southeast Asian conflict lasted only as long as World War I or Korea or World War II, but when it began to rival the Siege of Troy in its duration, upper-middle-class youth and collegiate youth rose in rebellion. They quite understandably didn't wish to be freighted to the Asian tropics to be returned home in a rubber bag.

The etiquette of our politics frowns on agitating on one's own behalf. Correct deportment requires that one's self-interest be disguised in a shimmer of outward altruism, so few protestors felt they could get up in public and say, "I'm against this war because I don't want to go into the army and I don't want to give my life for my country, I want to keep my life and enjoy it." To avoid having to say they were against the war on their own behalf, many assumed a radicalism they neither felt nor understood. Real radicals who also opposed the war were appalled, dismayed, and downcast at their vapid, theatrical leftism. Friends and critics alike would shake their heads at the young, incoherent, but awesomely ardent war protestors, and agree that they had no program, no realistic understanding of

the society they were angrily flinging words at, no organized
scaffolding of thought whatsoever.

In 1917 there were also such people. The confused Indians
and black and white tenant farmers of eastern Oklahoma who
took up arms when they heard that Big Slick, as they called
Wilson, was going to draft them followed only the dimmest
road map of political reality. After several days of cutting tele-
graph lines and blowing up a railroad trestle or two, the Green
Corn Rebellion was run to earth by the posse comitatus. Over
200 were tried, and 86 of them were sent to the penitentiary.
The governor of North Carolina reported that people in several
of the mountainous western townships in his state were in a
similar insurrectionary state of mind.

The center of antiwar opposition, though, was the far-left
International Workers of the World labor/political organization and the less flamboyant and less anarchistic but no less
antiwar Socialist party. The socialist parties in the combatant
nations in Europe had gone back on their pledge to resist capitalism's war and had been drawn into supporting their respec-
tive governments, but the party in the United States did not
yield to the call for national unity in the hour of crisis. A few
intellectuals chickened out under the social pressure and joined
the liberals in support of Wilson and war, but the mass of the
party did not.

The party's position on the war was drawn up at a special
convention in St. Louis that met only five days after Wilson's
war message. The chairman of the Committee on War and
Militarism, Kate Richards O'Hare, summarized the delegates'
feeling when she said, "I am a Socialist, a labor unionist and
a believer in the Prince of Peace *first* and an American second. . . . If need be I will give my life and the life of my mate,
to serve my call, but never with my consent will they be given
to add to the profits and protect the stolen wealth of the bankers, food speculators and ammunition makers."[16] Before too
much longer, Mrs. O'Hare would be sent to the penitentiary for
making such statements.

What made her and her confreres so dangerous was that a

lot of other Americans agreed. In the off-year elections of 1917, the Socialists began pulling 20, 30, and 40 percent of the vote. In many cities and towns of Ohio, their vote was so big that the *Akron Beacon-Journal* said there was "scarcely a political observer whose opinion is worth much but what will admit that were an election to come now a mighty tide of Socialism would inundate the Middle West."[17] In Chicago the party pulled 34 percent of the vote; in suburban Cook County it carried nineteen of twenty-nine towns. In a number of places, the Republicans and the Democrats revealed the shallowness of the divisions between them to unite with a fusion candidate to make sure the Socialist could not win. In New York City, the party's mayoral candidate, Morris Hillquit, got people listening when he told them, "We are for peace. We are unalterably opposed to the killing of our manhood and the draining of our resources in a bewildering pursuit of an incomprehensible 'democracy' . . . a pursuit which begins by suppressing the freedom of speech and press and public assemblage, and by stifling legitimate political criticism."[18] The socialist candidate got almost 22 percent of the vote, despite an antisemitic campaign directed against him by the *Tribune* which, in its series on "Who's Who against America," described him as "a Jew, born at Riga, the Milwaukee of Russia. . . . Now he is rich and lives on Riverside Drive."[19] And in Wisconsin, residents could read on fifty billboards scattered around Milwaukee the words,

WAR IS HELL CAUSED BY CAPITALISM.
SOCIALISTS DEMAND PEACE.
READ THE PEOPLE'S SIDE.
MILWAUKEE LEADER.
VICTOR L. BERGER, EDITOR.

Those so inclined might have had difficulty getting the people's side to read, since the government banned the magazine from the mails and banned delivery of mail to its editor. Nevertheless Berger entered the Senate race in 1918 and polled 110,000 votes, 26 percent of the total cast.

Everywhere there were large, impolite manifestations of resistance. Even in New England, which tended to be prowar and anti-Socialist, they had an antiwar parade in Boston made up of some four thousand union men and another four thousand members of various immigrant-group organizations. The signs they carried said things like

DEMOCRATIZE GERMANY?
A SIX-HOUR DAY IN SOCIALIST RUSSIA, WHY NOT
HERE?
IS THIS A POPULAR WAR, WHY CONSCRIPTION?
WHO STOLE PANAMA?
WHO CRUSHED HAITI?
LIBERTY BONDS ARE FIRST MORTGAGES ON LABOR.

WE DEMAND PEACE!

There was extensive antiwar sentiment among farmers in the upper midwest, the southwest, and a number of places in the south, and among industrial workers and immigrant groups. All of it was organized, or potentially organized, by nativist radical politicians who had both a coherent explanation as to how capitalism had brought this tragedy to the country and well-thought-out proposals as to how matters might be changed. The conspiracy, or effectively organized political opposition—the Justice Department is congenitally unable to distinguish between the two—which Presidents Johnson and Nixon descried during their war actually existed during Wilson's. The campaign that the administrations of the two later presidents began against the transitory and chaotic opposition failed because it was geared to smash a political entity that didn't exist; the same sort of campaign by the Wilson administration was far more successful because there was something solid to strike at.

The firm hand of stern repression that Wilson had promised was laid on the Socialist party, on the Wobblies, on any uppity union or other organization that might be accurately accused of stirring up the lower orders to defend themselves. Every level of government played its part in the repression, as did mob and vigilante violence. On July 11, 1917, gangs of armed men under the direction of Sheriff Harry E. Wheeler of Cochise County, Arizona, rounded up 1,186 strikers at the Phelps-Dodge Corporation copper mine in Bisbee. Many were taken from their homes at gunpoint; all were corralled at the baseball park and then driven onto the freight and cattle cars of a train headed toward Columbus, New Mexico, 180 miles away. At Columbus, the locals would not allow the train to be unloaded although many in the cars had been without food or water; so the train chugged into the desert where the men were abandoned at a place called Hermanas, New Mexico. This rather spectacular kidnapping, for which no one ever went to jail, was carried out under the color of patriotism. Strikes were being fomented by the Imperial German government, so the *Los Angeles Times* could declare, "The citizens of Cochise County, Arizona, have written a lesson that the whole of America would do well to copy." Many citizens did copy it and the hundreds of incidents of antiradical violence, of denial of the rights of speech and assembly, defy listing.

Against this background, the federal government conducted its more calculated supression not merely of dissent but of the noncapitalist political party of national scope and organization: the Socialists. The attack began by the passage of a series of laws which effectively ended free press and free speech. The first law provided for up to twenty years in jail plus a $10,000 fine —an enormous sum in those days—for anyone who "shall wilfully make or convey false reports or false statements with intent to interfere with the operation or success of the military or naval forces of the United States or to promote the success of its enemies . . . or shall wilfully obstruct the recruitment or enlistment or service of the United States." For practical purposes the language of this statute meant any remark critical of the war, no matter how obtuse, how obscure, could land you in jail.

Some years later, Zechariah Chafee, Jr., the civil-libertarian Harvard professor who lived and litigated through the period, made this summary of how federal district and appellate judges came to interpret the laws' applications:

> It became criminal to advocate heavier taxation instead of bond issues, to state that conscription was unconstitutional though the Supreme Court had not yet held it valid . . . to urge that a referendum should have preceded our declaration of war, to say that the war was contrary to the teachings of Christ. Men were punished for criticizing the Red Cross and the Y.M.C.A., while under the Minnesota Espionage Act it was held a crime to discourage women from knitting by the remark, "No soldier ever sees these socks." It was in no way necessary that these expressions of opinion should be addressed to soldiers or men on the point of enlisting or being drafted. Most judges held it enough if the words might conceivably reach such men. They have made it impossible for an opponent of the war to write an article or even a letter in a newspaper of general circulation because it would be read in some training camp where it might cause insubordination or interfere with military success. He could not address a large audience because it was liable to include a few men in uniform; and some judges held him punishable if it contained men between eighteen and forty-five, since they might be called into the army eventually; some emphasized the possible presence of shipbuilders and munition-makers. . . .
>
> One judge even made it criminal to argue to women against a war, by the words, "I am for the people and the government is for profiteers," because what is said to mothers, sisters, and sweethearts may lessen their enthusiasm for the war and our armies in the field and our navies upon the seas can operate and succeed only so far as they are supported and maintained by the folks at home."[20]

Reasoning like that might as well have come from the mouth of federal judge Julius Hoffman, the angry jurisprude whom the combined Johnson/Nixon administration used to convict the Chicago Seven, that odd assortment of radicals charged with crossing state lines to throw the 1968 Democratic National Convention into an uproar. In due time, those convictions were reversed and the whole famous and protracted affair came to be regarded as an example of how you can have justice even when persecuted by vindictive prosecutors and malevolent judges. And so you can, when the social and political consensus hasn't formed against you. Unlike the Chicago Seven, Charles T. Schenck, the general secretary of the Socialist party, had his freedom of speech taken away from him and had the decision to do it reaffirmed by Oliver Wendell Holmes. Schenck was arrested in August of 1917 when the cops raided a socialist bookstore. Because of his connection with the store and its inventory, which included a volume entitled *Long Live the Constitution of the United States,* Schenck was accused of obstructing recruitment and enlistment. For this he got six months in the pokey, with the Great Dissenter thinking up his "clear and present danger" idea as justification for not dissenting. Holmes's argument was a rationalization that shows that even the greatest of judges can find a way to justify injustice in the evil hour of patriotism and gore:

> The question in every case is whether the words are used in such circumstances and are of such a nature as to create a clear and present danger that they will bring about the substantive evils Congress has a right to prevent. It is a question of proximity and degree. When a nation is at war many things that may be said in time of peace are such a hindrance to its efforts that their utterance will not be endured so long as men fight and that no court could regard them as protected by a constitutional right.[21]

With the courts mobilized, along with every other institution, it was easy for the government to go after the Socialist party press. In an age of sluggish communication, it was the socialist newspapers which linked the locals in towns and cities across America and which also reached the untouched with seditious thoughts and converted them. By 1913 *Appeal to Reason* had a weekly circulation of more than 750,000; the *National Rip Saw,* aimed at radical farmers, had a circulation of about 150,000. Altogether the circulation of the many socialist journals, which included such diverse publications as the *Jewish Daily Forward* and the Dallas, Texas, *Laborer,* is estimated to

have exceeded two million. Five months after the war was
declared, every important socialist publication had been banned
from the mails at least once, many for weeks at a time. In due
course, this mass-circulation, noncapitalist, alternative press
was destroyed. The socialists were isolated from their fellow
party members, and membership fell off. Local chapters vanished in the midwest and southwest, the pre–World War I
centers of socialist strength. The party survived the war and the
raids and terrors of the immediate postwar period, but it had
lost its base in the American heartland. Before the war, the
foreign-born had been a minority in what was an anticapitalist,
but decidedly American, political organization; after the war,
the preponderance had shifted to immigrant members and
places like New York. Socialism was on its way to being
thought of as an alien religion. In that, the federal government's
destruction of the party's means of internal communication
played a major part.

The attack on First Amendment rights was designed to land
the mostly imaginary agents and sympathizers of the Central
Powers, and if, in nine cases out of ten, those attacked were
socialists, trade unionists, and the like, that doesn't mean the
administration was out-and-out antilabor. Prowar and procapi-
talist labor organizations were protected for the most part, but
to mobilize and/or cow a society it helps to have a degree of
irrational and pointless injustice. A tyrant who stays within his
rules, no matter how harsh and unfair the rules, is going to get
less frantic compliance than the one who occasionally lets the
whip fall on the slaves who have been doing what they're told.

Nothing has ever been unearthed to suggest that such was the
conscious or deliberate policy of the government during World
War I any more than evidence exists to show that the reason
the federal income-tax rules are incomprehensible is to make
the tax gatherers that much more frightening. But intentions
are less important than results. The arrest, trial, and conviction
of Robert Goldstein and his punishment of ten years in the
penitentiary plus a $5,000 fine wasn't, in all likelihood, part of
a campaign to teach the frightened onlooker to fear the govern-

ment and serve it, but it must have had that effect. The unlucky Mr. Goldstein was the producer of a motion picture, made before the declaration of war but released shortly after it, called *The Spirit of '76.* As you might imagine, it was about the American Revolution and therefore the English were portrayed as less than heroes; one scene reportedly showed a redcoat spiking an American baby on his bayonet and spinning the vastly discomfited infant around his head. The judge told Goldstein that such scenes caused people "to question the good faith of our ally, Great Britain."

After Postmaster General Albert Burleson stopped an issue of the *Nation* because of a remark in it making fun of Samuel Gompers, head of the AFL and one of the good, if not the best and most obedient of labor leaders, the magazine's editor, Oswald Garrison Villard, traveled to Washington to get his publication reinstated. At the White House, he found Joseph Tumulty, Wilson's confidential secretary, "incensed and profanely desirous of helping." With Tumulty's intercession, Wilson overruled the ban on the *Nation,* which was not a socialist publication. Villard wrote later that ". . . Burleson went on and actually suppressed the little publication *Unity* in Chicago for what? *For publishing a poem of Robert Browning's!* [emphasis is Villard's] . . . This whole censorship business was a clear illustration of the way the administration did not allow its right hand to know what its left hand was doing. Throughout the war, Mr. Wilson and his cabinet heads 'rode off in all directions.' "[22] Theodore Roosevelt, who loved the war but couldn't abide Wilson, wrote in May of 1918 that, "during the past year the action of the Administration, taken largely through the Post-Office Department, has been such as to render it a matter of some danger for any man, and especially newspapermen, to speak the truth, if that truth be unpleasant to the governmental authorities in Washington."[23]

How many thousands went to jail is not known. More than a thousand persons were convicted under the Espionage Act, not a single one of whom was ever shown to have committed an act of espionage. The better-known cases have been fairly well preserved. In the summer of July, 1917, Kate Richards O'Hare made her speech in Bowman, North Dakota, declaring "that the women of the United States were nothing more nor less than brood sows, to raise children to get into the army and be made into fertilizer." For that she served more than a year in the Missouri State Penitentiary. Wherever possible, censorship was made to look voluntary, as in the case of the English-language press, which agreed to censor itself; where not possible, it was made mandatory, as with the foreign-language press, which was required to submit translations of all material dealing with the government or the war. Wilson made his own prophecy to Josephus Daniels, just before our intervention in 1917, come true: "Every reform we have won will be lost if we go into this war. We have been making a fight on special privilege. . . . War means autocracy. The people we have unhorsed will inevitably come into control of the country for we shall be dependent upon the steel, ore and financial magnates. They will run the nation."[24]

9

Repression

If the repression had been limited to wartime, perhaps Americans might have relapsed into thinking of their government as it had existed before 1917. But after the Great War, the repression continued.

What was called the Red Scare has usually been treated like the 1918–19 influenza epidemic, as though political persecutions are like mass infections or infestations of the gypsy moth: natural phenomena, horrible, regrettable phenomena, which make their cyclic appearance and against which there is no immunity. All you can do is pay your dues to the American Civil Liberties Union and pray.

The Red Scare, during which thousands were rounded up, is sometimes attributed to postwar adjustment difficulties, hard times, the jitters, or, more plausibly, the big strikes which occurred shortly after the armistice and unnerved the middle class. They certainly played a part, but from the time of the Alien and Sedition Acts of 1798 to the McCarthy era, such vehement repression has been associated with war and foreign policy. Labor unrest may be met with repressive counterattacks, but it is never as methodical and national in scope as those in which foreign policy is a major motivating factor.

The Red Scare came about because even back then people were on guard against the Communist Menace. "The spirit of the Bolsheviki is lurking everywhere," quoth a spooked T.

Woodrow, to whom must go the credit for laying down the outlines of American foreign policy vis-à-vis Russian communism. If today many people assume that before Truman and Acheson and those types declared the Cold War, our relations with Russia were "normal," that is in part due to the wild, pro-Russian propaganda of the American right during World War II. In 1943, *Life* magazine, then the most influential mass medium in the country, ran a cover picture of the Muscovite despot with an explanation that it was a hard picture to snap because "Stalin's granite face kept breaking out into a grin." The same issue informed its readers that Lenin was "perhaps the greatest man of modern times" and that "If the Soviet leaders tell us that the control of information was necessary to get the job done, we can afford to take their word for it." Even the attendees at the 1942 convention of the Daughters of the American Revolution (DAR) learned from Tryphosa Duncan Bates-Batcheller (her very self) that "Stalin is a university graduate and man of great studies. He is a man who, when he sees a great mistake, admits it and corrects it." Herbert Hoover, who certainly ought to have known better, told the Republican National Convention in 1944, "The Communist internationalism has been driven out by the nationalist aspiration to free Mother Russia and expand the empire." And Winston Churchill, who did know better, told Parliament with an almost straight face, "The religious side of Russian life has had a wonderful rebirth."

All of this, plus the gemütlichkeit of victory, left a vague and false memory of a happy time between the two countries, so that we have come to think of the Cold War as an aberration. It wasn't. From the moment the Bolsheviks took power in 1917, relations between the two countries—excepting 1941–45—have ranged from nonexistent to putrid. But if Woodrow Wilson was the first American president to spy the Reds hiding behind the trees, he was also the first American statesman to find out that you must be very clever to fight Bolshevism successfully; you must stamp on it without squirting it all over. Wilson wasn't a simple-minded, Red-baiting yahoo;

and, although he ordered troops into Russia after the Revolution, at the ports of Archangel and Vladivostok and in Siberia, he was concerned lest their presence rally the Russians against foreign intrusion and lest American arms be used to establish some sort of bloody, illiberal, and counterrevolutionary tyrant. Wilson was the first of an ever-lengthening line who looked to defeat communism without backing fascism, which was only being born, or any other right-wing autocracy.

Wilson was consecrated to assuring American business access to world markets and raw materials, and he linked this goal to liberal institutions, as he explained in an address to, heaven help us, the Salesmanship Congress in Detroit: ". . . with the inspiration of the thought that you are Americans and are meant to carry liberty and justice and the principles of humanity wherever you go, go out and sell goods that will make the world more comfortable and more happy, and convert them to the principles of America."[1]

From the perspective of 1919, it did appear that America, home of Henry Ford and mass-produced wealth, would be able to confer the good life and the free life on the rest of the world. And if the men of 1945 shared the same perception of global, anti-Bolshevik geopolitics, it may have been because they often were the same men. Allen Dulles, one day to become the most powerful and prestigious of the CIA chieftains, was in the foreign service, serving in 1918 in Switzerland whence he was dispatching information on the Communist penetration of Western Europe to Washington; his brother, John Foster Dulles, was with Wilson at Versailles; and it was under Wilson that Herbert Hoover perfected the use of food as a weapon, as this passage from his memoirs about keeping the Reds out of power in Austria explains:

It was expected that the Communists would try to seize the government on May Day, 1919. . . . I authorized the authorities to post the city walls with a proclamation containing a statement signed by me that "Any disturbance of public order will render food shipments impossible and bring Vienna face to face with absolute famine." Things passed off quietly. Again, a Communist crisis arose when Hungary went Bolshevist. But fear of starvation held the Austrian people from revolution.[2]

Best was when we could find "our way into the great international exchanges of the world," while pushing back the Commies simultaneously. "While it is most important for us to dispose of this surplus in order to avoid difficulties in the United States," said Wilson, after explaining we were making more manufactured goods than we could consume, "it is most fortunate that we have this surplus which is necessary to save human lives and stem the tide of Bolshevism in Europe."[3]

Nearly the same words were used by Truman, Eisenhower, and Kennedy and their secretaries of state. So were the tactics, the need to bolster a defeated Germany so it could stop the redmen riding in from the east. To those brought up on the thinking of the Marshall Plan and the Truman Doctrine (economic and military aid to anticommunist lands) these remarks by Secretary of State Robert Lansing in 1919 have a familiar tone:

And now that the mighty conflict is ended and the great war engine of Prussia is crushed, we have new problems to solve, new dangers to overcome. East of the Rhine there are famine and idleness, want and misery.... We must change the conditions on which social unrest feeds and strive to restore Germany to a normal though it be a weakened social order. Two words tell the story—Food and Peace. To make Germany capable of resisting anarchism and the hideous despotism of the Red Terror, Germany must be allowed to purchase food; and to earn that food industrial conditions must be restored by a treaty of peace. It is not out of pity for the German people that this must be done and done without delay, but because we, the victors in this war, will be the chief sufferers if it is not done.[4]

There have been many disagreements about how to fight, where to fight, and when to fight, but no significant stream of opinion has ever wanted to love 'em up in the Kremlin. In 1944, after three years of the wartime pro-Russian propaganda, Hadley Cantril, FDR's pollster, found 20 percent of the population still were willing to tell a stranger they expected Communists to push into Europe after the war.

It wasn't only noncommunist leftists like pacifist A. J. Muste who gagged at FDR's concessions, the covering up of such Russian war crimes as the murder of over eight thousand Polish officers in the Katyn Forest, and the laughably laudatory depiction of the Soviet state. Liberals like Congressman John Dingell of Michigan were informing the White House by the summer of 1943 that "We Americans are not sacrificing, fighting and dying to make permanent and more powerful the Communistic Government of Russia and to make Joseph Stalin a dictator over the liberated countries of Europe."[5] Roosevelt, who had been sending a series of notes to Old Black Joe in the Kremlin hinting it would help with Congress if he turned the despotism down a couple of decibels, was worried enough about the issue to disavow Commie support in the 1944 election: "I have never sought and I do not welcome the support of any person or group committed to communism or fascism or any other foreign ideology which would undermine the American system of government or the American system of free competitive enterprise and private property."[6]

Given the American dislike, if not loathing, of Communism, and given the fact that after both wars—although not during the economic isolationism of the twenties and thirties—it seemed to be in our financial self-interest to seek out Reds around the earth and oppose them, it is obvious that we mislead ourselves if we say Wilson or Truman started the anti-Russian policy, the cordon sanitaire, the Cold War. Back in 1919, evangelist Billy Sunday was explaining that a Commie is "a guy with a face like a porcupine and a breath that would scare a polecat. If I had my way, I'd fill the jails so full of them that their feet would stick out the windows. . . . Let them rule? We'll swim horses in blood up to the bridles first."[7]

Both the Red Scare and the McCarthy-era repression coincided with an international military and economic push against Bolshevism abroad; both succeeded, by depriving the Communists of their civil rights, in depriving the whole spectrum of the left of its civil rights. In both instances, the repression was enthusiastically supported at the highest levels. In the Truman administration, William D. Leahy, chief of staff to the commander-in-chief, even thought Secretary of State Jimmy Byrnes, a South Carolina politician of unblemished conservatism, might be touched by the Reds in the State Department because Byrnes was just a mite slower than some of the others in understanding that the war was over and so was the romance with Moscow.

Four months after World War I had ended, Oliver Wendell Holmes was reading the Supreme Court's unanimous affirmation of Eugene Debs's conviction for making an antiwar speech. Congressman Victor Berger, the Socialist editor from Milwaukee, was expelled from the U.S. House of Representatives amid shouts of "Bolshevik" and "traitor." Promptly reelected by his Milwaukee constituency, Berger was again refused his seat, although the second time, instead of getting one vote on his side, six congressmen voted for him. In 1920, five members of the New York State Legislature were called up front by the Speaker and informed, "You, whom I have summoned before the bar of the house . . . have been elected on a platform that is absolutely inimical to the best interests of the State of New York. . . ."[8] Whereupon a vote was taken and the five of them were chucked out. Warren Harding and Charles Evans Hughes, seeing how this might get out of hand and eventually spread to Republicans and Democrats, protested the expulsions.

In Centralia, Washington, the attack on radicals was pursued with less restraint. There in November, 1919, in a nightmare that might have been directed by Sam Peckinpah, a bunch of American Legionnaires rushed the IWW hall. The Wobblies shot and killed several of their attackers before being overpowered and taken off to jail. One Wobbly, a certain Wesley Everest, escaped. Tracked down by a posse, he fired on his pursuers, killing one of them before he was taken. The posse knocked his teeth out with a rifle butt and threw him in jail. That night a mob broke into the jail, got Everest a second time, beat him again, and carried him off in an automobile. In the car, they castrated him; then, with Everest screaming, "Shoot me, for God's sakes, shoot me," he was hung by a rope from a railroad bridge. For some reason, the rope's short length offended the mob's aesthetics, so the wretched, still-alive Everest twice was hauled up and fitted with a longer noose. The mob prepared to drop him off the bridge again, but he was clutching onto it. "Tramp on the bastard's fingers," somebody said, and finally, this the third time, Wesley Everest hung till he died. Then in the feeble illumination of the automobile headlights of the Tin Lizzie, the mob filled his body full of rifle bullets.

Dreadful as was the vigilante violence against unions and left-wing opinion, such almost random cruelties pass off in time, often leaving the victims' organizations stronger than before. But the coordinated and thought-out attacks of the police state, which is what the Palmer Raids were, set out to destroy opposition, and they succeeded. A. Mitchell Palmer, whom Wilson named to succeed Attorney General Gregory and who made his predecessor's concern for civil liberties look almost fastidious, has given his name to the repressive raids following World War I and has also gotten much of the blame.

But Palmer was not alone. In 1919 many Americans, particularly in the ruling circles, thought the world was coming apart —or worse, was being blown apart. There were socialist labor riots in Boston, New York, and Cleveland and race riots in Chicago and Washington—which amounted to the same thing, since the upper classes were told by organs like the *New York Times* that "Bolshevist agitation has been extended among the Negroes."[9]

Bombs were going off all over that spring, but the politically most explosive was the one announced in the June 3 *Washington Star:*

BOMB EXPLOSION
AT ATTORNEY GENERAL'S HOME

STARTS A NATION-WIDE ROUNDUP OF ANARCHISTS

NONE OF MR. PALMER'S HOUSEHOLD INJURED
Perpetrator of Crime Blown to Shreds;
Man Who Was Italian, Believed to Have Tripped As He
Entered Yard Bringing Premature Explosion
Terrorist's Head Found on Roof of House.

You can see how today's television news follows in the great tradition of American journalism when you read the *Star*'s coverage:

RED'S BODY IS TORN INTO SHREDS

Fragments of the anarchist's body were literally driven into the back of trees, the woodwork of nearby houses, scattered over the pavements and smeared on the front roofs of houses, while a large portion of the man's torso was found hanging to the cornice of a house on S Street a block from the spot where the explosion occurred. A part of the man's liver was found on the top of an automobile standing 100 feet away. . . . Front windows at the home of Franklin Roosevelt, Assistant Secretary of War . . . were shattered.

FDR was assistant secretary of the navy, but if the *Star*'s facts were smudged, its entertainment value was clear enough. Then as now, the fashion in journalism is to solicit the views of famous people who have no pertinent knowledge to contribute. So the *Star* interviewed Postmaster General Burleson, whose specialty was press censorship:

Look for the woman in the case is the advice of Postmaster General Burleson, who frankly stated today that he expected the anarchists to make selection of himself for a victim. . . . Evidence that the fair sex is largely implicated is found in the fact that many of the anonymous letters received recently by Mr. Burleson are from women. These communications are couched in the bitterest terms. Sometimes they are profane, often obscene and always violent. . . . These amazons are located in many cities in the United States. . . . "Yes, I expect that they will try to get me," said Mr. Burleson. . . . "I have denied them admission to the mails and this has resulted in their ruin in a good many instances. The cowards are naturally resentful and would, if they dared, have run a knife into me or blown me up long ago. . . . I will try to find the leading woman anarchist and when she is found I think the whole plot will be laid bare. Let us find the woman in the case. . . ."

Despite finding a blood-smeared copy of an Italian-American dictionary and a hat with a sweatband from DeLuca Bros. Hatters in Philadelphia, no progress was made in identifying the anarchist. Police hopes of identifying the perpetrator through fingerprints were dashed when they learned that the digit they took to be a finger was a toe. All these details were reported with the same thoroughness they would be now, and printed along with stories such as:

MAY ROUND UP D.C.
"HIGHBROW" REDS

AUTHORITIES BLAME "PARLOR
BOLSHEVIKI" FOR MUCH OF AGITATION

SEEK EDUCATED MEN AND WOMEN

. . . "These people, men and women," said an official today, "are the ones we would like to land. They more than anyone else, are responsible. . . . Many of them are native-born Americans, mostly college-trained men and women. They are seekers after new sensations almost without exception. Once in a while one finds among these high-browed anarchists a crack-brained individual with a fancied grievance against society; but usually they are theorists and faddists with too much idle time on their hands."[10]

Amusing in retrospect, but like the television and newspaper coverage of the hippies, peaceniks, and protestors of the late sixties, when it is happening, it provides the political Muzak during which serious violations of civil liberties are sanctioned. Nothing on the scale of the Palmer Raids has occurred in

America since, for the reason that the American left, in an organizational sense, never recovered. The first raids took place on November 7, 1919, netting 250 people in eleven cities, all thought to be members of the Union of Russian Workers, an organization which described itself as being composed of "atheists, communists and anarchists." Newspaper reports said some of the arrested were beaten, but equally disturbing to liberty lovers of the time must have been the long incarceration of some of the victims, notably those in Hartford, Connecticut, who languished in the slammer five months before being granted a hearing.

The next day, November 8, New York State authorities raided no less than seventy-three Communist or Socialist or some-sort-of-radical offices, arresting over 500 persons and taking tons of printed material and Lord knows what else. The pattern of these raids, regardless of which political jurisdiction conducted them, was to give the aliens to the federal authorities, who could deport them without trial or any kind of due process, while American citizens remained in the hands of local authorities, who could try them for violating the criminal-syndicalism laws that the legislatures of many states had been passing ever since the murder of William McKinley. It was in this manner that 249 persons were scooped up and deported to Finland on the *Buford,* a ship that came to be better known as the "Soviet Ark." Two of its passengers were Emma Goldman and Alexander Berkman, Goldman's lover, lifelong friend, and the man who tried to murder Henry Clay Frick, the steel tycoon, during the Homestead strike of 1892.

The apex or the nadir came on January 2, 1920, when the Justice Department's Bureau of Investigation (the "Federal" hadn't been added on yet) seized—arrested is hardly the word, since there were no warrants in many cases—four thousand radicals. They were grabbed up everywhere, homes, meetings, club rooms; they were held incommunicado, often without lawyers, without food, without heat. One woman, Minnie Federman, a citizen with no radical connections at all, was taken from her bedroom at six in the morning.

The Palmer Raids represent the first successful large-scale use of tactics and practices that would be so widely excoriated under Nixon fifty years later. The reason so many Communists and other radicals could be picked up on the same night was that Bureau of Investigation agents, who had previously infiltrated these organizations, were ordered to call the meetings for that night. As Oswald Garrison Villard wrote in his 1939 memoirs,

> It was brought out . . . in court that under Mr. Palmer's instructions his spies and agents provocateur in the ranks of the Communist Party had not only called the meetings on January 2, 1920, which Mr. Palmer's federal agents raided all over the country, but had actually written the very portions of the Communist platform upon which the government based its prosecutions of the men it duped. In other words, the government manufactured the crime and then sent men to prison for doing what it had induced them to do.[11]

That was by no means all the Department of Justice was doing to fight radicals. The Department carried on a program of feeding the country's press with articles and cartoons for the inspiriting of the forces of 100 percent Americanism. Under the General Intelligence Division of the Bureau of Investigation, the dossiers of radicals began to be assembled. By the fall of 1919, some 60,000 names were in the files, which Palmer proudly called "a greater mass of data upon this subject than is anywhere else available." These files were part of a larger set of 200,000 which covered organizations, geographic divisions, publications, etc., all apparently intelligently worked out by a young man from the Library of Congress named J. Edgar Hoover. That Hoover should be doing the same things under Nixon that he was doing under Wilson ought to have been the cause of less surprise than it was; over a period of fifty years a person can get set in his ways.

Even without the government's help, the American left was doing a job on itself. Prior to 1919, the Socialist party had been *the* umbrella party of the left, under which rightists, leftists, and centrists lived, if not in harmony, at least in cooperation, much as people did in the capitalist parties. The wholly unexpected triumph of socialism in Russia caused serious repercussions among the American socialists, whose excitement over this event obscured how little they had in common with the antidemocratic, disciplined toughnuts who would be building their almost Oriental version of the worker's paradise in the very palace of the czars. Nor was the non-American aspect of the Communist victory lessened by the almost immediate and very real domination of the comrades in the United States by the Russians through the Third International. The splits and animosities this engendered were so great that by 1923 or '24, noncommunist groups on the left were already barring the door to Red participation, in a pattern that would be common until the late forties and early fifties, when this never-very-numerous breed would be reduced to a few faithful with too much psychic investment to quit, and a few FBI agents awaiting transfer to more interesting assignments.

It's impossible to guess what would have happened to American socialism in the face of the Communist split without the raids. What did happen was that the membership in left-wing parties declined. The Communists, harassed by police-state tactics, went underground and developed the conspiratorial mode which made them all the more suspect and difficult to work with. American Communists were victims in the 1920s and again in the 1940s, but part of the reason others on the left went to their defense with such lethargic energy was that they were, when the policy line dictated it, treacherous, devious disruptionists with whom it was impossible to cooperate. That they were truly oppressed does not make them the more lovable.

10

Silent Years

The differences between the Red Scare of 1919 and the Red Scare of the Truman-Eisenhower period reflect how completely the left had been smashed or had disintegrated in the interval. The McCarthy period reinforced the lesson that the walls had ears and the ears belonged to Uncle Sam, that it was not safe to be outwardly different. In the years following 1948 the kept professoriat complained of conformity and the Silent Generation. They were silent because they had seen what happens to the loner who acts in a conspicuous way or talks too much. McCarthyism was mostly accusing people of being secret Communist sympathizers, of being spies, agents, operators in stealth. The expression which was used time and time again was the Communist Conspiracy.

In the period ending in the early twenties it was just the opposite. They accused the Wobblies and the socialists and even the early Communists of every imaginable crime, but not clandestine subversion. What they were jailed for was open, flagrant sedition. Debs's crime was making a speech in Canton, Ohio, to a large assembly in front of the jail where three fellow party members were serving time for a political offense. Debs's famous speech to the judge before his sentencing are the words of a man schooled in a very tough, but an open and nonconspiratorial politics:

Your honor, years ago I recognized my kinship with all living
beings, and I made up my mind that I was not one bit better than
the meanest on earth. I said then, and I say now, that while there
is a lower class, I am in it, while there is a criminal element I
am of it, and while there is a soul in prison, I am not free. . . .
I ask no mercy and I plead for no immunity. I realize that finally
the right must prevail. I never so clearly comprehended as now
the great struggle between the powers of greed and the exploitation on the one hand and upon the other the rising hosts of
industrial freedom and social justice.[1]

Whether or not Debs spoke for the masses, masses of people,
loudly and publicly, harkened to his words. Five thousand
people in Toledo defied the mayor's ban on the use of Memorial
Hall to hear Debs speak his goodbye before he became convict
Number 9653 in the Atlanta Federal Penitentiary. Languishing
there two years after the war was over—Wilson was merciless
in his refusal to grant pardon or amnesty to the political prisoners in his jails—Debs still polled over 900,000 votes for the
presidency in 1920.

Even without the government's repression and the divisions
caused by Communism, a noncapitalist political party might
not have been able to survive the 1920s. It was then that Fi-
orello La Guardia, Progressive Republican congressman and
later mayor of New York, complained, "I tell you, it's damned
discouraging to be a reformer in the wealthiest land in the
world."[2] Whatever the might-have-beens were, the destruction
of the socialist press meant there was no competition for the
advertiser-supported mass media. Henceforth, there was one
view and one reality—or objectivity, as it came to be called—
accessible to the citizenry. Likewise, there might still be the
quasi-clandestine Communists, but there was no longer a noncapitalist or anticapitalist political party committed to democratic principles. The jailed Debs and the hundreds of overrun,
destroyed local chapters were proof of that.

In a political universe where the two remaining parties
shared the same basic perceptions and definitions, expressions
like "free-enterprise system" became synonymously inter-

changeable with "democracy." It was all one emergent corporate capitalism; knowing a man's political party might give you a clue to his religion or his geographical region but not to his convictions. This is one of the reasons that, contrary to the theory of the way it ought to work, groups like the blacks have found little profit in trying to play one party off against the other. The parties are too amorphous and too similar to permit such tactics to be effective. Which is why the largest changes accruing to blacks came first as a result of the Cold War, and then of the threat of disruptions completely outside of the political or legal institutions and processes.

A racially segregated society at home was too much to explain in what we fancied was a worldwide tussle between ourselves and the Russians for the affections of black- and brown-skinned people who, it has come about, don't have much time for either of us. But foreign-policy considerations only led us to such cosmetic changes as the Supreme Court's Brown decision; neither it nor many other laws and rules on the subject were carried out until blacks took first nonviolent and then violent action.

It wasn't only blacks who lost a party that might have fought for their interests. When Debs and the Socialists went kaput, so did any hope of trade unions becoming an integral part of any political movement. Without the support of a party that makes prolabor legislation one of its major reasons for existence, labor has been forced to rely on what it can coax out of the bipartisan consensus. Lacking a political base, labor has become less of an adversary to management and more of a junior partner. The unions lobby the management's position on environment, foreign trade, or energy, and they discipline the labor force, working with management to cut down absenteeism, sabotage, and wildcat strikes. This role for labor unions has become so generally accepted that a labor organization like the United Mine Workers is judged to be weak or strong, good or bad, as much on its ability to stop unauthorized strikes and get the membership to work on time as it is for any benefits it might secure for the miners.

If, in the years following the Red Scare, no serious alterna-
tives to the Republicrats existed, values like being against war
had nonetheless not dropped out of public life. William G.
McAdoo, Wilson's secretary of the treasury, son-in-law, and
longtime power in the Democratic party, once said that when
Warren Harding talked, it "left the impression of an army of
pompous phrases moving over the landscape in search of an
idea. Sometimes these meandering words would actually capture a straggling thought and bear it triumphally, a prisoner in
their midst, until it died of servitude and overwork."[3] One of
the ideas that Harding, who has been maligned by posterity,
bore off into captivity was that of peace and disarmament. In
their outward behavior and speech, Americans of that period
were moved and horrified by war in a way we are not. American
presidents of our era talk about peace every bit as much as they
did then—more so, perhaps—but their words seldom communicate the emotion Harding's did on a dock in Hoboken, New
Jersey, where he met the freighter *Wheaton,* whose cargo was
the coffins of 5,212 of the servicemen killed in Europe: "I find
a hundred thousand sorrows touching my heart, and there is a
ringing in my ears, like an admonition eternal, an insistent call,
'It must not be again! It must not be again!' "[4]

Harding wasn't alone in hearing that call. Beginning in the
early 1920s and lasting until 1937 or '38, there was a continuous
and stunning amount of antiwar activity. The fans the delegates
used at the 1924 Democratic National Convention had "Law,
Not War" printed on them; Ernest Hemingway wrote *A Fare-
well to Arms;* and Erich Maria Remarque's nauseatingly realistic description of trench warfare, *All Quiet on the Western
Front,* was a huge bestseller. Church groups petitioned for an
end to war and armaments; college students took the Oxford
oath, vowing they would never fight in another war; high-
school students' antiwar posters were exhibited at special show-
ings; on April 12, 1935, sixty thousand students took part in a
"strike" against war. By the mid-1930s, membership and attendance in antiwar organizations had never been larger.

All of this activity wasn't being directed toward a disinterested government. Harding and his secretary of state, Charles

Evans Hughes, invited the chief military powers of the world to an international conference in Washington in the fall of 1921 and then shocked the hell out of them by abandoning generalities to make specific proposals for disarmament. They required the proprietors of the world's three largest navies, the equivalent in that age of the ICBM, to scrap much of their battleship tonnage. Secretary of State Hughes had sunk more men o' war in his short speech making the proposals "than all the admirals of the world have sunk in a cycle of centuries," one of the people at the conference remarked. William Jennings Bryan, there as a reporter, wept. In the end the conferees signed a treaty providing that for every five battleships the English built, the Americans could build five too, the Japanese three, and the Italians and the French one and three-quarters each.

There were wrangles over the relative worth of submarines and fortified places, which should be easy to understand for a generation that has to listen to arguments about whether or not a Soviet tank in Poland is an offensive weapon or a cruise missile a strategic one. At length, on February 6, 1922, perhaps the most comprehensive set of antiwar treaties the United States has ever been party to were signed. Will Rogers, in a dispatch to the *Cleveland Plain Dealer,* seems to have caught the scene nicely:

> Today was the day for them to sign the treaties. Everybody signed but the Senate. Every man was allowed to keep the pen he signed with. England got six pens to our four. Belgium had a tough trip for one pen. China got three pens in exchange for Chinese Siberia, Indo-China, Shanghai and Mongolia. . . . France received two pens and no submarines. . . . Japan got all the islands north of the equator, Siberia, Mongolia, Battleship *Matsu* and protection and three pens. . . .[5]

The treaties were ratified with a minimum of fuss when you consider that the Senate as an institution doesn't like to ratify treaties. The proximate cause for the relative ease of passage was that the politically adept Harding had appointed Oscar W. Underwood, the Senate Democratic minority leader, to the official negotiating team. Harry Truman would do much the same sort of thing with Republican Arthur Vandenberg when the not-always-so-Cold War was being put into place. But such bipartisanship arises when the two political organizations so completely share the same values they aren't able to sustain a significant level of disagreement. Having run pell-mell into war together, they were now going as fast as they could in the direction of disarmament. In between, the parties did split on the question of American membership in the League of Nations, but that has as much to do with personalities, grudges, and Wilson's probably brain-damaged refusal to allow a comma in the document to be altered as it did with the policy objections raised by some of the anti-League senators such as Borah.

"Public sentiment was the real author of the move for disarmament," said Borah,[6] and it is certain that every kind of group spoke for it. One poll showed that 723 out of 803 newspapers were for ratification of the Harding-Hughes treaties.[7] It even had the support of Gen. John Pershing, the commander of the American Expeditionary Force in 1917–18. What must have been yet sweeter music to people's ears then was that even some of the merchants of death came out for disarmament. Charlie Schwab, whose Bethlehem Steel Corporation had cleaned up on the war, conceded in a speech given while the Harding-Hughes proposals were still being negotiated in Washington that the treaties might cost him money, but

> such a thing as financial loss can be of no consideration when compared to the inestimable boon to mankind which would be involved in the realization of that magnificent plan. What red-blooded American would not, indeed, make any sacrifice if the burden of armament could be lifted from the shoulders of humanity? ... But ... if the states now assembled in Washington ... should find it possible to bring about disarmament and permanent peace, gladly would I see the war-making machinery of the Bethlehem Steel Corporation sunk to the bottom of the ocean.[8]

In fact, only the smallest portion of steel-production capacity was then being devoted to arms, so Charlie's red-blooded American offer of sacrifice was largely theoretical. But it fit in nicely with the thoughts of the British foreign minister that were quoted by Hughes at the time:

> The increase of armaments, that is intended in each nation to produce consciousness of strength, and a sense of security, does not produce these effects. On the contrary, it produces a consciousness of the strength of other nations and a sense of fear. Fear begets suspicion and distrust and evil imaginings of all sorts, till each nation feels it would be criminal and a betrayal of its own country not to take every precaution, while every government regards every precaution of every other government as evidence of hostile intent. . . . The enormous growth of arms in Europe, the sense of insecurity and fear caused by them—it was these that made war inevitable.[9]

The same argument would be exhumed fifty years later and treated as a novel truth arising from the perfection of the atomic-tipped 15,000-mile missile. While by no means without merit, it's not the whole story, as *Bankers Magazine* pointed out in 1921:

> . . . The enthusiasts for immediate disarmament are attaching altogether too much importance to navies and armies as provocatives [*sic*] of war. . . . The seemingly ineradicable propensity of mankind [for conquest], racial hatred, religious prejudices, national vanity, territorial greed, personal ambition, and trade rivalries—these are the causes of war about which no dispute exists. . . . Why then, should we give up that in which our security rests (that is, armaments) until these real and known causes of war are stamped out or at least diminished . . .?[10]

Why then indeed? Part of the reason is that the only two political parties contesting for power were so inextricably intertwined with "the causes of war" the magazine cited, it is fatuous to have supposed they might have moved toward correcting them. A political party with a truly different perspective, a truly different constituency and set of interests to protect and advance, might have at least offered another view and alternative policies. That was not to be. America and the world proceeded with disarmament until the last great war precipitated by the old capitalist order so wasted the great powers that the way was prepared for the wars of political religion which have made our own lifetimes such a joy.

Without the internal friction of debate, objection, and opposition, America became vulnerable to a politics of successive excesses. Pendulum-swinging. Our political commentators are forever explaining a headlong rush one way or another as "the swing of the pendulum" back toward the White House, toward Congress, toward free enterprise, toward the Cold War, or away from any of the above. We are accustomed to thinking of these violent about-faces as the occurrences of nature. If it was mildly simple-minded to believe that guns or missiles cause war, it is no less simple-minded to think the absence of them does, but when the pendulum swings it can knock the best of brains fuzzy; quoth Walter Lippmann, "The preachment and the practice of pacifists in Britain and America were a cause of the World War. They were the cause of the failure to keep pace with the growth of German and Japanese armaments. They led to the policy of . . . appeasement."[11] The argument that arms are a deterrent to war has been used since Lippmann wrote that in 1942, through Korea, Vietnam, and beyond.

The antiwar movement between 1919 and 1939, being a peace-without-politics effort, fell to pieces for want of a political position that said anything more than "we hate war." During the late 1930s, an attempt was made to form a coalition of antiwar people, left and right. Composed of the remnants of the Senate "Irreconcilables" (the men who shot down the League of Nations), socialists, a newer generation of conservative isolationists, and a tinge of quasi-fascist persons with an antisemitic inclination, the America First Committee could not even enlist the support of most traditional pacifist groups, certainly not with a slogan like "Keep Out, Keep Ready." The massive antiarmament sentiment of the previous years was marching off to war with Lucky Strike Green.

During World War II more than forty thousand men declared themselves some form of conscientious objector. Tucked away in jails and hidden in remote work camps in forest and mountain, they made no splash, they didn't even make a quick plop in public attention. Yet they carried out hunger strikes and other nonviolent demonstrations for the racial integration of the dining facilities, first at the Danbury Federal Penitentiary and then elsewhere. The protestors existed, they were active, and word of them finally did get out to a few people. But what most of America heard were words like the ones Gen. George S. Patton, Jr., addressed to a Sunday School class in June of 1945: "You are the soldiers and the nurses of the next war," the general told the children, most of whom were about eight years of age. "There will be another war. There always has been."[12]

Outside of the pariah Progressive Party of 1948, there was no deviating from the biparty line, almost nothing in the way of protest, resistance, or debate. It was the Red Monolith versus the Red, White, and Blue Monolith. Who was going to dare to say nay when liberals like Earl Warren were explaining to the voters in the 1948 presidential campaign that "while we spend billions to halt the spread of the Communist conspiracy abroad, we find this same conspiracy reaching its stealthy fingers to grab the framework of our own free institutions and tear them down."[13] By the 1950s, Mr. Democratic Liberal, Sen. Hubert Humphrey, was introducing legislation to take care of the Reds by outlawing their emasculated, petite political party. "I am tired of reading headlines about being 'soft' toward Communism. . . . I want Senators to stand up and to answer whether they are for the Communist Party, or are against it," Humphrey told his colleagues in defending his proposal of legal outlawry. To the worry that this kind of thing might have a depressing, if not an oppressing, effect on deviant opinion, he replied, "Let them join the party of Mars or the party of Jupiter, if they want to be different."[14]

Such respectable political opposition as there was came from the right. Strangely enough, it did not advocate an atomic ultimatum. You would have thought that, if there ever was a time for the United States to intervene in the domestic affairs of another country, it was then, with Stalin on the throne, verily one of history's big-league butchers. America had the means and it had the motive to extinguish the messianic ugliness that dwelt in Moscow. But it appears that such thoughts were never seriously entertained. The nation that went to war in Southeast Asia, over the most trifling of incidents, and lost could not screw up its moral courage to off its most dangerous enemy while it safely could. Even in the few years of American atomic monopoly, it was not within us to commit such an act.

Instead, the right advanced a Fortress America approach, which never had a real chance. It may have been best stated by Republican Congressman (later Senator) George Bender of Ohio, when President Truman asked for aid to Greece and Turkey in 1947 and America began to move toward the formation of NATO and the institutionalization of the status quo:

> I believe that the White House program is a reaffirmation of the nineteenth century belief in power politics. It is a refinement of the policy first adopted after the Treaty of Versailles in 1919 designed to encircle Russia and establish a 'Cordon Sanitaire' around the Soviet Union. It is a program which points to a new policy of interventionism in Europe as a corollary to our Monroe Doctrine in South America. Let there be no mistake about the far-reaching implications of this plan. Once we have taken the historic step of sending financial aid, military experts and loans to Greece and Turkey, we shall be irrevocably committed to a course of action from which it will be impossible to withdraw. More and larger demands will follow. Greater needs will arise throughout the many areas of friction in the world."[15]

The difficulty with this position, particularly as it was espoused by Bender's leader, Sen. Robert A. Taft, was that it was the expression of a disparate faction of Republicans, not of a party, and that what it was reluctant to do in Europe, it was more than willing to do in the Far East to recapture "lost" China. Taft Republicans, the political residue of pre-1939 conservative anti-war sentiment, nursed a rancorous anger at both Roosevelt and Truman for the arrangements the two presidents had concluded with the Russians over the disposition of Europe. To Taftian eyes, it looked as if a chain-gang of countries, the so-called "captive nations," had simply been delivered into Communist hands for no good and many bad reasons. At the same time, their immediate political and partisan traditions made it difficult for them to see their way clear to backing entangling—oh fatal word!—alliances in Europe, even if those alliances were aggressively anticommunist in nature.

Nevertheless, the chagrin and shock of the Taft Republicans over the rapid ooze of the color red on the map needed some focus for action. The place they chose was China. Thus the foreign-policy battle of the period was fought not over the question of whether we should be doing this, but between the Eastern internationalist liberals, as they were called for no very good reason, and the midwestern isolationists, as they were called for no very good reason, over where the primary thrust of American international anticommunism should be directed, Europe or Asia. Without their realizing it, the Taftian small-government conservatives—who drew back from a military commitment for Europe, at least partly because they understood that mobilization for war always increases the power of the central government—went along with the same measures when undertaken in the name of chasing the Reds out of Asia so that the Oriental millions might become democrats, Christians, and integrated consumer/producers within the framework of western capitalism. Viewed from our time, such thoughts in connection with China sound crazy, but twenty-five years ago the "Miracle of Japan" was already beginning to take shape and the dream of China as a nation of 800 million Methodist homeowners hadn't yet taken on the coloration of an eccentric's dream.

With all political factions agreeing on the Cold War, although disagreeing on how it might best be prosecuted, the country was silent and without public demur about being put on a semipermanent war footing until June 15, 1955, when a certain Rocco Parilli, a shoeshine boy by occupation, became perhaps the first innocent victim of peace. Parilli, who had entered City Hall Park in New York for the lawful purpose of taking a drink of water from a fountain, was arrested with thirty members of the Catholic Workers, the War Resisters League, and the Fellowship of Reconciliation for failing to take cover during an air-raid drill. By the mid-1950s, the children of America were all being taught to get under their school desks and, in the proper position as illustrated in the civil-defense manuals, await the moment of the splitting of their own personal atoms. The protests against the air-raid drills used as a means of conditioning the populace to the idea of war continued every year until 1960, when a thousand or more persons joined the original thirty, and the city abandoned war practice.

Faced with thermonuclear nihilism, more people began to speak out. The National Committee for a Sane Nuclear Policy grew at a dizzy speed; huge rallies were held as all sorts of proper people like Eleanor Roosevelt and Alf Landon, the 1936 Republican presidential candidate, appeared to bless the multitudes. Then the problem of peace-without-politics again presented itself. Senator Thomas Dodd of Connecticut, a major Washington figure of the time, said one of the committee's chief staff organizers was a Communist. The organization was too weak and amorphous to resist. The head of the committee suspended the accused subversive and had the bad judgment to let Dodd announce this inglorious fact. Many local chapters split over the issue, and the organization began to shrivel. At length the United States and Soviet Russia did sign a test-ban treaty. No more atomic bombs were to be detonated above ground, where their dirty radioactive detritus could poison babies' milk. Admirable as this was as a public-health measure, it had no effect on the prospects for peace or disarmament, as both nations continued to test underground, only more often than before.

Ask not what the state can do for you, but what you can do

for the state. Pogo meets the enemy and finds he is us, as Simone Weil explained as early as February, 1945, when World War II was but ending. There was only a small, not very solvent magazine for her words, no political party, no way to convert her understanding to a force for bending events:

> Whether the mask is labelled Fascism, Democracy, or Dictatorship of the Proletariat, our great adversary remains the Apparatus—the bureaucracy, the police, the military. Not the one facing us across the frontier or the battle-lines, which is not so much our enemy as our brothers' enemy, but the one that calls itself our protector and makes us its slaves. No matter what the circumstances, the worst betrayal will always be to subordinate ourselves to this Apparatus, and to trample underfoot, in its service, all human values in ourselves and in others.[16]

Part 4

Government conscripted public opinion as they conscripted men and money and materials. Having conscripted it, they dealt with it as they dealt with other raw recruits. They mobilized it. They put it in charge of drill sergeants. They goose-stepped it. They taught it to stand at attention and salute.

Frank Cobb, editor of the *New York World,*
December, 1919

11

The All-American Medley

Throughout the wars of the twentieth century, the boast has been that the government has never, no, not even in times of direst national crisis, fastened censorship on the commercial press. The noncommercial, noncapitalist press didn't do so well, as we've seen, but with the exception of its vaporization as a mass medium, the boast is correct. Actually, it's uncharacteristically modest. The commercial mass media did more than exercise voluntary self-censorship in regard to troop movements or other military secrets. It functioned as conductor of the symphony orchestra playing the American Medley. The editors and reporters were pompom girls leading the society in a perpetual locomotive cheer for the free market, the two-party system, for a government of law not men, and the half-dozen sloganized ideas which made us great. It could scarcely be otherwise. The corporations that own the mass media are not going to direct their orchestra to play anarchist ragtime or even the gentler rhythms of the socialist waltz. He who pays the piper does call the tune, and when the pipers are persons like Barbara Walters, who receive salaries of a million dollars a year, they perform the music exactly as the notes are printed.

Countless others, although they don't make a million a year, do make enough to lift their voices in the song. With their standard of living, Americans have an answer to the question, If you're so smart, why aren't you rich? That Swedes, French, and Japanese, living in countries with far more meager natural resources, have come fairly close to equaling our material well-being has not persuaded Americans that luck or happenstance may account for a part of their wealth. It's not natural resources, the fertility of the land, the migratory millions providing cheap labor, nor the billions invested here by European capitalists; it's the nation's unique system of political economy which explains all. Once that is said, wealth becomes the universal verifier. Every assertion of a patriotic or ideological nature is regarded as a statement of fact verified and validated by the standard of living, by wealth. The two-party system, the metaphysics of the competitive ideal, the valor of our forefathers must be as it is said, or else why are we so rich?

Behind the tiered choir celebrating this certitude, there lies a set of convictions, a manner of viewing ourselves and the world that is not born of transitory government propaganda campaigns. In nonliterate society, the totality of seeing and thinking that provides the meaning, order, and limits of understanding is received and traditional. Not so in societies like ours, where they didn't wait for Big Brother and 1984 to mess with our minds, or at least to shape them for the economic tasks, the productive arrangements, and the technological activities that occupy so much of our waking lives. The modern American was consciously engineered, as an 1828 report of the Boston School Committee on mass public education makes clear: "its effects on the habits, character and intelligence of youth are highly beneficial; disposing their minds to industry, to readiness of attention and to subordination, thereby creating in early life a love of order, preparation for business. . . . "[1]

The efforts to mass-produce the ideal employee have been massive and continuous. A reader prepared in 1912 for German immigrant workers at an International Harvester plant obviously had another objective as well: "I hear the whistle. I must hurry. I hear the five minute whistle. It is time to go to the shop. I take my check from the gate board and hang it on the department board. I change my clothes and get ready for work. The starting whistle blows. . . . I eat lunch. It is forbidden to eat until then. The whistle blows at five minutes of starting time."[2]

Thought control and engineering the human personality have gotten themselves a smutty reputation with the rise of the modern, technological, totalitarian state and the recognition that we here in America are pygmies in the skyscraper forest of organizational and corporate trees. Thought control, or molding the character, is an ancient and not necessarily nefarious activity. Once a society abandons raising its children purely by unquestioned, inherited, and traditional practices, people have to ask what kind of adults we want to train up and how we adjust our child-rearing practices to make them that way. That's what the professor of education at the University of Wisconsin meant in 1909 when he wrote that the purpose of schooling was to bring the individual "into harmony with the customs, ideals, and institutions of present-day society. Intense individualistic feelings and actions must be brought under control and cooperation must largely take the place of original tendencies to opposition and agression."[3] Individual initiative may be praised in the abstract, but for office, factory, civil service, the army, and the laboratory, American children are taught teamwork. From nursery school on they learn that the virtuoso genius is temperamental, eccentric, and impossibly disruptive in any system where work is thought to "flow." In our imaginations we think about great men and great deeds; we adore a Winston Churchill—but only for England. Cynical and irreverent personalities of such unique distinction aren't trusted on this side of the Atlantic and are not entrusted with high office. In 1912, William McAndrew, the superintendent of the New York City public school system, remarked that one "unsocial custom persisting from feudal times is the award of prizes for superiority in scholarship. There is no social service secured by the selection of the best scholar for special honor. It is rank individualism."[4] Early in the century, Bell Labs, the research organ of AT&T, abandoned incentive rewards. Frank Jewett, head of the lab, explained, "It created a situation where men would not work with each other . . . yet the problem which was before us was a problem which required team action. . . . so some way had to be found to get over that."[5]

Public education's success in training children to grow up to be workers and consumers is incontestable. Tens, perhaps hundreds, of millions of dollars are spent on every imaginable vocational and psychological preparation for adding pliant young people to the labor force. The family as a carrier of social values outside of and superior to those of the cash economy is too weakened to interpose a different ideal than that of the worker-consumer-acquirer-owner. Fewer and fewer families find they can afford to have an unemployed parent at home tending to child-rearing; the public school system, the corporate crêche, the halfway house, and the youth center take over the job. From sex education to lessons on unit pricing to making sure the kid gets a hot lunch and an adequate breakfast, civil servants assume the responsibility while the mothers and the fathers take an evening course at the community college on "parenting."

Within a century or less a true novus homo, an authentic new human, has been designed, fabricated, and is now being mass-produced. Without ties to place, community, or family, this is the disposable human at the disposal of large-organization logistics. The newest and most advanced models come in any color and either gender; when they marry, if they marry, they are content to see their spouses once a week or once a month —work comes first. Their politics is nebulous but they have learned that you make your own breaks in life through hard work, prayer—Christian or Buddhist meditation—and the perfection of your own psychology. Few are called to greatness, but all can learn to deal with it, to relate to it, to master coping skills, as they say in clinic and classroom.

Human engineering like the mechanical and electronic kind is not always so certain in its outcomes. Dams do break, bridges sometimes fall, and the pioneers in the universities and corporate-owned factories in discovering how to motivate and manipulate could not have foreseen how their work would contribute to the reworking of the soul. The conversion of the majority of the population from a largely self-sufficient farming life to a totally cash-dependent, job-desperate work force played a part;

the perfection of mass production and the creation of a new advertising to push the goods the industrial cornucopia was disgorging helped persuade the populace to abandon the values of thrift, utility, and frugality; people who live on credit aren't the same as those who pay cash. Those who consciously worked at effecting the new American person may not have anticipated all that happened and may not be pleased by it, but from about the turn of the century onward the leaders of the corporate industrial society have tried to extend their dominance to the mind and the spirit. Before World War I, Harvard psychologist Hugo Münsterberg was adjuring his colleagues to put their discipline at the service of industry. By the 1920s, innumerable attempts to increase production and lower costs by tinkering with the employees' minds were under way. The most famous were the experiments run at AT&T's Hawthorne Western Electric plant on Chicago's west side. The work at Hawthorne went on for decades as relays of some of the best-known names in American psychology, sociology, and anthropology consecrated themselves to the task of making the worker as reliable and predictable as the machine. That ubiquitous, albeit quietly conspicuous, American institution, the counseling center, can trace part of its origins back to Hawthorne. Today the society is as interpenetrated with these repair shops for broken spirits as it is with McDonald's and Midas Muffler shops; the purpose is the same—to get the busted robot off alcohol, off drugs, off the marital blues, off depression, and back to functioning at his or her work. The very use of the word functioning suggests how far we've gone in thinking of ourselves as inanimate mechanisms that don't get sick but suffer "down time."

At the same time, academics in service to the corporations —working to keep the human machines on stream and producing—also got into the testing business. During World War I the IQ test was administered to every draftee and, as blacks and other minority groups chanced to find out many, many years later, the power to label some people smart and other people dumb is power indeed. Nor did it take long for men like Dean P. F. Walker of the University of Kansas to appreciate the tool that had been delivered into the hands of the powerful and their technological and scholarly servitors. Writing in 1919, he said,

> The war gave a great impetus to the idea of testing and grading men as a means of estimating their capabilities. The intelligence or psychological tests and the trade test were most in evidence, along with the system of grading on personality characteristics. . . . There is a strong tendency in the schools to take up the matter. From the beginning the weeding out of the unfit and the adjusting of the pegs . . . to fit the industrial openings, have been among the difficult problems. Educators are disposed to welcome any system which promises assistance.[6]

Through the American Council on Education, testing programs were broadened to govern admissions to every imaginable kind of school and subsequent occupation. Since those who devise the tests ultimately dictate what must be taught in order to pass them, the Educational Testing Service, where testing in America is centralized, in effect controls much of the content of instruction. While leaving the appearances of free choice and local self-determination, in fact uniformity is inescapable.

In 1930 the General Board of Education of the Rockefeller Foundation put up a large amount of money to perfect and further the development of the testing system. Doubtless neither the Rockefellers themselves, nor the philanthropic bureaucrats in their employ, and certainly not the recipients, considered the half a million dollars given to the work an investment in social control. In recent years, the obvious connection between foundation money and political power has gone largely unremarked except by right-wingers, many of whom could be dismissed as Birchites or the next thing to it. But back in the days of the Taft administration when the Rockefeller people first asked for federal incorporation of their foundation, this one-hundred-million-dollar proposition was vehemently opposed by Attorney General George Wickersham, who wrote President Taft that there never before had been submitted to Congress, or any legislative body, such an indefinite scheme for perpetuating vast wealth as this; and personally I believe it to be entirely inconsistent with the public interest that any such bill should be passed. . . . The power which, under such a bill, would be vested in and exercised by a small body of men, in absolute control of $100,000,000 or more, to be expended for the general indefinite objects described in the bill, might be in the highest degree corrupt in its influence. The medieval statutes against mortmain were enacted to prevent just such perpetuation of wealth in a few hands under the cloak of such charitable purpose as this. . . . It was not without much reason that the English common law and English statutes required bequests for charitable purposes to be definite and specific in their terms. Such legislation was the result of experience with the indefinite charities which the monastic and other medieval institutions erected, and which were the occasion of so much scandal and corruption. . . . the underlying evil was the centralization of wealth in a few hands under the guise of charity.[7]

By the time Wickersham wrote this letter to Taft, who agreed with it, there had already been demonstrations of the power of the philanthropic trust to influence and change institutions many times its own size. The Carnegie Foundation had been able to use the promise of providing retirement annuities for faculty members as a lever to get a host of colleges to renounce their denominational affiliations and secularize themselves. Religiously oriented schools were the slowest to teach the values and technology most suited for the new world of corporate organization. The connection between a given school's general political tendencies and its principal benefactors was visible enough by 1923 for Upton Sinclair to be calling Columbia "The University of the House of Morgan" and Chicago "The University of Standard Oil."

The power of the purse was early recognized as a more serious threat to dangerous flirtations with the heterodoxy than was censorship. James McKeen Cattell, a professor of psychology who got himself fired from Columbia University for needling the hierarchies of learning and scholarship for being too, too obedient, made these observations in 1917:

It is not academic freedom in the classical sense which is seriously in question, but the limitations in speech and conduct
which university routine imposes. It is not dismissal which is the
difficulty, but the dependence on favor for advancement in position and in salary and for the little offices and honors about the
institution which serve in lieu of salary. . . . It seems at times as
though the whole organization of the university is better suited
to the courtier, the adventurer or the mediocrity than to the man
of genius or fine temperament.[8]

Although colleges and universities are sometimes regarded as
hothouses of heresy, instances of academic men and women
turning heretical have been quite rare. Either the teachers have
quietly decided it's not prudent to be different or, more likely,
very few of them harbor subversive thoughts. ROTC programs
were welcomed onto campuses before the First World War;
throughout the whole 1914–18 period university teachers and
administrators took the lead in clamoring for war. When America finally entered the conflict, Nicholas Murray Butler, the
president of Columbia, announced, "This is the University's
last and only warning to any among us . . . who are not with
whole heart and mind and strength committed to fight with us
to make the world safe for democracy."[9] Only the tiniest number of people in higher education were disposed to be against
the war or show less than rabid enthusiasm for it.

Failure to cheer loudly and with the eyes bulging could get
you fired. That's what happened to William A. Schaper, a
political scientist at the University of Minnesota. He opposed
the war until the American entrance into it, whereupon he
subsided and supported it even to the extent of counseling
several students to enlist; that wasn't good enough. With fifteen
minutes' warning, he was pulled before the Board of Regents,
which informed him they didn't like his "attitude of mind" and
canned him forthwith.

Who is the real patriot anyhow, the man who waves the flag and
shouts on the side that will profit him the most or the man who
risks the loss of old and dear friends, the ill-will of his superiors,

the abuse of the press, and finally his only source of income to keep his country out of the most awful war in all history? No one who has ever known me will ever doubt my devotion to my country. It was because of my intense Americanism that I tried to keep my country out of the European war.[10]

Few came to his aid, not from fear but because they had no sympathy for him. The war was so wholeheartedly supported on campus that on October 1, 1918, 140,000 students at 516 colleges and universities were simultaneously inducted into the armed forces under the Students' Army Training Corps. Henceforth, they marched to class and stood at attention when called upon by their teachers, who were required to carry military passes and show them to the sentries posted at the doors of university buildings.

When the anti–Vietnam War protestors complained that university aid in the southeast Asian struggle was a perversion of the schools' traditional role, they were wrong. The schools have never been the sanctuary some mistakenly imagined them, never been incubators of dissent, never been the ivory-towered citadels anti-intellectual cavemen call them. During the worst of the McCarthy period they purged themselves of seditionists and subversives. As with those who were blacklisted in Hollywood, those who got into trouble and were fired were conspicuous—but, as in World War I, there weren't very many. Nor was the behavior of the schools or their teaching staffs during the Vietnam upheaval at particular variance with the past. College and university faculty members may have turned against the war a little sooner and in somewhat larger numbers than the others in their social class, but if the war had to wait for the teachers to end it, the boys would still be gook-shooting in the rice paddies.

American higher education is run by businessmen and -women and/or people of inherited wealth, as a glance at the affiliations of the members of any board of trustees demonstrates. The great state universities have corporate control somewhat diluted by the appointment of people representing other interest groups to the schools' ruling bodies; the same effect is achieved in private schools by the influence of federal money. But the differences between schools lie mainly in geography, living standards for the students, and the classiness of the faculty, not in values or educational philosophy. The interchangeability of the parts is so advanced they can accept each other's credits with almost no difficulty.

But if the schools provide the base of like-thinking graduates, it is still the ruling classes—the country is too large and too diverse to speak of *the* ruling class—that decide what that thinking should be. Lunching together, intermarrying, chitchatting after tennis at the country club, the ruling circles can produce a consensus on a community or a regional level; for bringing cohesion and agreement on broader questions, there are institutions like Bohemian Grove, the 2,700-acre private camp in the northern California redwood forest. There, for two weeks every summer, hundreds of the most powerful businessmen recreate with major national politicians, university professors, movie stars, and other white male members of the American nobility. In the cool and beautiful woods, camping out quite literally with the assistance of their French chefs and their valets, they put on expensive amateur theatricals with names like *Cremation of Care.* No business is conducted, although there are formal speeches, which some members listen to and others sleep through. The primary idea is to have fun and it is in the course of having fun by mixing a PGA champ with a Chief Justice and the board chairman of a multinational construction corporation that major topics are chewed over and a cohesive, shared outlook evolves.

Such get-togethers help set a way of thinking on an issue or validate one just coming into vogue; by having their favorite professors and writers come and pollinate them, the power men undoubtedly do get ideas and are inspired to launch projects they might not have thought of, but in certain critical areas a more formal mechanism for deciding on the party line is needed. That is the job of an institution like the Council on

Foreign Relations. It brings together the Wall Street lawyers, the international bankers, the foundation heads, and the other power types to work in concert for the kind of foreign policy it advocates. For the last forty years or so, it has been successful because it has had the ear of presidents, has placed its people in the most important government positions, been able to dispense money to its most favored academics to get the research it wanted done, and been able to have the mass media broadcast its party line to the virtual exclusion of all others.

The council was begun shortly after the First World War by men like ex-Republican cabinet officers Elihu Root and George Wickersham, who left Washington to practice law on Wall Street. Root had also served as the president of the Carnegie Endowment for International Peace in that intertwining of philanthropy and politics that Wickersham had opposed as attorney general. With Root was his protégé, Henry L. Stimson, who had been secretary of war under Taft and who would serve as Hoover's secretary of state and again as secretary of war under Franklin Roosevelt and Harry Truman. Also active at the beginning was Edwin F. Gray, an official in the Wilson administration and the first dean of the Harvard Business School. Recommended to the council by a Morgan associate, Gray was the first of many professors who would, like Henry Kissinger so many decades later, be given money and would in turn supply the staff work and the propaganda for the council's foreign policy. It was Gray, years before the council was formed, who summed up where it wanted to go. In 1898, he wrote, "When I think of the British Empire as our inheritance, I think simply of the natural right of succession. That ultimate succession is inevitable."[11]

The ability of the Council on Foreign Relations to put its men in the top policy-making positions grew from the Hoover administration on. It made no difference if the president happened to be a Republican or a Democrat, a man considered liberal or conservative; the administration drew from the council's talent pool. "Whenever we needed a man we thumbed through the roll of Council members and put through a call to New York,"[12] said John J. McCloy, who was Stimson's assistant secretary during World War II, a president of the World Bank, American High Commissioner to occupied Germany, and at one time chairman of both the council and the Ford Foundation. (At one point in the early seventies, the majority of the board members of America's four largest foundations were council members.) It has been calculated that under Truman and Eisenhower, who was himself a card-holding member, no less than 40 percent of the persons occupying top foreign policy jobs were council members; under Kennedy and Johnson, the number rose to over 50 percent; Nixon wrote for the council's prestigious magazine, *Foreign Affairs;* Kissinger worked for the council, where he came into contact with the likes of the Rockefellers, who have played an important role in the council for many years. Under Carter we find council members in Secretary of State Cyrus Vance and National Security Adviser Zbigniew Brzezinski. Matching the council's interlock with business, academia, and the foundations is its contacts with mass media. These include the membership of the Sulzberger family, who control the *New York Times,* and Katherine Graham, who controls the *Washington Post.* Working journalists like the *Times*'s James Reston and CBS's Marvin Kalb also belong to the council.

The council has been accused of running what amounts to a conspiracy, although what it does is easily obtainable public knowledge. Nor do all its members always agree with the prevailing opinion. Toward the end of the Vietnam war, its members, like so many others, split over what to do about the situation. The organization was unable to play its usual cohesive, policy-leadership role. But if the council isn't a conspiracy or an especially sinister organization, its makeup and its activities underscore the fact that things happen because people make them happen, and in our society those people are often the great interests, symbolized by names like Rockefeller, magnifying and coordinating their power through organizations like the Council on Foreign Relations.

The council is of particular importance not only because foreign affairs is inherently important, but also because so many different strings run into its Pratt House headquarters. Given its connection with the universities, the think tanks, the foundations that fund them, and the mass media, the council can do more than influence the outcome of foreign-policy debate. It can limit the debate, define what is respectable and what is disreputable opinion. It can determine what the world of thought and discourse will be. Which is not to say there are no scholars with different ideas, no deviating thinkers. There are, but they don't get as much money or the high-status teaching jobs. Bereft of any institutional or organizational support, their ideas seldom get wide dissemination. The United States isn't Russia, so these sorts aren't jailed and are offered a living. Harmless and without influence, even when one occasionally makes the best-seller list, they reassure us that the First Amendment still exists. How would one know speech was free if there were no divergent opinion? Just as you pinch yourself to know you're awake, occasionally somebody has to say "I disagree" for you to know you're still free.

Over the decades, the process of securing a uniform mass media seems to have grown smoother and more automatic. In part this is because of the audience. A population that for all practical purposes attended the same school and had the same curriculum won't look at or read anything that visibly deviates from the norm. It has been taught that standard-brand news is the news, and, while people sometimes don't trust it and get mad at it, the mass audience will not watch or read anything else. The most maddeningly depressing part of being a reformer or a radical in America is that most of the people you want to help don't want to hear what you have to say.

A dozen or so corporations, which provide all the national and international news Americans get, reinforce the prevailing orthodoxies. To listen to executives of corporations in other industries you would think the mass media are out to do capitalism in, but in reality nothing is less threatening to the established order than consumer complaints on television. Crusades to get flammable children's nighties off the market convince people that the avenging reporter-hero figure really lives. The belief in journalism as the universal ombudsman who protects us against crooked building inspectors and venal congressmen is helpful, especially when the journalists aren't independent, modern knights errant, but quickly replaceable employees. The press, like the public-opinion polls, are part of the vastly numerous feedback systems a society like ours must have in order to run; the occasional complaints and exposés lend the local newspaper a degree of authenticity.

In addition to the oceans of words and images supplied by the corporate news organizations, news and information that is defined as being detached, objective, or unbiased, there is an immeasurably large propaganda effort by the government. This effort dates, like so much else, from World War I and the creation of the Committee on Public Information, a government body that inundated the nation with posters, pamphlets, and speakers.

Herbert Hoover, of all people, was probably the first thoroughly modern mass-media politician. As the food dictator under Wilson, he learned the value of sloganeering and was so successful at it that voluntary food and energy conservation was called Hooverizing. It is he whom every generation of children since has to thank for being told, "Finish your supper. Think of the poor starving children in (fill in the blank)." He also understood the power of broadcasting and was the first candidate and then president to use it as we're accustomed to having it used on us, but, although he knew "that the world lived by phrases," he was too stiff a personality to project himself via the new medium of radio. It was left to his successor, Franklin Roosevelt, to communicate with radio waves as none have since.

With Pearl Harbor the government went back into propaganda in a big way and hasn't been out of it since. There was a short-lived experiment in having the Office of War Information, but it grates on American sensibilities to have Washington obviously and overtly in the propaganda business. So Congress, with Roosevelt's blessings, cut off virtually all money for domestic propaganda activity. Telling foreigners fibs was another matter; appropriations for that were allowed to continue. For domestic consumption the preferred method was voluntary co-operation in truth-telling between the private and public sectors, as FDR put it in 1942 to the Advertising Federation of America, "For the duration . . . there are many messages which should be given the public through the use of advertising space. . . . If the members of your organization will . . . assist in the war program and continue the splendid spirit . . . which they have shown, . . . advertising will have a . . . patriotic place in the nation's total war effort."[13] That splendid spirit continues to this day through the Advertising Council, in which executives from the major news corporations and advertising agencies meet with government officials to decide what campaigns will be pushed. Will it be the fight against inflation or infection, for productivity or clean air? On superduper drives and campaigns, like efforts to discourage addiction to drugs of pleasure, Hollywood and television entertainment producers will be contacted to do their part. In this manner, mass-media news and drama can follow the sinuosities of the All-American party line with the same fidelity as in a totalitarian state, but with the quite truthful claim that it all comes about by the free will of the private sector.

With an electorate whose ears have been trained to hear only one tune, it's no wonder politics in the United States seems so dissatisfying and indecisive. The blame is ordinarily placed on the decline of the two-party system, but in its best days it never amounted to much. In 1912 Teddy Roosevelt was telling the masses that the two parties were "husks, with no real soul within either, divided on artificial lines, boss-ridden and privilege controlled." His new party, TR said in words that have ceased to sound very new, was going to "put forth a platform which shall be a contract with the people and we shall hold ourselves under honorable obligation to fulfill every promise it contains as loyally as if it were actually enforceable under penalties of law."[14] Thirty-two years later, cousin Franklin could be heard declaring, "We ought to have two real parties —one liberal and the other conservative."[15] And thirty years after him we heard Gov. George Wallace of Alabama tell us, "You can take all the Democratic candidates for President and all the Republican candidates for President. Put them in a sack and shake them up. Take the first one that falls out, grab him by the nape of the neck, and put him right back in the sack. Because there is not a dime's worth of difference in any of them."[16]

Party differences have been so unimportant that two Republican presidents, Hoover in 1920 and Eisenhower in 1948, were offered the Democratic nomination by powerful elements in that party. Both men, under the misapprehension that there is a profound difference between the two political organizations, decided to wait and win as Republicans. Hoover, after his defeat, grew embittered by the often very unfair things that were said about him and became intensely partisan, but in the years of his great popularity he, as well as Eisenhower, preferred to assume the nonpolitical, nonprofessional-politician pose.

It may have appeared to the voters that Barry Goldwater was offering them "a choice not an echo" in 1964, but this man who strove so hard to be the conservative opponent to the liberal Lyndon Johnson could not make a meaningful distinction on what, retrospectively at least, was the most important question in the campaign. The *New York Times* editorial of August 6, 1964, on the decision to expand the war, says it neatly: "Ranks have been closed in the United States with Senator Goldwater's open support for Administration action. If Hanoi's attacks were an attempt to exploit political and racial division in the United States, the American reaction has proved this futile. Vietnam, in fact, has been taken out of the Presidential campaign for the moment." The moment never ended, inasmuch as the war ended without it becoming a partisan issue that would have allowed people to tell themselves that a vote for one party was a vote for the war, a vote for the other a vote against it. Eugene McCarthy's failure to become the Democratic party candidate in 1968 kept the issue out of that election. Four years afterward, the Democrats did indeed nominate an avowed and unequivocal antiwar candidate, but President Nixon and Secretary of State Kissinger, with the China trip glowing in the background and Kissinger announcing that "Peace is at hand," campaigned against George McGovern on already having ended the war and, as a bonus, having done it "with honor." McGovern, whose mob seized the party by squatters' rights when the legitimate owners were away visiting relatives, had no stable organization and so lost control of the party as soon as he got it. Although the man was more left-wing aura than substance, his merely looking different frightened many traditional Democrats into backing Nixon so that they could get their party back.

Since Bryan versus McKinley in 1896, American national elections have seldom decided anything. The Democratic Bryan, while not entirely a populist, was the explicit and sworn enemy of eastern, corporate capitalism. Had he won, he might well have brought in a Congress sufficiently of the same mind to have made significant change. But offering the voters no choice may not be as debilitating to the electoral process as tricking them into thinking they have one and then double-crossing them. In 1916, the Wilson forces put ads in the leading newspapers around the country proclaiming:

YOU ARE WORKING—NOT FIGHTING!

ALIVE AND HAPPY—NOT CANNON FODDER!

WILSON AND PEACE WITH HONOR?

OR

HUGHES WITH ROOSEVELT AND WAR?

• • •

THE LESSON IS PLAIN:

IF YOU WANT **WAR, VOTE FOR HUGHES!**

IF YOU WANT PEACE WITH HONOR

VOTE FOR WILSON

AND CONTINUED PROSPERITY[17]

Five months later America was at war, and in the next couple of elections, voter turnout rates slumped horribly. With FDR and Eisenhower they crawled back up, although never to pre-Wilson levels; in recent years they've fallen back down.

The presidential elections in the 1920s were as splendidly issueless as any modern contest. There was prohibition to argue about, and high tariffs, but we can see from the distance of fifty or sixty years that it didn't matter which side won. Even the question of joining the League of Nations got muzzed over by Harding in the 1920 election, so pro-League and anti-League people could both vote for him, confident that once in the White House he would do what they wanted. In 1928 it was Al Smith's Catholic religion more than his politics that distinguished him from the Quaker Hoover, and although Hoover was too big a man to use bigotry to get himself elected, this unspoken issue was the closest thing the campaign had to an important division.

If the nomination of Franklin Delano Roosevelt in 1932 heralded the abrupt beginning of a new dawn, the candidate was so absentminded about his own significance he forgot to tell the voters about it. FDR sounded like every candidate running against every other incumbent president when he told a Sioux City, Iowa, audience "I accuse the present Administration of being the greatest spending Administration in peace times in all our history. It is an Administration that has piled bureau on bureau, commission on commission, and has failed to anticipate the dire needs and reduced earning power of the people."[18] What FDR was asking the people of the country was so clear and readily understandable that Elmer Davis, one of the most respected newsmen of the epoch, said of the candidate's performance, "You could not quarrel with a single one of his generalities; you seldom can. But what they mean (if anything) is known only to Franklin D. Roosevelt and his God."[19] Hoover called him "a chameleon on plaid."[20] But even with benefit of hindsight it's impossible to imagine FDR saying anything which would have separated him from Hoover and the Republicans in a clear way. His party didn't stand for anything that different.

After FDR's nomination, the Democratic millionaire faction, which had supported Smith for another nomination, came on board with a $50,000 love offering. When Raymond Moley, one of Roosevelt's two or three closest aides, heard about it, he wrote a note to himself saying, "So it goes—first the radicals will be betrayed then the conservatives. So everyone is ultimately sold out. . . . The Republicans of course are selling out just the same."[21] What he describes here may be mistaken for corruption and ex parte privilege, but what it is is a process by which a one-party reality in a two-party aspect realizes itself.

In FDR's three subsequent elections, so close were his opponents' views to his own on the major questions of the day that one wonders why the Republican party spent money on opposing him. In 1940 Wendell Willkie accepted the Republican nomination for president and took the war issue out of the campaign while doing so when he put a paragraph in his speech saying, "I promise, by returning to those same American principles that overcame German autocracy once before, both in business and in war, to outdistance Hitler in any contest he chooses in 1940 or after. And I promise that when we beat him, we shall beat him on our own terms and in our American way."[22] During the course of the campaign Willkie and Roosevelt were even in indirect communication with each other over sending aid to Britain. Through intermediary William Allen White, the famous newspaper editor, Willkie signaled that he agreed but dared not say so for fear of the isolationist-antiwar wing of his party. Those gentlemen were the first Republicans to raise the plaint of "Me-Tooism." But if they thought their champion and the other side's champion agreed a mite too much, so did others who heard the Willkie acceptance speech that day: "Norman Thomas, Socialist candidate for President, in commenting on the acceptance speech of Wendell L. Willkie, declared it left the public no real choice between the major party candidates. The speech put Mr. Willkie so much in agreement with President Roosevelt that 'any debate [between them] would involve little more than personalities and oratorical generalizations,' Mr. Thomas declared," according to the *New York Times.*[23]

After the elections, these two irreconcilable opponents dis-
cussed the idea of reorganizing the two parties along conservative and liberal lines, whatever those two slippery words meant
to the gentlemen. In practice they mean that one party is somewhat more free-handed in distributing alms to the poor than the
other. The parties are so astonishingly alike even partisan zea-
lots despair of explaining how they differ except that one favors
elephants and the other donkeys. In the 1930s and 1940s the
differences appeared much greater, to the Republicans' disadvantage. In 1976 Jimmy Carter campaigned on the promise that
he could impart a higher moral tone to the White House than
his opponent, and he squeaked over the finish line only a few
millimeters ahead of a fellow family man and Christian Jerry
Ford. The degree to which the candidates themselves have
rigged elections to purge them of disagreement and debate is
described by President Truman, writing about his 1948 tussle
with Republican Thomas E. Dewey:

> One of the things I tried to keep out of the campaign was foreign
> policy. There should be no break in the bi-partisan foreign
> policy of the United States at any time—particularly during a
> national election. I even asked that a teletype machine be set up
> on the Dewey train so that the Republican candidate personally
> could be informed of all the foreign developments as they pro-
> gressed, and I did so because I did not want to encourage the
> possibility of a partisan, political approach to foreign policy.[24]

In domestic matters he also strove to strike the appearance of
a difference that did not exist. He went out of his way to make
himself look liberal in contrast to his Republican opponent by
running against the fictitiously paleolithic Herbert Hoover and
the specter of breadlines and evictions. He knew better. "I
didn't mean a word of it," he said after the elections, "Hoover
didn't have any more to do with the Depression than you and
I did."[25] To fortify his reputation as a liberal, Truman called
Congress back to Washington after the parties' nominating
conventions to what was called the Turnip Day Special Session,
so named after some obscure Missouri fertility rite. It wasn't

turnips but a parcel of welfare legislation that the president demanded of the Republican-controlled Congress. He would have been mortified if the Congress had said yes and passed the laws he claimed he wanted, but they didn't and the Republicans went into November looking like hardhearted reactionaries.

To some extent this mildly hypocritical mickeymouse was owing to the third-party candidacy of former Vice-President (1941–45) Henry Wallace. Wallace had also been FDR's secretary of agriculture for eight years as well as secretary of commerce, a post from which President Truman sacked him in 1946 for making a speech advocating a more accommodating policy toward the Russians at a time when the rest of the government was getting up running speed for the Cold War. Although Henry Wallace's name is now completely obliterated by George Wallace's, then the ejected cabinet member was seen as FDR's true heir by at least a moderate-sized multitude. Thousands of people around the country paid their way in to hear Wallace speak. Charging admission to political rallies and getting people to pay it was as unheard-of then as it is now, so Truman and the Democrats tilted ever so slightly to the left, or at least appeared to tilt, in order to discourage the liberals from following Wallace into the catch-as-catch-can Progressive party his supporters wanted to build around him.

The problems that defeated the third-party effort of Wisconsin's Robert La Follette twenty-four years before were now compounded. La Follette, running on a ticket that was a mishmash of old Progressives and bewildered socialist types, got almost five million votes—more than 16 percent of the total. By 1948 nothing was left of the Socialist party; the noncapitalist news media had vanished; and Wallace had no hope of obtaining the labor-union support that La Follette had gotten. Nor was Wallace able to handle the accusation that he was a Communist stooge, albeit an unknowing one. La Follette had been able to disavow the Reds but Wallace couldn't, not only because he wasn't nimble enough but because the essence of his campaign was a resistance to a repetition of the antiradical horrors of the Wilson period and a strenuous insistence that if

the Russians were allotted a sphere of influence in Eastern
Europe they would settle down to being good, peace-loving
chaps. The Wallace position as it was given to radio interviewer
Edward R. Murrow is tepid by today's standards:

> According to the newspapers, I'm getting a lot of support from
> Communists, and the Communist leaders seem to think they
> have to endorse me every day or so. There's no question that this
> sort of thing is a political liability. The Communists oppose my
> advocacy of progressive capitalism. They support me because I
> say that we can have peace with Russia. I will not repudiate any
> support which comes to me on the basis of interest in peace. The
> Communists are interested in peace because they want a suc-
> cessful socialist experiment in Russia. I am interested in peace
> because I want our American system to demonstrate the enor-
> mous vitality of which it is capable. That vitality which is being
> wasted in preparations for war. . . . If you accept the idea that
> Communists have no right to express their opinions, then you
> don't believe in democracy. And if you accept the notion that
> it is impossible to live in a world with sharply differing ideas,
> then you accept the inevitability of war. I don't believe in the
> inevitability of war. I do believe in democracy.[26]

At any given time the range of discourse permitted in polite
politics is exceedingly narrow, and in 1948 such a speech was
over the boundary. When you get on the other side of that
border, you are the target for nonstop fusillades of old boots
and orange rinds. With a unanimity of opinion that should have
commanded admiration in the ministries of information in
Eastern Europe, the mass media razed Wallace, his Progressive
party, and their Philadelphia convention. *Time* magazine
called the man "the centerpiece of U.S. Communism's most
authentic looking facade"; the *Des Moines Register* told its
readers, "The Communist manipulators of the Progressive
party went back to New York Monday with the party control
locked in their satchels"; the *Philadelphia Inquirer* called it a
"mongrel party . . . a made-to-order instrument of Communist
policy"; *New York Times* columnist Anne O'Hare McCormick

compared the convention's greeting for Wallace on his appearance before it to the Nazi and Fascist rallies for Hitler and Mussolini; as the convention opened, the *Detroit Free Press* told its readers,

> Every type of crackpot, every known kind of malcontent, every species of hate-blinded neurotic, every element of anti-Americanism will be on hand to jeer and sneer at all this Nation has ever stood for in its most exalted moments of service and sacrifice.
>
> They are glorifiers of Russia and totalitarianism. They preach the New Deal doctrine that the 'people are too damned dumb to understand.' They are disciples—or pretend to be—of the strange, wild creature who might have been President of the United States—Henry Wallace. . . . In Russia they would all be shot before they could meet, not because of their Marxian vagaries but because the Stalin gangsters would look upon them as possible rivals in their racket.[27]

Oddly enough, Wallace proved he was a strange wild creature by coming to agree with some of his enemies' assessments of himself. At least he went so far some years later as to tell Truman in public that it was a good thing that Harry and not he was elected in 1948.

After Wallace there were no significant names to enter a demurral on foreign-policy questions, and the society which regards "polarizing" as a form of treason could feel that one threat had passed.

12

Tweedledum and Tweedledumber: Cracking Open the One-Party State

It is true that no society, regardless of how strong its commitment to civil liberties, can allow unlimited dissent. Unless a few basic rules of political conduct are agreed upon, all disagreements are in danger of being settled by a chaotic form of violence. Free speech, the sanctity of the ballot—a few such things make up the ground rules that everyone abides by; but we have whittled permissible conduct down to much less than that. By denominating any dissent that questions first principles of policy as "irresponsible," "ideological," "radical," or "extremist," political debate can be stopped and dismissed as pathological zealotry. No major forum is open to you unless what you have to say is defined as responsible, middle-of-the-road, and pragmatic. The practical, nonideological workman who is thus exalted turns out to be the Dr. Strangelove of our satirical literature and the Bob Haldeman of real political fact. The road on the middle of which so many walk to avoid the perils of fuzzy fanaticism can lead to Oz and beyond to the land of the Hobbits. The practical, hard-nosed, tough minded, no-nonsense, realistic military men who explained they had to destroy the South Vietnamese city of Hue to save it from the Communist enemy gave America a cliché phrase that reminds us that where there is no right and no left, where the discussion of politics is limited to means, never ends, the people we call moderates, gradualists, and practitioners of the pragmatic can be stark, staring crackers, and we won't know it. Politics, the men of the middle repeat and repeat, is the art of the possible. Yet in Vietnam the most practical men of affairs attempted the impossible, squandering American power as Athenian power was wasted before Syracuse. Opposition sharpens judgment and forces men and women in high places to be practical; a yes-man ambiance enervates the faculties needed to recognize reality. This, as much as that nebulous phrase, the arrogance of power, explains why these people did what they're always accusing their opponents, the ideologues, of doing—they acted impractically.

Franklin Roosevelt once remarked, "There's one issue in this campaign. It's myself, and people must be either for me or against me."[1] That is the issue in almost every campaign, the character of the candidates. In a political system which excludes broad policy questions from the electoral process, what else is there to fasten on than the candidates' individual traits? Of necessity people assess the contenders, not on what they believe, since they both believe the same thing, but on how good a job they might do. In political campaigns, it's performance, not policy, which the voters are asked to pass judgment on.

The characters and private lives of the great have always been of as much interest to the historian and the biographer as to the gossip, but the more recent invention of psychohistory and psychopolitical science may reflect the presidency as primarily a managerial post. The more narrowly limited the power of the office, the more important the personality of the officeholder. Presidential style and image become matters of great media interest, but the president, the chairman of the board of America, Inc., the presiding officer, doesn't decide substantive questions by himself. If a Jimmy Carter gives what may seem like an excessive amount of time to striking poses in public, he's not being hollow and manipulative as much as he's trying to live up to the exigencies of his position.

Television makes this sort of posturing intrusively visible. Carter's carefully-done plebeian inauguration, walking hand in hand with his family and inviting the wash-and-wear multitudes to his balls, is in line with what many of his predecessors did for effect. His gesture of walking on Pennsylvania Avenue was much more vivid thanks to television. Though TV isn't the cause of personality politics, which far antedates the medium, it facilitates it. It's ever so much better to make your evaluation of the man by seeing him—something less than one percent of the population probably got to do before TV—than by being told what he's like.

Electoral politics, like farming and many another activity, has gone from being a labor-intensive to a capital-intensive business. Television, as well as expensively computerized mail-order, money-solicitation operations, has put the paid political worker, the old-time precinct captain, into the museum next to the exhibit of the interurban trolley car. It is possible to reach more people for less money through radio and television than it is through paying people to knock on doors. Since advertising, especially what is considered garish advertising, is slightly déclassé among upper-middle-class Americans, many think using such techniques and tactics denigrates the dignity of the presidency. Perhaps it does, but with candidates who basically agree with each other, what are you going to do if you don't conduct the campaign with singing commercials and minor theatrical diversions? The singing commercials will vanish as soon as the boys and girls disagree. With bread, soap, beer, and gasoline, advertising takes the form it does not because the products are different but because they are the same. That is also true of politics.

If elections don't bear heavily on the decision-making processes, they are nonetheless indispensable to the symbol system, that elaborate arrangement of signs, values, metaphysical propositions, and myths that distinguishes one nation from another just as much as the grossest of national products. We have elections, ergo we know we are a democracy. In truth, the United States is as much of a democracy as any comparable nation, but its representational system isn't especially dependent on electing our magistrates. Representation comes primarily through organizational affiliation—the brokered government that political scientists write about—and through feed-back devices like the public-opinion polls and the journalistic springer spaniels and Irish setters who course the countryside, coming to attention and pointing at each new trend and tremor of taste and opinion. As for elections, it may be that America would be no more or less democratic without them.

The elective process does work in getting rid of abusive or unworthy public officials who become personally unpopular, but kicking the rascals out is decision-making in only the most meager sense. The next set will undoubtedly have to be given the bum's rush also. Twirling rascals around the revolving door isn't as important as simply having the election, any election. Having the election validates our democratic authenticity, par-ticularly for the upper classes that have not only a larger mate-rial but also a greater psychic stake in our political institutions. That's why corporations, churches, every sort of respectable institution sanctions and even sponsors get-out-the-vote, voter-registration drives. "Vote for anybody, but vote," is the slogan heard on radio and television in the closing weeks of every important election. "It doesn't matter who you vote for, just vote"—which, if you stop to think about it, is a bald and public way of saying it's the election, not the result of the election, that matters. In countries like France, Portugal, or Italy where there are large Communist and Socialist, as well as capitalist, parties, will the electorate be told it doesn't matter whom you vote for so long as you vote? Whether their way or our way is better, their elections are truly decisive; they do decide important po-litical disputes. On this side of the ocean it sometimes seems that the most closely watched number on election night is the total turnout figure. How many will reaffirm their credo by voting? Will tens of millions disappoint us by not casting a ballot, in much the same way we are disappointed when church attendance falls off?

The significance of elections is not enhanced by the general aversion to anything thought to smack of "partisanship" or "partisan advantage." These words have an even smellier repu-tation than the adjective "political," so it's no surprise that, excepting Nixon, the progression from administration to administration is so reassuringly smooth. A Jerry Ford goes and a Jimmy Carter comes and appoints not only the same old people but also the same new people. Younger persons—even from such heretical places as the Ralph Nader organizations and the anti–Vietnam-War groups—may join the government, but the institutional weight and arrangement make them like those who sat at the desks before. Carter himself has disappointed many who worked for him and hoped for him. He was not the true, new man after all, but working within the system deprives one of new possibilities. If there is no thesis and if there is no antithesis, there can be no synthesis. In an organizational universe of managers and problem-solvers, there's no dialectic, no dynamic.

No ideas, no change can be generated by such politics. It was long ago commented on that the two parties are sterile, unable to conceive, invent, or create, and have depended on third parties for new ideas. In the sixties and the seventies, the civil-rights movement and the antiwar people provided the agenda and framed the debate. Left to the law courts, the national legislature, or the electoral process, Rosa Parks would still be riding the streets of Montgomery, Alabama, in the back of a bus; the B-29s would still be attempting to interdict the military supplies moving into South Vietnam on the Ho Chi Minh Trail. You can't work within the system, because the system doesn't work. To effect change you have to threaten a slave rebellion, start a riot, set off a mini-revolution, induce a galvanic event outside the marble-pillared buildings with concussion waves severe enough to disturb the eternally mortuarial tranquillity within.

Elective or electoral politicians can't make such loud noises. Even to force change into the public discussion, much less realize it, puts one beyond the pale. In the lingo of the pros, "issue-oriented" people destroy their own political effectiveness, i.e., they make it impossible for themselves to get elected. The paradox is that the politically effective people can't get anything done, while the ineffective people, a Martin Luther

King, a Ralph Nader, a Saul Alinsky, can't get elected but can get things done.

A Jimmy Carter is almost prototypical then. Effective at getting elected, he is ineffective at realizing the changes candidate Carter seemed to have been promising the voting multitudes. In actuality, the Carter campaign was the traditional one of whichever party does not control the White House. His anti-Washington theme is hoary with age, going back at least as far as Andrew Jackson, another Southern boy who ran as an outsider. In the destruction of the Bank of the United States, Old Hickory could be said to have lived up to his egalitarian, anti-Eastern campaign posture, but, although comparisons between presidents separated that far in time are meaningless, they show how some thematic matter endures more as a cultural attitude than a political position. Whether Jimmy the Baptist and his advisors consciously chose an anti-Washington stance or merely drifted into it, they were reciting the classic lines of the challenger in our election rituals. Where Carter has gotten into trouble is that, as Big Brother has grown to manhood, a larger proportion of the electorate may have come to expect him to do something about Washington than was the case when a Woodrow Wilson was making the same campaign promises. A detached reading of Carter's stump locutions will show that he never suggested a new relationship between government and the individual or the society, something implicit in the demands of those who worry about Big Brotherism. That would entail a decentralist upheaval of near-revolutionary proportions, something for which there is great support among individual Americans and none among organized power groups —and Jimmy Carter is assuredly a power-group person. Jimmy Carter in 1976 was well to the right of William Jennings Bryan, who told America in 1919, "Our greatest task today is to protect the God-made man from the man-made giant. The God-made man has natural rights; the corporate giant has no rights except those conferred by the law."[2] Bryan was one of the last major national politicians willing to disestablish the government-corporate connection, but he died in 1925. By the time

Carter took it up a half century later, the anti-Washington attitude was purged of any suggestion of institutional change and was defined as administrative adjustments, such as "zero-based budgeting," a minor business-school fad. During his presidential vote canvass, Carter told the country he expected to realize palpable administrative efficiencies through ZBB. The fact that such trifles were made so much of testifies to how little was left for the soon-to-be-president and his opponent to argue over. In large measure the campaign that saw Jimmy Carter enter the White House consisted of the two opponents waiting for the other to trip into a slip of the tongue. The least lapsus linguae, devoid of any significance, was grabbed hold of by the one man or the other, in the hopes that sheer accident could produce the disagreement between them that intentional statements of policy could not.

Even for the elaborate electoral game of America's one-party politics, the Carter-Ford contest was particularly without readily discernible meaning. The ruling circles of the country are not composed of think-alike robots; their members do disagree enough on the details, if not the fundamentals, so that intelligent men and women, caught up in the excitements and ambitions of politics, can convince themselves that chasms of principle separate them from the people on the other side. If Carter fits too embarassingly well as the classic example of the bipartisan, nonpartisan problem-solver president, this may be explained by the fact that both he and many others believe that the nation had been rent, torn, divided, and set against itself so deeply that the healer-unifier was an exigent necessity. Nixon started to play that role after the Johnson years but ended by aggravating the very divisions he said he would soften and smooth out. During the interregnum, Ford also tried to play physician-president, but just as the kings of France had to be crowned and anointed in the Cathedral of Rheims, so a president of the United States must be elected if he is to lay on hands with therapeutic effect.

Some doubt exists that the nation was ever as torn apart and rent as was suggested in the months after Nixon's fall. After all, scarcely 50 percent of the eligible voters participated in either the '68 or the '72 election. Thus one out of two Americans of voting age didn't care enough about the disgraced president to vote for him or against him. Like the divisions over Vietnam, the battle to chase Nixon out of Washington was enjoyed as entertainment more than it was suffered over as "the gravest constitutional crisis since the Civil War," as the television news readers portentiously described it. The movies, novels, and television dramas built around or suggested by Watergate reenforce the proposition that most Americans, if they gave it much thought at all, took it as good theater with the most distant connection to their own lives.

This was not the case with the ruling classes. The painful injuries they projected on the nation were the ones they felt. Not since Franklin Roosevelt's second term had there been such division among the members of the higher circles as there were in the late sixties and early seventies. It was their wounds which needed the ointment and for this a Wheatena man like Carter was most suitable. They needed reuniting, and Carter, the Baptist of richly conventional piety, the member of the Trilateral Commission (an international Council on Foreign Relations whose membership includes leading Japanese and European capitalists and politicians), Carter the engineer, businessman, and quiet-speaking problem-solver president was acceptable if not desirable.

Election under these circumstances is hardly more than a mandate to be—be nice, be honest, be good, be quiet. The political terms of Carter's ascension were that he confine himself to proposals and initiatives that would not disturb institutional arrangements or long-established practices. This was the reason for the contorted Ptolemaic economics of something like his energy program. He was trying to limit consumption without limiting the industry's traditional marketing prerogatives. Future presidents, and even Carter himself, may be given more latitude than he enjoyed in the first two years of his first term. It is highly inconvenient to have a man in the White House who dares little more than ribbon-cutting and smiling platitudes, but he has to be viewed as the inheritor of a clipped and humbled presidency.

A Democrat who has learned that having his party control Congress avails him little more than it did his Republican predecessors, Carter has been forced into the old pattern of continuing the work and direction of the man he vanquished in 1976. This president lives out his administration in a flat, uneffervescent moment. He has been taxed with breaking a campaign promise here and there, of being a jot clumsy, but mostly he has had to suffer being accused of that all-purpose sin, lack of leadership. But where is he to lead in a time when no one puts forth any strong claim to know where to go? Presidents reflect their times, they do not rise above them. Carter, like his predecessors, must pick up his clues as to what to do from the power circles hedging him in and supporting his office. Lyndon Johnson no more invented the Great Society than Franklin Roosevelt invented the New Deal. They did not even name them. Their gift, and the reason they're given the credit or the blame, is that they were able to see which were the politically and socially potent ideas, the ideas backed by the power configurations, and to go along with them. In the 1920s it was the idea that gave birth to the NRA—of cooperation—that was being talked of in business circles. It is not that Carter is ignoring today's dramatic and necessary ideas. There aren't any.

In the eyes of most, present arrangements are minimally satisfactory if not outright splendid. We may feel vexed by too much government, overtaxed, annoyed, and cheated by one huge institution or another, but on balance, people don't think their wishes are unrepresented. They do not cherish a dream of another, different America. The American Dream now is of an idealized past. Our grandparents dreamt of a bigger, better, farther, a more perfect nation. We have moderated our hopes and dream only of a future that is as good as the past.

For turn-of-the-century Americans the recognition of the coming end of the frontier was a gloomy metaphysical fact. As we cannot conceive a no-growth economy, they could not imagine a no-growth society. People who otherwise might not have supported the Spanish-American War may have done so out of the conviction the nation had a spiritual need for expansion. The continent conquered, the Philippines would provide the sense of new space. The frontier, at least as a metaphor for a large and future destiny, remained a popular word until John Kennedy proclaimed a new one and it turned out to be our last. Kennedy's New Frontier wasn't the pushing forward of boundaries but the maintaining of them—guarding the physical extremities of empire, manning the tropical marches to hold back the Red infiltration.

The outer bounds have been established. The future is prologue no more. The past worked before, and it will work again, but beyond the ups and downs and bumpsy-daisies of war and peace and boom and bust, every day everything got a little better because the nation got richer. The per capita income in the United States cannot jump in the next seventy-five years as it did in the last. The central material fact on which our political economy has rested, the rapid and infinite growth in wealth, has changed.

We have not, and this closed universe we have constructed for ourselves makes it excessively hard for us to do so. The formal mechanisms for debate and decision have failed us in the great issues of the post-1945 era, but even in smaller matters the arthritis of politics increasingly forces the courts to try to do what the legislative and executive branches cannot make themselves do. Where every interest is strong enough to veto every other, turning to the judges to rule by fiat has a great appeal, but the Great Impasse extends to the judiciary. One judge nullifies another and the attempt to use the judiciary to legislate in any broad way fails.

Raise the taxes, cut the taxes, increase the budget deficits, lower them, centralize HEW to increase coordination, decentralize HEW to decrease excessive centralized coordination. Government becomes the choice among a very small number of finite acts or combinations of acts repeated without end. Management or tinkering replaces politics; that works well enough as long as all other things stay equal, which they are not doing. A society thus petrified and repetitive places itself in peril of becoming as obsolete as the short-lived gadgetry it must manufacture and sell in spite of its own desires to build true and forever.

For that we must replace management with politics. We must understand we can be manipulated as much by false harmonies as we can injure ourselves with the love of discord. Politicize, polarize, ignite the rancors of politics, disunite, crack open the one-party state; no change, no democracy is possible without friction.

The American tautology of politics and economics is not watertight. Wisps of other ideas and other values have not been completely voided from the hermetical social sphere. Some among us can still cause trouble, so we can hope that some among us will.

Notes

Part 1

Chapter 1: The Captive Presidency

1. Jules Archer, *The Plot to Seize the White House* (New York: Hawthorne Books, 1973), pp. 213–14.
2. Arthur S. Link, *Wilson Campaigns for Progressivism and Peace, 1916–1917* vol. V (Princeton: Princeton University Press, 1965), pp. 43–47.
3. Henry F. Pringle, *The Life and Times of William Howard Taft* Vol. 2 (Hamden, Conn.: Archon Books, 1964), pp. 817–18.
4. Henry F. Pringle, *Theodore Roosevelt: A Biography* (New York: Harcourt, Brace & Co., 1931), pp. 339–40.
5. Charter Day address at the University of California at Berkeley, March 23, 1911, as reported the next day in the *San Francisco Examiner* and quoted in Miles P. DuVal, Jr., *Cadiz to Cathay* (Stanford: Stanford University Press, 1940), p. 438.
6. *Reader's Digest,* March 1968, pp. 88–92.
7. Richard P. Nathan, *The Plot That Failed: Nixon and the Administrative Presidency* (New York: John Wiley & Sons, 1975), pp. 83, 69.
8. Ibid., p. 83.
9. John Newhouse, *Cold Dawn* (New York: Holt, Rinehart and Winston, 1973), pp. 203–16.
10. Jimmy Breslin, *How the Good Guys Finally Won* (New York: Ballantine Books, 1975), pp. 14–15.
11. Herbert E. Alexander, *Financing the 1972 Election* (Lexington, Mass.: D. C. Heath and Co., Lexington Books, 1976) pp. 458–59.
12. Ibid., p. 473.
13. Ibid.
14. Ibid., p. 525.
15. Report of the Special Review Committee of the Board of Directors of Gulf Oil Corporation, John J. McCloy, chairman, in *Securities and Exchange Commission v. Gulf Oil,* Civil Action No. 75–0324, December, 1975, p. 44.
16. William Safire, *Before the Fall* (Garden City, N.Y.: Doubleday & Co., 1975), p. 262.
17. Charles W. Colson, *Born Again* (Old Tappan, N.J.: Fleming H. Revell Co., Chosen Books, 1976), p. 35.
18. J. Anthony Lukas, *Nightmare: The Underside of the Nixon Years* (New York: Viking Press, 1976), pp. 18, 19.
19. Bob Woodward and Carl Bernstein, *The Final Days* (New York: Simon and Schuster, 1976), p. 89.

20. John W. Dean III, *Blind Ambition* (New York: Simon and Schuster, 1976), pp. 147–48.
21. Final Report of the President's Task Force on Governmental Organization, June, 1967, as quoted in Nathan, *Plot That Failed,* p. 88.
22. Nathan, *Plot That Failed,* p. 89.
23. Peter Polenberg, *Reorganizing Roosevelt's Government: 1936–1939, The Controversy over Executive Reorganization* (Cambridge, Mass.: Harvard Univeristy Press, 1966), p. 154.
24. Lukas, *Nightmare,* p. 559.
25. Nathan, *Plot That Failed,* p. 40.
26. In both 1970 and 1971, the Pentagon's budget, even when figured in current dollars, dropped below the preceding year: the Total Obligational Authority for 1969 was $78,495,000,000; 1970, $76,035,000,000; 1971, $74,336,000,000. (Figures from the Office of Assistant Secretary of Defense, Comptroller, under the Deputy Comptroller for Program and Budget, the Pentagon)
27. Lukas, *Nightmare,* p. 356.
28. *Washington Post,* 19 June 1977.
29. From a transcript of *The MacNeil/Lehrer Report,* WETA 26, Washington, D.C., May 10, 1977.
30. Joseph P. Lash, *Roosevelt and Churchill, 1939–1941* (New York: W. W. Norton & Co., 1976), p. 182.

Part 2

Chapter 2: The NRA: Mobilizing America

1. Daniel R. Fusfeld, *The Economic Thought of Franklin D. Roosevelt and the Origins of the New Deal* (New York: AMS Press, 1970), p. 204.
2. William E. Leuchtenburg, "The New Deal and the Analogue of War," in *Change and Continuity in Twentieth Century America,* ed. John Braeman, Robert Bremner, and Everett Walters (Columbus: Ohio State University Press, 1964), pp. 105–6.
3. Ibid., p. 103.
4. Ibid., p. 105.
5. William E. Leuchtenburg, *Franklin D. Roosevelt and the New Deal* (New York: Harper and Row, 1963), p. 30.
6. George Creel, *Rebel at Large: Recollections of Fifty Crowded Years* (New York: G. P. Putnam's Sons, 1947), p. 277.
7. Bernard Bellush, *The Failure of the NRA* (New York: W. W. Norton & Co., 1975), p. 27.
8. T. Harry Williams, *Huey Long* (New York: Bantam Books, 1970), p. 666.
9. Ronald Radosh, "The Myth of the New Deal," in *A New History of Leviathan: Essays on the Rise of the American Corporate State,* ed. Ronald Radosh and Murray Rothbard (New York: E. P. Dutton & Co., 1972), p. 170.
10. Hugh S. Johnson, *The Blue Eagle from Egg to Earth* (Garden City, N.Y.: Doubleday, Doran, 1935), p. 260.

11. *The New York Times,* 8 September 1933.

12. Ellis W. Hawley, *The New Deal and the Problem of Monopoly* (Princeton: Princeton University Press, 1966), p. 54.

13. Sidney Fine, *The Automobile under the Blue Eagle* (Ann Arbor: University of Michigan Press, 1963), p. 80.

14. Arthur M. Schlesinger, Jr., *The Coming of the New Deal* (Boston: Houghton Mifflin Co., 1958), p. 114.

15. Johnson, *Blue Eagle,* p. 265.

16. Ibid.

17. *New Republic,* November 14, 1934, p. 9.

18. Hawley, *New Deal and Monopoly,* p. 77.

Chapter 3: *"Competition Is War and Was Is Hell"*

1. Harold U. Faulkner, *The Decline of Laissez Faire, 1897–1917* (New York: Rinehart & Co., 1951), p. 173.

2. Gabriel Kolko, *The Triumph of Conservatism* (Chicago: Quadrangle Books, 1967), pp. 69–70.

3. Ibid., p. 88.

4. George E. Mowry, *The Era of Theodore Roosevelt, 1900–1912* (New York: Harper & Bros., 1958), p. 55.

5. From Wilson's *Constitutional Government,* quoted in William Diamond, *The Economic Thought of Woodrow Wilson* (Baltimore: Johns Hopkins University Press, 1943), p. 65.

6. Quoted in Kolko, *Triumph of Conservatism,* p. 68, and elsewhere in Joseph B. Bishop, *Theodore Roosevelt and His Time* vol. 1 (New York: Charles Scribner's Sons, 1920), p. 184.

7. Faulkner, *Decline of Laissez Faire,* p. 202.

8. Gabriel Kolko, *Railroads and Regulation, 1877–1916* (New York: W. W. Norton & Co., 1970), pp. 146–47.

9. For tourists wishing to hunt down the descendants of free-market heroes, our chap's name was Hugo Richard Meyer, and his signally unsuccessful book was entitled *Government Regulation of Railway Rates* (New York: The Macmillan Co., 1905).

10. Kolko, *Railroads and Regulation,* p. 37.

11. Albro Martin, *Enterprise Denied: Origins of the Decline of American Railroads, 1897–1917* (New York: Columbia University Press, 1971), p. 170.

12. Ibid., p. 319.

Chapter 4: Inspector America

1. James Weinstein, *The Corporate Ideal in the Liberal State, 1900–1918* (Boston: Beacon Press, 1968), p. 45.

2. Kolko, *Triumph of Conservatism* p. 103.

3. John Braeman, "The Square Deal in Action: A Case Study in the Growth of the 'National Police Power,' " in *Change and Continuity in Twentieth*

Century America, ed. John Braeman, Robert Bremner, and Everett Walters (Columbus: Ohio State University Press, 1964), p. 73.

4. Weinstein, *Corporate Ideal,* p. 131.

5. Ibid., p. 132.

6. James Weinstein, *The Decline of Socialism in America: 1912–1925* (New York: Monthly Review Press, 1967), p. 21.

7. Pringle, *Roosevelt,* p. 258.

8. Ibid., p. 192.

9. Kolko, *Triumph of Conservatism,* pp. 13–14.

10. Quoted in Melvin I. Urofsky, *Big Steel and the Wilson Administration* (Columbus: Ohio State University Press, 1969), pp. xxix–xxx.

11. Kolko, *Triumph of Conservatism,* p. 174.

12. Gerald D. Nash, *United States Oil Policy, 1890–1964* (Pittsburgh: University of Pittsburgh Press, 1968), p. 94.

13. Ibid., p. 23.

14. Joan Hoff Wilson, *American Business and Foreign Policy, 1920–1933* (Boston: Beacon Press, 1971), p. 187.

15. Nash, *U.S. Oil Policy,* p. 84.

16. *Daily Oklahoman,* 5 August 1931.

17. Hawley, *New Deal and Monopoly,* p. 374.

Chapter 5: When Big Brother Was a Baby

1. Pringle, *Roosevelt,* pp. 381–82.

2. G. Wallace Chessman, *Theodore Roosevelt and the Politics of Power* (Boston: Little, Brown, & Co., 1969), p. 168.

3. Diamond, *Economic Thought,* p. 80.

4. Chessman, *TR and Politics of Power,* pp. 175–76.

5. Diamond, *Economic Thought,* p. 92.

6. Mowry, *Era of TR,* p. 93.

7. Arthur S. Link, *Wilson: The Road to the White House* vol. I (Princeton: Princeton University Press, 1947), pp. 381–82.

8. Diamond, *Economic Thought,* p. 94.

9. Ibid., p. 122.

10. Kolko, *Triumph of Conservatism,* p. 206.

11. Pringle, *Taft,* p. 791.

12. Ibid., pp. 789–90.

13. Otis L. Graham, Jr., *An Encore for Reform: The Old Progressives and the New Deal* (New York: Oxford University Press, Galaxy Books, 1967), p. 24.

14. Arthur S. Link, *Wilson: The New Freedom* vol. II (Princeton: Princeton University Press, 1956), p. 81.

15. Robert H. Wiebe, "Business Disunity and the Progressive Movement, 1901–1914," *Mississippi Valley Historical Review* 44 (March 1958): 673.

16. Robert K. Murray, *The Politics of Normalcy: Governmental Theory and Practice in the Harding-Coolidge Era* (New York: W. W. Norton & Co., 1973), p. 15.

17. Wilson, *Hoover,* p. 115.

18. Jordan A. Schwarz, *The Interregnum of Despair* (Urbana: University of Illinois Press, 1970), p. 31.

Chapter 6: To Market, to Market, to Sell a Small Pig

1. Diamond, *Economic Thought,* p. 132.
2. Albert U. Romasco, "Herbert Hoover's Policies for Dealing with the Great Depression: The End of the Old Order or the Beginning of the New?" in *The Hoover Presidency: A Reappraisal,* ed. Martin L. Fausold and George T. Mazuzan (Albany: State University of New York Press, 1974), p. 71.
3. H. Roger Grant and L. Edward Purcell, eds., *Years of Struggle: The Farm Diary of Elmer G. Powers, 1931–1936* (Ames: Iowa State University Press, 1976), pp. 15, 17, 18, 20, 22.
4. Elliot A. Rosen, *Hoover, Roosevelt and the Brains Trust* (New York: Columbia University Press, 1977), p. 289.
5. 1978 Budget Document, p. 437.
6. Fusfeld, *Economic Thought of FDR,* p. 230.
7. Ibid., p. 248.
8. Grant and Purcell, *Years of Struggle,* p. 36.
9. *Chicago Tribune,* 25 August 1933.
10. Roland M. Jones, in *The New York Times,* 27 August 1933.
11. Saul Alinsky, *John L. Lewis* (New York: G. P. Putnam's Sons, 1949), p. 177.
12. Thurman Arnold, *The Folklore of Capitalism* (New Haven: Yale University Press, 1937), p. 220.

Part 3

Chapter 7: "Do Not Make Peace Until We Get Porto Rico . . ."

1. William E. Leuchtenburg, "Progressivism and Imperialism: The Progressive Movement and American Foreign Policy, 1898–1916," *Mississippi Valley Historical Review* 39 (December 1952): 484.
2. Moorfield Storey, "Marked Severities," in *Philippine Warfare, Secretary Root's Record: An Analysis of the Law and Facts Bearing on the Actions and Utterances of President Roosevelt and Secretary Root* (Boston: George H. Ellis Co., 1902), p. 95.
3. Ibid., p. 27.
4. Ibid., p. 10.
5. Ibid., p. 25.
6. *The New York Times,* 3 May 1901.
7. *The New York Times,* 15 April 1902.
8. Daniel B. Schirmer, *Republic or Empire: American Resistance to the Philippine War* (Cambridge, Mass.: Schenkman Publishing Co., 1972), p. 72.
9. Ibid., p. 54.
10. Faulkner, *Decline of Laissez Faire,* p. 81.

11. Charles A. Beard, *Giddy Minds and Foreign Quarrels* (New York: Macmillan Co., 1939), p. 36.

12. David F. Healy, *The United States in Cuba, 1898 to 1902* (Madison: University of Wisconsin Press, 1963), p. 34.

13. Pringle, *Taft*, p. 678.

14. The following is a list of American military interventions in the Caribbean, Central America, and Mexico between 1900 and 1920, from Paul Jacobs and Saul Landau with Eve Pell, *To Serve the Devil* vol. 2, *Colonials and Sojourners* (New York: Random House, 1971), pp. 348–52.

1901—Colombia (State of Panama), November 20–December 4. To protect American property on the Isthmus and to keep transit lines open during serious revolutionary disturbances.

1902—Colombia, April 16–23. To protect American lives and property at Bocas del Toro during a civil war.

1902—Colombia (State of Panama), September 17–November 18. To place armed guards on all trains crossing the Isthmus and to keep the railroad line open.

1903—Honduras, March 23–30 or 31. To protect the American consulate and the steamship wharf at Puerto Cortez during a period of revolutionary activity.

1903—Domincan Republic, March 30–April 21. To protect American interests in the city of Santo Domingo during a revolutionary outbreak.

1903–1914—Panama. To protect American interests and lives during and following the revolution for independence from Colombia over construction of the Isthmian Canal. With brief intermissions, United States Marines were stationed on the Isthmus from November 4, 1903 to January 21, 1914, to guard American interests.

1904—Dominican Republic, January 2–February 11. To protect American interests in Puerto Plata, Sosua, and Santo Domingo City during revolutionary fighting.

1904—Panama, November 17–24. To protect American lives and property at Ancon at the time of a threatened insurrection.

1906–1909—Cuba, September, 1906–January 23, 1909. Intervention to restore order, protect foreigners, and establish a stable government after serious revolutionary activity.

1907—Honduras, March 18–June 8. To protect American interests during a war between Honduras and Nicaragua; troops were stationed for a few days or weeks in Trujillo, Ceiba, Puerto Cortez, San Pedro, Laguna, and Choloma.

1910—Nicaragua, February 22. During a civil war, to get information of conditions at Corinto; May 19–September 4, to protect American interests at Bluefields.

1911—Honduras, January 26 and some weeks thereafter. To protect American lives and interests during a civil war in Honduras.

1912—Honduras. Small force landed to prevent seizure by the government of an American-owned railroad at Puerto Cortez. Forces withdrawn after the United States disapproved the action.

1912—Panama. Troops, on request of both political parties, supervised elections outside the Canal Zone.

1912—Cuba, June 5–August 5. To protect American interests in the Province of Oriente, and in Havana.

1912–1925—Nicaragua, August–November 1912. To protect American interests during an attempted revolution. A small force, serving as a legation guard and as a promoter of peace and governmental stability, remained until August 5, 1925.

1913—Mexico, September 5–7. A few marines landed at Ciaris Estero to aid in evacuating American citizens and others from the Yaqui Valley, made dangerous to foreigners by civil strife.

1914—Haiti, January 29–February 9, February 20–21, October 19. To protect American nationals in a time of dangerous unrest.

1914—Dominican Republic, June and July. During a revolutionary movement, United States naval forces by gunfire stopped the bombardment of Puerto Plata, and by threat of force maintained Santo Domingo City as a neutral zone.

1914–1917—Mexico. The undeclared Mexican-American hostilities following the *Dolphin* affair and Villa's raids included capture of Veracruz and later Pershing's expedition into northern Mexico.

1915–1934—Haiti, July 28, 1915 to August 15, 1934. To maintain order during a period of chronic and threatened insurrection.

1916–1924—Dominican Republic, May 1916 to September 1924. To maintain order during a period of chronic and threatened insurrection.

1917–1922—Cuba. To protect American interests during an insurrection and subsequent unsettled conditions. Most of the United States armed forces left Cuba by August 1919, but two companies remained at Camagüey until February 1922.

1918–1919—Mexico. After withdrawal of the Pershing expedition, our troops entered Mexico in pursuit of bandits at least three times in 1918 and six in 1919. In August 1918, American and Mexican troops fought at Nogales.

1918–1920—Panama. For police duty according to treaty stipulations, at Chiriqui, during election disturbances and subsequent unrest.

1919—Honduras, September 8–12. A landing force was sent ashore to maintain order in a neutral zone during an attempted revolution.

1920—Guatemala, April 9–27. To protect the American Legation and other American interests, such as the cable station, during a period of fighting between unionists and the government of Guatemala.

15. Robert H. Wiebe, *The Search for Order, 1877–1920* (New York: Hill & Wang, 1967), p. 245.

16. John Lewis Gaddis, *The United States and the Origins of the Cold War, 1941–1947* (New York: Columbia University Press, 1972), pp. 24–25.

17. *The New York Times,* 6 August 1964.

The editorial continues:

> Moreover, the language of the resolution tends to be that proposed by the White House. Amendment is virtually impossible in a crisis atmosphere. It is regrettable, for example, that the Southeast Asia Resolution did not incorporate more of the language contained in the Presidential message that accompanied it. That message, unlike the resolution, said that the United States "intends no rashness, and seeks no wider war." It defined the American peace aim as

"restoration of the international agreements signed in Geneva in 1954 (and) 1962," and it contained the assurance that "we shall continue ready to explore any avenue of political solution" for the war in Vietnam.

The nation will expect that President Johnson is as firmly attached to these policies as to the commitments in the resolution itself. He now has proof of a united Congress and a united nation; he has demonstrated his own capacity for toughness. And the Communists have been left in no doubt about American determination. This is a position of strength from which the administration can and should now demonstrate that it is as resolute in seeking a peaceful settlement as it is in prosecuting the war.

18. *The New York Times,* 8 August 1964.

19. Arthur M. Schlesinger, Jr., *The Imperial Presidency* (Boston: Houghton Mifflin Co., 1973), p. 187.

20. Edward M. Bennet, "Joseph C. Grew: The Diplomacy of Pacification," in *Diplomats in Crisis: United States-Chinese-Japanese Relations, 1919–1941,* ed. Richard Dean Burns and Edward M. Bennet (Santa Barbara, Calif.: Clio Press, 1974), pp. 76–77.

21. Noam Chomsky, *American Power and the New Mandarins* (New York: Pantheon Books, 1967), p. 173.

22. Lloyd C. Gardner, "New Deal Diplomacy: A View from the Seventies," in *Watershed of Empire: Essays on New Deal Foreign Policy,* ed. Leonard P. Liggio and James J. Martin (Colorado Springs: Ralph Myles Publisher, 1976), pp. 102–3.

23. Ibid., p. 113.

24. Lloyd C. Gardner, *Economic Aspects of New Deal Diplomacy* (Madison: University of Wisconsin Press, 1964), p. 149.

25. *New York Daily News,* 11 January 1940; quoted in Gardner, *Economic Aspects,* p. 143.

26. Wallace C. Chessman, *Theodore Roosevelt and the Politics of Power* (Boston: Little, Brown & Co., 1969), pp. 118–19.

27. Link, *Wilson: The New Freedom* vol. II, p. 289.

28. In fairness, Wilson was the first president to appoint a Jew to the Supreme Court.

29. Lawrence S. Wittner, *Rebels against War: The American Peace Movement, 1941–1960* (New York: Columbia University Press, 1969), p. 105.

30. *The New York Times,* 29 January 1939.

31. *The New York Times,* 2 February 1939.

32. Ibid.

33. Gardner, "New Deal Diplomacy," p. 121.

34. Paul A. C. Kostinen, "The 'Industrial-Military Complex' in Historical Perspective: World War I," *Business History Review* 41:4 (Winter 1967):385.

35. For more tales of civilian blackmarketeering and getting rich while the soldier boys were getting dead, see John Morton Blum, *V Was for Victory: Politics and American Culture During World War II* (New York: Harcourt Brace Jovanovich, 1976).

36. Wittner, *Rebels Against War,* p. 110.

37. Franklin D. Roosevelt, press conference #523, February 3, 1939, as reported in *The New York Times,* 4 February 1939.

38. Richard Hofstadter, *Great Issues in American History: A Documentary*

Record vol. 2 (New York: Random House, Vintage Books, 1958), pp. 400–401.

39. *The New York Times,* 25 July 1941.

40. Arthur H. Vandenberg, *The Private Papers of Senator Vandenberg,* ed. Arthur H. Vandenberg, Jr., with Joe Alex Morris (Boston: Houghton Mifflin Co., 1952), pp. 10–11.

Chapter 8: "America First, Let It Cost What It May"

1. Link, *Wilson: The New Freedom* vol. II pp. 386–87.

2. Ibid., p. 395.

3. Ibid., p. 404.

4. Diamond, *Economic Thought,* p. 163.

5. Woodrow Wilson to Frank I. Cobb. April 2, 1917, as quoted in H. C. Peterson and Gilbert C. Fite, *Opponents of War, 1917–1918* (Madison: University of Wisconsin Press, 1957), p. 11.

6. C. Roland Marchand, *The American Peace Movement and Social Reform, 1898–1918* (Princeton: Princeton University Press, 1972), pp. 155–56.

7. *The New York Times,* 5 April 1917.

8. Ibid.

9. Peterson and Fite, *Opponents of War,* p. 234.

10. Ibid., p. 233.

11. Ibid., p. 231.

12. Ibid., p. 203.

13. Ibid., p. 204.

14. Woodrow Wilson's speech calling for the declaration of war, April 2, 1917.

15. Harry N. Scheiber, *The Wilson Administration and Civil Liberties, 1917–1921* (Ithaca: Cornell University Press, 1960), p. 27.

16. Weinstein, *Decline of Socialism,* pp. 125–26.

17. Ibid., p. 149.

18. Ibid., p. 151.

19. Ibid., p. 153.

20. Zechariah Chafee, Jr., *Thirty-Five Years with Freedom of Speech,* ACLU, Roger N. Baldwin Civil Liberties Foundation pamphlet, May 1952, pp. 6–7.

21. *Schenk v. United States,* 249 U.S. 47.

22. Oswald Garrison Villard, *Fighting Years: Memoirs of a Liberal Editor* (New York: Harcourt, Brace & Co., 1939), pp. 357–58.

23. Scheiber, *Wilson and Civil Liberties,* p. 30.

24. Robert K. Murray, *Red Scare: A Study in National Hysteria, 1919–1920* (New York: McGraw-Hill Book Co., 1964), p. 9.

Chapter 9: Repression

1. N. Gordon Levin, Jr., *Woodrow Wilson and World Politics: America's Response to War and Revolution* (New York: Oxford University Press, 1968), p. 18.

2. Walter Cohen, "Herbert Hoover Feeds the World," in *The Trojan Horse: A Radical Look at Foreign Aid,* ed. Steve Weissman et al., rev. ed. (Palo Alto, Calif.: Ramparts Press, 1975), p. 155.
3. Levin, *Wilson and World Politics,* p. 14.
4. Ibid., p. 138.
5. Gaddis, *Origins of the Cold War,* p. 139.
6. Ibid., p. 60.
7. Murray, *Red Scare,* p. 83.
8. Ibid., p. 236.
9. Ibid., p. 178.
10. *Washington Star,* 4 June 1919.
11. Villard, *Fighting Years,* pp. 463–64.

Chapter 10: Silent Years

1. Peterson and Fite, *Opponents of War,* p. 254.
2. Robert K. Murray, *The 103rd Ballot* (New York: Harper & Row, 1976), p. 261.
3. Robert K. Murray, *The Harding Era* (Minneapolis: University of Minnesota Press, 1969), p. 70.
4. Ibid., p. 144.
5. Betty Glad, *Charles Evans Hughes and the Illusions of Innocence* (Urbana: University of Illinois Press, 1966), p. 281.
6. Marian C. McKenna, *Borah* (Ann Arbor: University of Michigan Press, 1961), p. 178.
7. Murray, *Harding Era,* p. 158.
8. Wilson, *Business and Foreign Policy,* p. 37.
9. Glad, *Hughes and the Illusions of Innocence,* p. 279.
10. Wilson, *Business and Foreign Policy,* p. 33.
11. Wittner, *Rebels Against War,* p. 101.
12. Ibid., p. 98.
13. Richard M. Fried, *Men Against McCarthy* (New York: Columbia University Press, 1976), p. 16.
14. Ibid., pp. 301–2.
15. Ronald Radosh, *Prophets on the Right: Profiles of Conservative Critics of American Globalism* (New York: Simon & Schuster, 1975), p. 158.
16. From *Politics II* (February 1945), pp. 54–55, as quoted in Wittner, *Rebels Against War,* p. 95.

Part 4

Chapter 11: The All-American Medley

1. Joel H. Spring, *Education and the Rise of the Corporate State* (Boston: Beacon Press, 1972), p. 46.
2. Stuart Ewen, *Captains of Consciousness: Advertising and the Social Roots*

of the Consumer Culture (New York: McGraw-Hill Book Co., 1976), pp. 223–24.

3. Spring, *Education,* p. 2.
4. Ibid., p. 49.
5. David F. Noble, *America by Design: Science, Technology, and the Rise of the Corporate State* (New York: Alfred A. Knopf, 1977), p. 101.
6. Ibid., p. 234.
7. Pringle, *Taft,* p. 662.
8. Carol S. Gruber, *Mars and Minerva: World War I and the Uses of the Higher Learning in America* (Baton Rouge: Louisiana State University Press, 1975), p. 211.
9. Ibid., p. 199.
10. Ibid., p. 183.
11. Laurence H. Shoup and William Minter, *Imperial Brain Trust: The Council on Foreign Relations and U.S. Foreign Policy* (New York: Monthly Review Press, 1977), p. 19.
12. Ibid., p. 59.
13. John Morton Blum, *V Was for Victory,* p. 18.
14. Pringle, *Roosevelt,* pp. 396–97.
15. James MacGregor Burns, *Roosevelt: The Lion and the Fox* (New York: Harcourt, Brace & Co., 1956), p. 467.
16. George Wallace, *Stand Up for America* (Garden City, N.Y.: Doubleday & Co., 1976), p. 121.
17. Arthur S. Link, *Wilson Campaigns for Progressivism and Peace, 1916–1917* vol. V (Princeton, N.J.: Princeton University Press, 1965), p. 111.
18. Leuchtenburg, *Roosevelt,* p. 11.
19. Burns, *Roosevelt,* p. 143.
20. Ibid., p. 144.
21. Elliot A. Rosen, *Hoover, Roosevelt, and the Brains Trust: From Depression to New Deal* (New York: Columbia University Press, 1977), p. 312.
22. *The New York Times,* 18 August 1940.
23. Ibid.
24. Harry S. Truman, *Memoirs* vol. 2, *Years of Trial and Hope, 1946–1952* (Garden City, N.Y.: Doubleday & Co., 1956), p. 211.
25. Robert J. Donovan, *Conflict and Crisis: The Presidency of Harry S. Truman, 1945–1948* (New York: W. W. Norton & Co., 1977), p. 427.
26. Curtis D. MacDougall, *Gideon's Army* vol. 2, *The Decision and the Organization* (New York: Marzani & Munsell, 1965), p. 423.
27. Ibid., p. 491.

Chapter 12: Tweedledum and Tweedledumber: Cracking Open the One-Party State

1. Burns, *Roosevelt,* p. 271.
2. Lawrence W. Levine, *Defender of the Faith, William Jennings Bryan: The Last Decade, 1915–1925* (New York: Oxford University Press, 1965), p. 150.

Index

A

B

About the Author

Nicholas von Hoffman's career, first as a reporter for the *Chicago Daily News* and later for the *Washington Post,* included coverage of a broad spectrum of stories, from the civil-rights movement and the Mississippi summer of 1964 to Watts; from student riots and the Chicago Democratic Convention to Watergate. He has been a radio commentator for CBS news, and in the early seventies debated James J. Kirkpatrick weekly on *Sixty Minutes.* His column, now distributed by King Features Syndicate, appears three times a week in 150 newspapers across the country.

Von Hoffman is the author of numerous books, which range from an investigation of the drug culture to a work of fiction. His two most recent books, *Fireside Watergate* and *Tales from the Margaret Mead Taproom,* were co-authored with Garry Trudeau.